CW00455135

The Stuarts' Secret Army

The Stuarts' Secret Army

ENGLISH JACOBITES, 1689–1752

Evelyn Lord

PEARSON

Longman

Harlow, England • London • New York • Boston • San Francisco • Toronto
Sydney • Tokyo • Singapore • Hong Kong • Seoul • Taipei • New Delhi
Cape Town • Madrid • Mexico City • Amsterdam • Munich • Paris • Milan

PEARSON EDUCATION LIMITED

Edinburgh Gate
Harlow CM20 2JE
United Kingdom
Tel: +44 (0)1279 623623
Fax: +44 (0)1279 431059
Website: www.pearsoned.co.uk

———————————————

First edition published in Great Britain in 2004

© Pearson Education Limited 2004

The right of Evelyn Lord to be identified as author
of this work has been asserted by her in accordance
with the Copyright, Designs and Patents Act 1988.

ISBN 0 582 77256 7

British Library Cataloguing in Publication Data
A CIP catalogue record for this book can be obtained from the British Library

Library of Congress Cataloging in Publication Data
A CIP catalog record for this book can be obtained from the Library of Congress

10 9 8 7 6 5 4 3 2 1
08 07 06 05 04

Set in 9.5/14pt Melior by 35
Printed in China
PPLC/01
The Publisher's policy is to use paper manufactured from sustainable forests.

In Loving Memory
of
Katie Lord 1969–2003

Contents

Acknowledgements

We are grateful to the following for permission to reproduce copyright material:

Plates 1, 2, 4, 5, 7 and 15 courtesy of the National Portrait Gallery, London; plates 3, 6, 9 and 16 courtesy of the Ashmolean Museum, Oxford; plate 14 © The Trustees of the National Museums of Scotland; plates 10 and 11 courtesy of The Drambuie Collection; plate 8 courtesy of Lord Petre's Estate; plate 12 © University of Cambridge Institute of Continuing Education and plate 13 courtesy of Richard Elliott.

In some instances we have been unable to trace the owners of copyright material, and we would appreciate any information that would enable us to do so.

Foreword

Much of the 17th century was a turbulent time for England, a time of revolutions: the last revolution, in 1688–89, was called 'Glorious' by the winners, and its settlement proved enduring. The principal losers, however, made many attempts to overthrow that settlement: they are the Jacobites – supporters of the Stuart King James II ('Jacobus' in Latin) and his successors – a fascinating collection of individuals for whom the status quo was repellent, and further revolution remained a desirable aim, if not always a practical policy.

The Jacobites might well have succeeded. The restoration of Charles Stuart in 1660 would have seemed a very distant prospect a few years beforehand; why should his brother James not also be restored in triumph? The rule of Cromwell was arguably stronger and more secure than that of William III or the Hanoverian usurpers. A fair assessment of Jacobite hopes and personalities can be coloured by our knowledge that, in fact, they did not succeed – in the words of T.S. Eliot, 'What might have been is an abstraction/Remaining a perpetual possibility/Only in a world of speculation.' More and more historians are trying to re-enter that world of speculation, to ask not just 'what?', and 'when?', and 'why?', but 'what if . . . ?'. The concept is sometimes called 'virtual' or 'counterfactual' history, and not everyone likes it; but its central question is pure common sense – from the participants' point of view, all historical events are part of an uncertain future that could have turned out in many different ways. The English Jacobites are a good example of people whose hopes were repeatedly dashed, but who still deserve to be remembered by us, and whose stories can still seize the attention of modern readers.

We, too, live in a world where the future is uncertain. In terms of the British monarchy, there is often a debate about the future: will Prince Charles ever take the throne? Will we have a King Charles III? One answer is that we already have had one: he reigned, in theory, from 1766 to 1788 (and is better known as 'Bonnie Prince Charlie'): king by right, according to his followers, but never in practice. Would he have dealt any better with the American revolution than George III? That revolution succeeded, while Charles's didn't: could it have been the other way around?

Again, looking at our own times, we cannot tell what chaos politics will throw at us. At the time of writing (20 November 2003) we have just seen the fall of one Conservative leader, the 'coronation' of another; Mr Blair hangs on to power, with enemies next door and farther afield. Will the situation be similar when you read this, or totally different? I have no idea – and nor did the English people of two or three centuries ago.

Who better to guide us through the maze of past loyalties and ambitions than a historian who specialises in local history? Not the history of any particular locality (though of course she knows many of them as well), so much as the methods needed to explore the past of every location and group. History, according to Thomas Carlyle, is 'the essence of innumerable biographies'. Some of those countless past lives are illuminated by this study, and Dr Lord provides guidance for further investigation of the topic. The English Jacobites were spread throughout the kingdom. Some were famous scholars, churchmen, landowners; others are barely known to posterity. Many were not quite as loyal – to either side – as they seemed. If we ignore them, we will have a distorted picture of our country's past. We are in need of a clear and readable guide to their England, so similar, and yet so different, to our own. Welcome to a world of plots and poetry, piety and passions – the English Jacobites.

Dr David Money
University of Sunderland

Preface

Much has been written about 'Bonnie Prince Charlie' and the Scottish Jacobites, less about Jacobite supporters in England. For over one hundred years as spies, secret agents and politicians they carried on a secret war on behalf of the exiled Stuarts. In 1715 they joined with their Scottish colleagues in rebellion against the House of Hanover, and were defeated. The tragic and charismatic Earl of Derwentwater lost his life as a result of this, and the repercussions of the 1715 rebellion were felt at all levels of society.

In 1745 the English Jacobites stayed at home. Why was this? They have been accused of self-interest and cowardice, but were these the only reasons for their non-appearance? This book looks at the motivations of the English Jacobites, from the flight of James II into exile to the last visit of his grandson, Prince Charles Edward, to England in 1752.

This book is aimed at the reader interested in history in general and the Jacobites in particular. In view of this it is written as a straightforward narrative, and includes a gazetteer for those who wish to visit some of the sites mentioned in the book, a glossary and chronology to aid understanding of the historical dimension, and lists of known English Jacobites for the family historian. For those wishing to pursue the subject further there is a detailed bibliography, a discussion of debates on the English Jacobites, and an account of the location of primary source material available for the student working on the English Jacobites. The interpretation of evidence and events represent the author's own conclusions, and any mistakes are her own.

In writing this book I would like to thank Edward, Gabriel and Katie Lord for practical assistance and helpful comments, the University of Cambridge's Institute of Continuing Education for enabling me to have a sabbatical to complete the work, the staff of Cambridge University Library, the Friends of the Ashmolean Museum, Lord Petre, James Kilvington of the National Portrait Gallery, Robin Nicolson of the Drambuie Liquor Company, Helen Nicoll of the National Museum of Scotland, Lionel Munby for sharing his work on Charles Caesar of Hertfordshire, Paul Walford for supplying photographs of Madingley Hall and Richard Elliott and other descendants of the Hynde Cotton family. Finally, thanks must go to Heather McCallum and her editorial team at Pearson Education for their patience and understanding during what has been a difficult and traumatic time for the author.

Notes on dates and titles used in the text

Until 1752 when England changed from the Julian to the Gregorian calendar the new year was dated from 25 March and the period between 1 January and 24 March given a double date, for example 22 February 1744/5. In order to avoid confusion in this book the new year is deemed to have started on 1 January, so 22 February 1745.

Although James Francis was never crowned king he was recognised by his supporters as James III. For ease of expression following the death of James II he will be referred to as James III. His son Prince Charles Edward, or 'Bonnie Prince Charlie' as he is popularly known, will be referred to as Prince Charles throughout the book.

Chronology of English Jacobite events

1688

10 June	Birth of James Francis Stuart (James III)
5 November	William III lands at Torbay
10 November	James Francis taken to France
11 December	James II throws the Great Seal in the Thames
18 December	William enters London
23 December	James II leaves for France

1689

25 January	Parliament declares James abdicated and offers crown to William and Mary
11 April	William and Mary crowned by the Bishop of London
20 April	Clergy and government office holders required to take a new oath of allegiance

1690

1 February	All clergy who refused to take the new oath of allegiance deprived of their livings
1 July	William defeats James at the Battle of the Boyne
December	Preston Plot discovered

1692

May	Franco-Jacobite invasion of England planned, but abandoned

1693

April	The Earl of Middleton defects to the Jacobites

1694

October   The Lancashire Plot

1696

February   The Assassination Plot discovered

1697

September   Peace of Ryswyk. France recognises William as King of England

1701

April   Act of Settlement protecting the Protestant succession of the English crown

6 September   Death of James II

1702

March   Abjuration Act requiring formal renunciation of oath of allegiance to James III
                 Death of William III

1703

                 The Lovat Plot

1707

                 The Act of Union suspending the Scottish Parliament

1708

April   The Scottish Plot

1709

November   Dr Sacheverell's pro-Jacobite sermon in St Paul's Cathedral

1710

                 Riots when Sacheverell indicted for high treason

1711

January   Founding of the Tory/Jacobite October Club

1714

1 August	Death of Queen Anne
10 August	James III seeks French help in order to restore the House of Stuart on the English throne
20 October	Pro-Jacobite riots on George's coronation day

1715

July	Viscount Bolingbroke defects to the Jacobites
August	The Duke of Ormonde defects to the Jacobites
6 September	The Earl of Mar raises the Stuart standard at Braemar
6 October	The English Jacobites gather in Northumberland
9 November	The Jacobites reach Preston
14 November	The Jacobites surrender to the government troops
25 November	Jacobite prisoners taken from Preston to London
9 December	The prisoners arrive in London
22 December	James lands at Peterhead

1716

9 January	Impeachment of the Earl of Derwentwater
19 January	Trial of the Earl of Derwentwater
3 February	James returns to France
9 February	Derwentwater sentenced to death
24 February	Derwentwater and Lord Kenmure executed on Tower Hill
16 March	Display of the Aurora Borealis as Derwentwater's body travels north

1717

January	The Swedish Plot

1718

March	The Spanish Plot

1719

9 September	James marries Clementina Sobieska of Poland

1720

20 December	Birth of Prince Charles

1722

November   The Layer Plot

1723

Discovery of the Atterbury Plot
First of the Black Acts passed

1730

Jacobite Tory MPs instructed to bring down
Sir Robert Walpole

1731

The Cornbury Plot

1740

May   Jacobite Tory MPs make contact with James

1741

September   James tells them to bring Walpole down

1742

February   Walpole resigns

1743

August   Butler visits England to gauge support for the Jacobites
November   France begins to make invasion plans. Delayed by
                  Sir John Hynde Cotton
30 December   Prince Charles Edward leaves Rome secretly for France

1744

14 February   De Bussy reveals the invasion plans to the
                  British government
24 February   French fleet dispersed by a storm
28 February   French abandon invasion plans

1745

5 July   Prince Charles sails from Nantes for Scotland
23 July   Lands at Eriskay

19 August	Stuart standard raised at Glenfinnan
17 September	Jacobites reach Edinburgh
21 September	Government army defeated at Prestonpans
8 November	Jacobites enter England
9 November	Siege of Carlisle
15 November	Jacobites take Carlisle
29 November	Jacobites at Manchester
1 December	Jacobites at Macclesfield. English Jacobites make overtures to the French
4 December	Jacobites at Derby
6 December	Retreat from Derby
11 December	Engagement at Clifton
25 December	Main Jacobite army reaches Glasgow
30 December	Jacobite garrison at Carlisle surrenders to the Duke of Cumberland

1746

2 January	Jacobites besiege Stirling Castle
17 January	Battle of Falkirk
30 January	Siege of Stirling Castle abandoned
16 April	Battle of Culloden
30 September	Prince Charles reaches France

1747

September	Pro-Jacobite demonstrations at Lichfield Races

1750

May	Pro-Jacobite rioting in the Black Country
September	Prince Charles in London

1753

	The Elibank Plot

1766

1 January	Death of James III. The Pope refuses to acknowledge Charles as king

1788

30 January   Death of Charles III

1807

13 July   Death of Cardinal Prince Henry of York, last of the
Stuarts

Introduction

On 11 December 1688, James II, anointed king of England, Ireland, Scotland and Wales, threw the Great Seal into the Thames and fled towards the coast. Apprehended at Sheerness, James must have thought his fate was sealed. Like his father, he too would make the short walk to the scaffold and the headsman's axe. But his subjects did not want his blood. They wanted a Protestant monarchy and free parliaments. James's son-in-law, William of Orange, who was Charles I's eldest surviving grandson, fitted the bill. William entered London on 18 December 1688. On 23 December 1688 James left for France, never to return. James's supporters took for themselves the Latin version of his name *Jacobus* and became Jacobites, a term that first appears in the State Papers in May 1690.[1]

As he had promised, William summoned a Parliament and accepted responsibility for the civil administration of the realm. On 28 January 1689 the 'Convention Parliament' declared James had abdicated and offered William and Mary his wife, James's eldest daughter, the crown. They were to hold this jointly for the term of both their lives, and on the death of the last of them, if they had no heirs, the crown would pass to Mary's younger sister Anne.

This coup has become known as the 'Glorious Revolution'. It ushered in a new limited monarchy, bound by the Bill of Rights to recognise parliamentary control of law making, taxes and the standing army, obliged to call regular parliaments, and to allow free debates in these.

In France, James, who had not given his consent to the abdication, still considered himself king of England and his infant son, James Francis, as Prince of Wales. As anointed king James believed that only God could unthrone him, not his subjects. He ruled by divine right, and not by the will of the people. In his mind and those of his supporters he would always be the king of England.

James made one last attempt to regain his kingdom but was defeated by William at the Battle of the Boyne in 1690 and returned to the continent. But this was not the end of the Stuarts and their claim to the British crown. From their courts in France and Italy they reigned as parallel kings of Britain. Throughout the 18th century they and their supporters were a constant threat to the security and peace of Britain, attracting political malcontents, soldiers of fortune, Roman Catholics, and those who firmly believed in the divine right of kings to their side.

Usually, the Jacobites are associated with the Highlands of Scotland, heather-clad hills, Bonnie Prince Charlie, the clans and the tragedy of Culloden. This is only part of the story. In England there were many Jacobite supporters who came from all sections of society. Bishops, peers, smugglers, tradesmen, clerics and the gentry were all represented in their ranks. They plotted in secret using coded messages, they formed clubs, wore special emblems and drank the health of 'the king over the water'. They published newspapers, pamphlets and journals arguing their case, and they hired ballad singers to sing seditious songs in the streets.

Was this an elaborate theatre without real substance? Did the Jacobite cause represent a haven for disaffected politicians to go to grumble about Walpole and the Whigs, high churchmen to inveigh against the upstart dissenters, or tradesmen to complain about new taxes? When Jacobite rebellion was raised in 1715 and 1745 many English Jacobites failed to respond. Perhaps when faced with the reality of the return of a Catholic king influenced by the Pope and supported by a French army they thought better of becoming involved. Political reality, the romance of a secret life and the promise that things would be better under the Stuarts never synchronised with reality for the English Jacobites. Nevertheless, they were a recognisable force in the political and social life of 18th-century England. This book will uncover their secrets and illuminate those individuals who wore the white rose of the Jacobites, and the plaid for the Stuarts.

Note

1   W.J. Hardy ed., *Calendar of State Papers Domestic, William and Mary, May 1690–October 1691*, London: HMSO, 1898, 282.

CHAPTER 1

Life in 18th-century England

The Jacobite drama was played out in a century of change, during which England changed from an agricultural nation to one in which industry was taking over. Silk and cotton mills spread along the valleys of Derbyshire and the north-west of England. Iron works belched smoke and fumes over Coalbrookdale and the Severn Valley. Daniel Defoe on his tour through Great Britain during 1724–26 noted in Newcastle upon Tyne 'a view of the inexhausted store of Coals and Coal Pits, from whence not only London, but all the South Part of England is continually supplied . . . we see the prodigious heaps, I might say, Mountains of Coal, which are dug up at every Pit'. Defoe also observed the great increase of the Yorkshire woollen trade.[1]

Canals, turnpikes and coastal shipping tied industry and markets together, closing the gap between the north and south, east and west of England, and helping to create a coherent nation state. The turnpike facilitated travel, and Defoe devoted an appendix in the account of his tour to the benefits of the turnpike, noting that keeping the roads in good repair was essential for trade and for 'the Ease and safety of Gentlemen riding to London'.[2]

Life was short in the 18th century, but the population was growing inexorably. Although vulnerable to disease and starvation, a steady increase in the number of people can be discerned from 1750 onwards. In 1701 the population was estimated to be about 5 million, by 1801 it was 8.6 million and rising. This was despite 25 mortality crises in the 18th century, when the death rate peaked and outstripped births.[3] As the population increased efforts had to be made to feed the many hungry mouths, efforts which changed the landscape of England. Open fields were enclosed by hedges and walls, so that new crops could be tried and new livestock breeds introduced. Common land was ploughed up and cultivated, fens and marshes were drained, and wasteland brought into production. Eighteenth-century England was a hive of activity.

Society was organised according to rank and status. At the top were the temporal and spiritual lords, the peers and the gentry. In the upper middle section were the clergy, the professionals such as lawyers, and the wealthy tradesmen and yeomen farmers. In the lower middle were the craftsmen, shopkeepers and farmers with only a few acres. At the bottom were the labourers and the paupers. In 1688 Gregory King, a political economist, drew up a scheme of income and expenditure for all levels of society. His calculations show that at the top were 160 families with an income of at least £3200 a year, at the bottom 849,000 families who lived on £2 a head per year.[4]

In the countryside these inequalities were becoming more visible as the structure of the old village communities changed. The gentry withdrew further behind their park fences, and employed landscape gardeners such as Humphrey Repton or Capability Brown to design managed wildernesses for them. At their gates the poor struggled to live on what they were allowed from parish relief. Laws prevented them from moving in search of work unless they had a certificate promising to pay any poor relief should they need it from the parish in which they were born, or had married into. If they moved without permission and fell on hard times they were hauled up before the Justices of the Peace and examined under oath as to where they had come from, and what they had been doing. They were then sent back to their original parish of settlement. Widows with children and women expecting children out of wedlock were especially vulnerable.

Defoe observed the contrast between rich and poor on his travels. He also noted how the two interacted. In his description of the town of Sudbury in Suffolk he noted that the town was 'very Populous and very Poor. They have a great Manufacture of Says . . . but Multitudes of poor almost ready to eat up the Rich.'[5]

Cesar De Saussure from Lorraine, who visited England in the 1720s, noted that the gentry had large country houses, and he observed that there was a strong network of country gentry who met regularly at assemblies for the purpose of dancing.[6] The assembly room became the hallmark of civic pride and polite society. It was part of the urban renaissance of the 18th century as towns and cities rebuilt their public areas. The rules of the assembly rooms show that they were run on strict lines that mirrored the divisions in society as a whole. At Derby, for example, when the assembly rooms opened in 1714 attorneys' clerks, shopkeepers and tradesmen were forbidden to enter, and there was a strict dress code in force with fines for anyone contravening it.[7]

Eighteenth-century society was one of contrast as well as change. It was the age when the population moved into the towns, to live in overcrowded courts and tenements, but it was also the age when great country houses were built: Castle Howard, Saltram, Stourhead and Stowe were 18th-century edifices. The elegant squares and crescents of Bath and other spa towns were built to house the leisured classes during the 'season'. Defoe observed them gossiping and drinking tea in Tunbridge Wells, Epsom and Hampstead.[8]

Although the 18th century could boast a vibrant provincial culture, it was London that dominated the country. One in ten of the population lived in London. From London newspapers, fashions and ideas spread out across the country. London was the seat of government, and the superior courts of law. London with its anonymous teeming streets provided ideal cover for the English Jacobites who could come and go unnoticed. They were helped in their endeavours by the fact that 18th-century England was a clubbable society. Coffee houses and taverns abounded, each with its own political stance and clientele. The Jacobites knew where to go to find other supporters. De Saussure described London's coffee houses with some distaste: 'In London there are a great number of coffee houses, most of which, to tell the truth, are not very clean, or well furnished, owing to the quantity of people who resort to these places and because the smoke quickly destroys good furniture.'[9] He quickly learnt that some coffee shops were not all they seemed; '. . . many others are temples of Venus. You can easily recognise the latter, because they frequently have as a sign a woman's arm or hand holding a coffee pot.'[10]

Despite their shortcomings coffee houses were an essential feature of 18th-century social life. Diaries kept by men such as John Byrom or Dudley Ryder show that they visited the coffee houses daily to meet with like-minded people, and to engage in debates on the scriptures, or discuss the events of the day. As well as the coffee house, in the years 1715–16 Ryder was a member of six different clubs.[11] The clubs and coffee houses were part of a flourishing intellectual life in London and in the provinces. Circulating libraries were popular, where those that could afford it could borrow volumes of improving sermons or the latest novels. Most urban areas of any size had a theatre where the patrons could watch actors such as David Garrick perform Shakespeare, or participate in the exuberant production of John Gay's *The Beggars' Opera*. First performed at the Lincoln's Inn Theatre in 1728, this was a satire on the corruption of the legal profession, as well as pandering to the public's taste for crime and sensational heroes. Strung together with ballads using recognisable popular tunes it was an instant success with all classes of society.

The Beggars' Opera is contemporary with the courtly and devotional music of Handel. Handel arrived in England in 1712, and dominated the music scene from then on with his anthems, concertos and oratorios, culminating in *The Messiah*, first performed in Dublin in 1742. Handel was the court musician who composed the music for the Hanoverians' coronations, and for other royal events that have remained in the classical music repertoire ever since.

The same comparison between popular and high culture can be seen in art. The cartoons and portrayals of low life by William Hogarth (1697–1764) can be compared with the urbane middle-class figures of Thomas Gainsborough (1727–88) and the patrician portraits of Joshua Reynolds (1723–92).

Another genre of 18th-century painting illustrated new developments in technology and scientific thought. Joseph Wright of Derby's paintings of scientific experiments such as *An Experiment on a Bird in a Bell Jar*, 1760 or *A Philosopher Giving a Lecture on the Orrery*, 1766, show new intellectual inquiries in action, while industrialisation with its furnaces working round the clock gave artists new sources of light and inspiration.

Joseph Wright was associated with the Lunar Society, a group of Midland intellectuals who met at each other's homes when the moon was full to discuss education and literature, and to perform scientific experiments. Their number included Erasmus Darwin and Josiah Wedgwood. The Lunar Society was one of many similar societies that grew up in the 18th century, which were the result of critical analysis of society, mankind and the universe that characterised the 18th-century Enlightenment. By the end of the century most towns had a Literary and Philosophic Society. This spirit of inquiry led to collections being made of antiquities, fossils and historical documents that form the basis of many provincial museums. Economic and social theory were also being placed onto a legitimate and rational footing in the 18th century with the publication of works such as *The Wealth of Nations* by Adam Smith in 1776.

Change was also taking place in politics. Although the Houses of Parliament were still dominated by the landed interest, this had split into parties. After the Hanoverian succession the Tories, who were the country party, were denied office and were continually in opposition. Denied political power many Tories looked towards the Jacobites to restore this for them. However, the court party, the Whigs, led by Robert Walpole, were firmly entrenched and supported by George I who heartily disliked the Tories. De Saussure wrote that the Tories believed in the absolute prerogative of the sovereign, and that all subjects must submit to him or her. The Whigs thought this created despotism, and they believed that a subject only owed obedience to the sovereign as long as the sovereign maintained the conditions under which power was given to him. He added that the two parties were so opposed to each other that it would be a miracle if they agreed.[12]

Few people were allowed to vote for members of parliament, but all were subject to its laws, and the taxes it imposed. The 18th century saw an increase in the harshness of the law. Capital offences multiplied, and these included acts against property as well as against person. The gallows or transportation became the common fate for the thief, the poacher and the forger. De Saussure described criminal law at work in 1726. In London, after the criminals were arrested they were taken to Newgate or one of the other government prisons. There they remained until the assizes. When the case had been heard the judge summed up, and if the prisoner was found guilty he or she was taken back to gaol, but this time loaded down with chains. Those sentenced to death were put onto a list given to the king for his approval. On the day of the execution the condemned prisoners, dressed in white linen shirts with white caps on their heads, were taken on carts to Tyburn. Once there they were placed on a wide cart under the gallows. The chaplain prayed and said a psalm and then the prisoners' relatives were allowed to mount the cart to say goodbye. After about a quarter of an hour the chaplain and relatives got down from the cart, the executioner covered the prisoners' eyes with the caps they were wearing and lashed the horses that pulled the carts, which slipped away from under the condemned men's feet. De Saussure saw the friends and relatives tugging at the prisoners' feet so that they would die quickly and not suffer, and afterwards there were undignified scuffles between the relatives of those hung and the London surgeons who arrived to take away the bodies for dissection.[13] De Saussure reported that executions took place in London every six weeks with between five and fifteen hung at a time. He remarked that hanging was no deterrent as 'there are a surprising number of footpads in this country, and a surprising quantity of robbers'.[14]

An alternative to robbery was to join the army. During the 18th century England was involved with the War of Spanish Succession from 1702–13, the War of Jenkins' Ear 1739–43,[15] the War of Austrian Succession 1740–48, the Seven Years War 1756–63, the War of American Independence, and of course wars with republican France at the end of the century. The early 18th-century army was at its most effective under the Duke of Marlborough, who planned the victory of Blenheim in 1704.

Finally, despite it not appearing to be centre stage, religion was still of fundamental importance in 18th-century social and political life. The Church of England was secured in 1688, but at the same time its place as the established church was weakened. The Toleration Act of 1689 gave dissenting worshippers the right to hold meetings provided they had a licence. This meant that Baptists, Congregationalists, Presbyterians and Unitarians were able to meet legally, and to build chapels. These became the focus of many 18th-century riots; when whipped up by priestly rhetoric the mob attacked the dissenting meeting houses and sometimes destroyed them.

The Church of England itself was split between the high churchmen who favoured the reforms put in place by Archbishop Laud, and the performance of old rituals that smacked of popery, and the low church, moderate evangelicals. De Saussure described a high church as having altars covered with velvet, silk or damask cloths, candlesticks upon them, and pictures hung above. Communion was taken kneeling.[16] The ministers themselves reflected the religious politics of whoever held the living. A high churchman was unlikely to appoint a low church rector. Many of the local clergy ministered to their flock conscientiously, taking on social responsibilities for the poor. Others collected livings to increase their income, appointed low-paid curates and lived in London. Some Jacobite clergy were notorious in this respect. Against this background John Wesley started his mission to bring salvation to all. At first he hoped to stay within the Church of England, but the split was inevitable. Methodism attracted the more lowly members of the population. Wesley may have helped to defuse the situation during the 1745 rebellion as he issued a letter to his followers advising against social disorder.

On the outside of this and worshipping illegally were the Catholics, many of whom supported the Catholic Stuarts. But not all Jacobites were Catholic. The core of English society – the country squire – was unequivocally Protestant, and as many of them also supported the Stuarts therein lay their dilemma and perhaps one of the reasons that they did not give practical support during the Jacobite rebellions.

However, despite the Stuarts' Catholicism, it was from the Church of England that the early Jacobites emerged – men of honour, who were Jacobites not by choice, but through their principles. They are the subject of the next chapter.

Notes

1 D. Defoe, *A Tour Thro' the Whole Island of Great Britain 1724–6*, facsimile edn, London: Frank Cass, 1968, 611, 658.

2 Defoe, 529.

3 E.A. Wrigley and R.S. Schofield, *The Population History of England and Wales, 1541–1871*, Cambridge: CUP, 1989, 338–9, 577.

4 P. Laslett, *The World We Have Lost*, London: Methuen, 2nd edn, 1971, 36–8.

5 Defoe, 48.

6 C. De Saussure, *A Foreign View of England in the Reigns of George I and George II*, translated by Madame van Muyden, London: John Murray, 1902, 306.

7 E. Lord, *Derby Past*, Chichester: Phillimore, 1996, 38.

8 Defoe, 38.

9 De Saussure, 161–2.

10 De Saussure, 165.

11 W. Matthews ed., *The Diary of Dudley Ryder 1715–1716*, London: Methuen, 1939.

12 De Saussure, 348.

13 De Saussure, 117–27.

14 De Saussure, 127.

15 The War of Jenkins' Ear started 1739; sometimes known as the Anglo-Spanish War. Spain and Britain were long-term rivals for power in areas such as the Caribbean. The catalyst for war came when Spanish coastguards cut off the ear of Captain Robert Jenkins during a fracas in the West Indies. He pickled it and took it to Parliament to demand redress.

16 De Saussure, 319.

CHAPTER 2

Principles, plots and discoveries, 1689–1703

Non-jurors

Identifying the English Jacobites is difficult. 'English Jacobites needed to be discrete. No one could be trusted.'[1] But the first group to be associated with the exiled Stuarts, deprived of their offices and estates, and accused of treason were well known to William III's government. They were open in their refusal to acknowledge William as the lawful king because of their principles. The oath of allegiance they had taken to James bound them to him as their rightful anointed king. William, they believed, had no lawful right to their allegiance, and taking an oath to him would perjure them. They became known as non-jurors.

Not all non-jurors were active Jacobites. Many of them abhorred plots against William but they refused to recognise him as their king, making their protest known through passive resistance. Other non-jurors were involved in conspiracies against William, and later against the Hanoverian Georges.

John Evelyn's diary shows that even before William accepted the crown, the question of the oath of allegiance was being discussed by churchmen. On 5 January 1689 Evelyn dined with the Archbishop of Canterbury and some of his principal bishops. After dinner they discussed the political situation. 'Some would have the Princess [Mary] made Queen, some were for a Regency. The Tory party was for inviting his Majestie [James] upon conditions, and Republicans would make the Prince of Orange [William] a Stadtholder. The Romanists busy amongst all, the several parts to bring into confusion.' Eventually the clerics declared for a regency, 'thereby to salve their consciences of the oaths, and so all public matters to proceed in His Majesty's [James] name.'[2]

The Archbishop of Canterbury, William Sancroft, and most of the bishops were absent from the House of Lords when William was offered the crown. The Archbishop remained firmly closeted in Lambeth Palace, and on 11 April 1689 it fell to the Bishop of London to crown William and Mary.[3] A number of satirical verses appeared about this, some praising him for his principles, others attacking him. The anonymous *Marvell's Ghost* accuses the Archbishop of allowing William to take the crown through his policy of passive resistance, when he might have prevented it.

> *When holy prelacy, from court withdrawn,*
> *Lies sick at Lambeth, in a shroud of lawn,*
> *Who, fearing now compliance with the Prince*
> *Should better men to equal power advance*
> *Withholds his hand, and in the very nick,*
> *The humorous prelate willingly falls sick!*[4]

The new oath of allegiance that all clergy and government office-holders were to take was prepared by 26 April 1689. Anyone who had not taken the oath by 1 August would be suspended from office for six months. If at the end of that time they still refused to take the oath they were to be permanently deprived of their offices and livings.[5]

Most is known about the clergy who refused to take the oath, because they were rigorously pursued, and ejected from their livings. Eventually, they were to form their own branch of the Church of England, which was to outlive the Jacobites and survive until 1804.

Clerical non-jurors

Four hundred clerics and college fellows refused to take the oath. They were in good company. William Sancroft (1617–93), Archbishop of Canterbury, and seven of his bishops refused to take it. The seven bishops were Francis Turner (1636–1700), Bishop of Ely, John Lake

(1624–98), Bishop of Chichester, William Thomas (1613–89), Bishop of Worcester, Thomas White (1628–98), Bishop of Peterborough, William Lloyd (1637–1710), Bishop of Norwich, Robert Frampton (1622–1708), Bishop of Gloucester, and the well-known hymn writer, Thomas Ken (1637–1710), Bishop of Bath and Wells. They were all high churchmen, elder statesmen and elderly men. A few years earlier they had all refused to recognise James's *Declaration of Indulgence* which gave freedom of worship to Catholics and Dissenters, and been confined to the Tower of London for this. Ironically, now they were being persecuted as James's supporters. They were, indeed, men of iron principles, and Dr Goldie suggests may have welcomed this further trial because they had 'a self-image of martyrdom to a purer Anglicanism'.[6]

The youngest of the bishops, Francis Turner of Ely, was soon involved in one of the earliest Jacobite plots, the Preston plot. In December 1690 a customs-house pinnace stopped and boarded the smack *Thomas and Elizabeth*. Under the hatches, lying on the ballast and surrounded by the remains of a meal consisting of a 'great piece of roast beef, a mince pie and a fowl' were Lord Preston, Edward Elliott, John Ashton and a servant. When they were discovered Preston threw Ashton a bundle of letters, which he was prevented from throwing in the sea. The letters, in code, were bound for James in France.

Despite protestations that they were bound for Flanders, not France, the smack's owner gave evidence that the boat had been hired to take them to France. The smack's captain had betrayed them to Lord Danby, a member of the government. The letters showed an early attempt at using a code. James and his queen were referred to as Mr and Mrs Redding or A & B, with

C = Prince of Wales
D = Prince of Orange
E = Cannon and the Scottish Officers
F = Duke of Berwick
G = Duke of Tyrconnel
H = Major-General Sarsfeld
I = Lieutenant-General Sheldon
L = King of France
M = Marshall Luxemburg

N = Marshall Belfort
O = Duke of Powis
P = Duchess of Powis
Amsterdam = Brest, Rotterdam = Dieppe, Hague = Havre de Grace,
Brill = Dunkirk, Harlem = Calais, Germany = Scotland, and
Spain = Ireland.[7]

On 4 January 1690/1 John Evelyn recorded that Lord Clarendon, Lord Preston and others were sent to the Tower, and the Bishop of Ely was searched for.[8] The Bishop of Ely had fled to Flanders with eleven others, including a strange bedfellow for a high churchman, William Penn the Quaker. On 5 February a proclamation was issued for the apprehension and arrest of both of them. By 3 March Turner was reported to be in Ireland.[9]

The non-jurors claimed that the plot was a fabrication designed to discredit the bishops. But if that was the case why had Turner fled? Two of the letters addressed to Mr and Mrs Redding appeared to be in Turner's hand, and appeared to offer the support of the Archbishop of Canterbury, his 'elder brother', and the other bishops 'his nearest relatives'. From this time onwards Turner was in constant correspondence with James, and spent much of his time flitting between England and the continent disguised as a Mr Harris. In June 1698 he was recognised in London attending Bishop White's funeral, but was not arrested. He was to die in England two years later.[10]

Only Ashton was executed as a result of the Preston plot. Richard Grahme, Viscount Preston saved himself by obligingly implicating anyone the government wanted removed. This illustrated the problems that were to dog the English Jacobites throughout their later careers – they could not trust each other, especially if the threat of execution for treason was hanging over them.

Meanwhile, Archbishop Sancroft sat on in Lambeth Palace, refusing to take the oath to William or to move out of the palace to allow the new Archbishop, William Tillotson, to move in. Eventually, Queen Mary ordered him to leave, and in July 1691 John Evelyn visited the palace and found all Sancroft's possessions packed up. Sancroft had departed, leaving his nephew in possession of the palace, who was thereupon arrested and imprisoned.[11] Sancroft retired to a cottage in his birthplace, Fressingfield in Suffolk.

William appointed new bishops to fill dioceses that the non-jurors did not consider vacant. This created a situation similar to that between William and James, who both considered themselves King of England. A parallel set of bishops now existed, both believing themselves to be the legal holders of the office. To complicate matters further, the non-juroring bishops, realising they were elderly men, began to consecrate their own bishops, creating another tranche of bishops and reviving dioceses that had fallen out of use such as Thetford. The split with the mainstream Church of England was complete.

Although the first two non-juroring bishops had nominal dioceses, those consecrated later had no diocese attached to them. The non-juroring congregations met in private houses where they created oratories. Holborn in London was one non-juroring centre, Manchester and Newcastle others. In April 1717, 20 male non-jurors were listed as belonging to the oratory in the Newcastle Iron market, and this oratory was to survive until 1784.[12]

The non-juroring clergy provided a focus for the Protestant Jacobites in England, but the non-juroring church's strength was to be weakened by an argument over the liturgy, 'the usages controversy' which split the church in two. What the non-jurors wanted was a return to a way of worship that existed before the Roman church came into existence. To achieve this some non-jurors started to negotiate with the Eastern Orthodox Church. Coupled with the highly intellectual debate over the usages, this did nothing to attract the ordinary churchgoer to the cause.

The non-juroring clerics themselves came from every diocese in England. Using a compilation taken from different lists, Overton arrived at the number of 360 ordinary clerics who lost their livings, and 101 Oxford and Cambridge fellows who refused to take the oath. Loss of livelihood meant severe hardship for some of these men, and a fund was set up to relief their suffering. Management of this was in the hands of the deprived bishops, who added the proviso that clerics relieved from it were not to be seen in coffee houses if they came to London.[13] The favourite coffee house of the non-jurors was the Essex Coffee House in the Strand, and many stormy meetings over the usages controversy took place here.[14]

The largest number of clerics came from the Norwich diocese, and the largest number of non-juroring fellows from St John's College, Cambridge. But it was a fellow of Peterhouse, John Talbot, who when he was ejected went as a non-juroring missionary to America, visiting New Jersey and Pennsylvania and setting up a non-juroring church in 1703. He was to become the bishop of the American church, and there is a record of his work and a monument in the Old Church at Burlington.[15] The lists show that at least 15 per cent of the clerics were pluralists with more than one living. Other features in common which emerge by linking the lists with other records are that many of them had at one time or another been chaplains in the household of the royal family or a nobleman's household, and many of them were antiquarians, collecting books and artefacts, while George Hicks, the first non-juroring bishop, was a noted Anglo-Saxon scholar.

These were scholarly men, unfitted for physical combat. Despite this, the conspirators in the 1695–96 assassination plot planned to raise a troop of non-juroring parsons to fight for James, commanded by the sinister-sounding Colonel Slaughter. In the event the role of the non-juroring clerics was to accompany those convicted of treason on their last journey to the gallows, to help them write their last speeches, and to absolve them of sin.

On 19 April 1696 both John Evelyn the Tory and Narcissus Luttrell the Whig recorded in their diaries that great offence had been taken at the ministers who absolved Sir John Friend and Sir William Parkin at Tyburn. Luttrell added that warrants were out for the clerics, Shadrach Cook, Jeremy Collier and William Snatt. Snatt was the son of Evelyn's tutor. Cook and Snatt were arrested immediately. Collier 'kept out of the way'.[16]

In August 1701 James II died. In Paris, his infant son, James Francis, was proclaimed James III, King of England. William's government produced another oath of allegiance that required clerics and office holders to abjure James III. This produced a second generation of non-jurors, while the oath demanded by George I on his accession in 1714 produced a third. By this time there were non-juroring clergy who had never been in the Church of England, but had been ordained straight into the non-juroring congregation. One of these was Thomas Deacon, a physician and pastor in Manchester. Deacon's sons show that the next generation were not prepared to accept passive resistance, but wanted action. Three of them were to enlist in the rebel army in 1745. One died in prison, one was transported and died soon after arriving in the West Indies, a third was executed for high treason. They fulfilled the self-image of martyrdom for the cause that had informed the principles of the original non-jurors.

The oratory of which Deacon was pastor survived until 1804. Aston's *Guide to Manchester* records that it still had a congregation of 30 souls at that date, in the care of Mr Booth in Long Millgate.[17] Although small in number, and in terminal decline by the 19th century, one of the lasting legacies of the non-jurors and their insistence on a liturgy that looked beyond the Roman church to the beginnings of Christian worship was their influence on the Oxford Anglo-Catholic movement of the 19th century.

Lay non-jurors

Historians have tended to concentrate their attention on clerical non-jurors, partly because lay non-jurors are more difficult to trace. The laity only had to take the oath if they held a government post or taught in school, and on the whole the authorities were less interested in them. Many of those involved in plots and conspiracies would have been non-jurors, but this cannot be proved.

Some lay non-jurors have been traced. Francis Cherry (1665–1713) of Shottesbrooke Park in Berkshire made his home into a haven for non-juroring clergy. He was a country gentleman and sportsman, who also collected manuscripts, coins and antiquities. He believed in passive resistance and refused to become involved in any of the late 17th-century plots against William III.[18] Another country gentleman who was a non-juror was the poet Elijah Fenton (1683–1730), from a Staffordshire county family. The lawyer Roger North (1653–1734), who had been James II's attorney-general, refused to take the oath but also refused to become involved in any plotting. He retired to his estates at Rougham, Norfolk and worked on improving these.[19]

There were a number of non-juroring gentry in Norfolk. Notable among these was the L'Estrange family of Hunstanton, including Sir Nicholas who was banned as a justice of the peace when he refused to take the oath in 1696, and Roger who was arrested in Ireland and had connections with the 1690 Preston plot. Their cousin Sir Christopher Calthorpe of East Baston, Norfolk was also arrested in 1690, but released. In that year he wrote that the oath he had taken to King James obliged him not to oppose him by force or prevent him from reigning as king. If he swore an oath to another sovereign while James was still alive he would commit the sin of perjury. He was fined £5 at the assizes for refusing to take the oath. He maintained a non-juroring cleric, Thomas White, as his chaplain.[20]

Norwich and Norfolk were to remain riddled with Jacobite cells until 1745. Another centre of non-jurors and Jacobite resistance was Lancashire, and it is in Lancashire that the next conspiracy unfolded.

The Lancashire plot

Lancashire had long been recognised by the government as a hotbed of Catholics, who accepted fines and persecution in order to worship as they wished. They were part of a county network, united by kinship, faith and marriage, and a natural place for a Jacobite cell to emerge. In 1694 a group of Lancashire gentry was arrested, accused of treason, tried and acquitted. The evidence against them was discounted, and the witnesses for the prosecution tried for perjury. The Lancashire plot was deemed to be a sham, and for 63 years its existence was denied, until a remarkable discovery led to the truth.

Disentangling truth from lies, identifying double agents and informers is one of the hazards of deconstructing a Jacobite conspiracy. What emerges is often a dark and confusing tale. However, it is one that shows that any attempt to restore James to the throne would not be a spontaneous uprising, but an orchestrated military operation. James sent officers' commissions to his supporters in the gentry and nobility, which empowered them to raise a secret army. In the eyes of the Jacobites this legalised proceedings, and made any attempt to put James back on the throne a legitimate act of war.

In 1694 when the Lancashire plot was uncovered, William was engaged in a war against France in Flanders. A rising in Lancashire would mean that he would be fighting a war on two fronts. A diversion in the north would give the French a chance to defeat him on the continent, and follow this by an invasion of England to place James back on the throne. Two birds would be killed with one stone. France would win the war, and James would retrieve his crown.

The plot came to light in 1694, but to find its origins we must return to the night of 13 June 1689 when a small ship, the *Lion of Lancaster*, came from Ireland and lay off the Lancashire coast at Cockerham, at the mouth of the river Lune. On board was a cargo of iron pots, barrels of beef and two anxious passengers, John Lunt and Edmund Threlfall. A little before sunrise, and before the customs-house boat came, the passengers were rowed ashore. Henry Knowles, one of the seamen who took them, said that as they neared the shore Lunt remembered he had left a bag on the ship. He asked Knowles to land him and Threlfall, and go back for the bag. Before Knowles could fetch the bag the customs officers arrived and searched the ship. In the hold they found Lunt's bag, and in it blank officers' commissions signed by James, declarations by James to his people, and other incriminating papers.[21] Had Lunt left these behind on purpose?

Lunt, whom Knowles described as 'low of stature, and wearing his own hair', is one of the key figures in the Lancashire plot. Threlfall was a Lancashire Catholic from Goosnargh. Having evaded the customs they made their way to Mr Tyldesley's of the Lodge at Myerscough, where the commissions were divided. Lunt took his into Lancashire, Cheshire and Staffordshire, Threlfall went to Yorkshire. Having distributed all his papers, Lunt then made his way to London to buy arms for the Lancashire Catholics, and to enlist men for James. On his way back to Lancashire in August 1689 the government spies caught up with him at Coventry and threw him into prison, where he was identified by the son of the ship's captain as one of the men who came from Ireland with commissions.[22] It is possible that in order to gain his release Lunt agreed to become a double agent.

Rumours of a rising in Lancashire began to circulate. John Kelly told the mayor of Evesham that 500 Irish soldiers were hidden in that county, ready to rise with the Catholic gentry.[23] Kelly was described as a wanderer and his evidence was discounted, but a more reliable witness came forward to testify to a rising: Robert Dodsworth of Ravensworth in Westmorland, a Catholic gentleman. He said on oath that there was a treasonable conspiracy in his neighbourhood, and that commissions had been received from James, brought over by Edmund Threlfall. At the same time as Lancashire rose the French would invade Cornwall, and the Duke of Berwick would create a diversion in Scotland. James himself was to land in Lancashire from Ireland. Dodsworth's motive in making these accusations may have been his lack of success in getting a commission for himself, but the government gave him a reward, and he obligingly provided a list of names for them.

Dodsworth's List

Regiments under Colonel Thomas Tyldesley of Fox Hall, Myerscough	
Lieutenant-Colonel John Girlington	Protestant
Captain Thomas Tyldesley of Fox Hall	Catholic
Captain Ralph Tyldesley	Catholic
Captains Henry and Richard Butler of Rawcliffe, Yorks.	Catholic, but related by marriage to Girlington
Captain Alexander Butler	Protestant
Captain Thomas Carus of Halton	Catholic related to the Butlers by marriage
Lieut. William Westby	Catholic
Mr Goodwin	a Catholic priest
Lieut. George Carus of Halton	Catholic
Lieut. Thomas Butler	
Cornet Knipe	Protestant but related to Carus
Cornet Coale	
Under Colonel Townley of Townley	Catholic
Lieut.-Colonel Standish, Standish Hall	Catholic
Captain Brierley	Catholic
Captain Barlow	Catholic
Cornet Woodfall of Aughton	Catholic
Quartermaster Ducket	Catholic
Under Colonel Molyneux of Sefton	Catholic
Lieut-Colonel Gerard	Catholic
Captain Westby	Catholic
Captain Harrington Aigburth	Catholic
Captain Molyneux	Catholic
Captain Penny	Catholic
Captain Carus	Catholic
Lieut. Stanley	Catholic
Lieut. Penalt Welsh	Catholic
Cornet Carus	Catholic

In Yorkshire
Colonel Tempest of Broughton   Catholic
Colonel Dalton[24]

At the time nobody believed Dodsworth. Even after the Lancashire plotters had been arrested Edward Finch wrote to Roger Kenyon referring to the 'sham plot being built upon by Dodsworth'.[25] But there is evidence that Dodsworth's information was correct. On 5 November 1693, Dodsworth, who had moved to London to be under the protection of Parliament, 'came reeling into an alehouse in Bloomsbury, and immediately died, having 2 fresh bleeding wounds in his body'.[26] Mrs Dodsworth believed that the Jacobites had revenged themselves on her husband with a knife in the dark, and she applied to the government for compensation.[27]

This would appear to show that the Lancashire plot was not a sham. However, Paul Hopkins has argued that the accusations against the Lancashire gentry were part of an elaborate conceit to acquire lands that were in the hands of the Catholic church. Witnesses who could prove that these lands had been conveyed to the Catholic church received a percentage of the income from the lands. Some of the most important witnesses against the Lancashire plotters were engaged in perjuring themselves to the Superstitious Lands Commission. John Lunt and his brother-in-law Mr Taaffe, who both gave evidence against the Lancashire plotters, were paid witnesses for the Superstitious Lands Commission.[28] Dodsworth may also have been trying to cash in on this.

The next stage of the conspiracy comes in 1692 when Colonel John Parker slipped across the channel from France. Parker was one of James's most important agents, an ex-army officer who had been wounded at the Battle of the Boyne. He was described as 'below middle stature, with a long face and sharp chin and a complexion blemished by small-pox'.[29] Parker was arrested on landing, but escaped and made his way to Lancashire. The plot was gradually changing focus. It was no longer a diversionary episode in a European war but was instead to concentrate on ridding England of William III by murdering him.[30] This was to be accompanied by a French invasion, and the French fleet was gathering in readiness.

The destruction of the invasion fleet at La Hogue by the English stopped the plot in its tracks, and the conspiracy lay dormant until 1693 when the Lancashire gentry sent an envoy to James at St Germains to discuss what they should do next. The envoy was none other than the ubiquitous John Lunt. The plans they discussed once more hinged on the assassination of William, and a French invasion. Lunt returned to England to put things into motion with Walter Crosby. Crosby was arrested in May 1694 carrying plans for the invasion and a list of Cheshire gentry allegedly favourable to James.[31] Perhaps this made up Lunt's mind that he could not be party to treason, or perhaps he was already in touch with William's ministers. On 15 June 1694 he disclosed the details of the Lancashire plot to Sir John Trenchard, secretary of state. He named the ringleaders of the plot as Lord Caryll Molyneux, Sir William Gerard, Sir Rowland Stanley, Sir Thomas Clifton, William Dicconson, Philip Langton, Bartholomew Walmsley, William Blundell and William Standish. Lunt also produced other witnesses who could testify to the plot: George Wilson, who confirmed he had seen James's commissions and had been present at the conspirators' meetings, and John Wombell, a bankrupt carrier who had delivered the arms that Lunt purchased in London to addresses in Lancashire.[32]

Ironically, the first 'conspirator' to be arrested was not on Lunt's list, and neither was he a Catholic. Early on the morning of 19 July 1694, Mr Clarke the King's messenger, John Lunt and 14 Dutch troopers rode to Lyme Park in Cheshire to search the house and to arrest its owner, Peter Legh. Of all the conspirators Peter Legh is thought to be the most innocent. Hopkins suggests that he was included in the arrests because Lunt wanted to get his hands on Legh's estate. Legh was acquitted of the charge of treason and released. But was he innocent? Other sources show that he was intimately connected with the other conspirators, visiting their houses and dining with them. Although his main residence was at Lyme Park he had extensive property in Lancashire, and considerable political influence in that county.[33]

One by one, those named by Lunt were arrested and taken to London to be lodged in the Tower of London. Eventually, they were returned north to be tried at Manchester. Holes soon appeared in Lunt's evidence. He was unable to identify the individual members of the conspirators, and the defence produced evidence that he was a man not to be trusted, known as a highway robber, confidence trickster and bigamist. It was shown that he could not have been where he claimed he was at the time. The other witnesses too were shown to be false. John Taaffe changed sides during the trial, claiming he had been bribed to testify against the accused. The jury acquitted all the conspirators; Lunt, Wilson and Wombell were charged with perjury.[34]

In Lancashire there was rejoicing when the conspirators were acquitted.

> May the Lancashire hornpipe their countrymen's praises
> Sound forth, and their fame which their honesty raises
> Their abhorrence of State (which false witnesses foster)
> Of Kensington tyrants and Lambeth imposters
> For if they had not
> Disgraced the sham plot
> Many innocent Englishmen would had gone to pot
> Then under oppression, good men to support all
> Whoever gets the crown, be the juries immortal[35]

The Lancashire plot was clearly a sham, as its contemporaries claimed. There the matter might have rested, but in 1757 the Old Coppice Wall at Standish Hall was taken down. Here a bundle of papers was found consisting of 35 letters dated 1692, and blank officers' commissions signed by James II. Here was the evidence that the Lancashire plot was real.[36]

The letters revealed the central part that Colonel Parker played in the plot. Five of the letters from James II were addressed to him, and yet he was not mentioned in the Manchester trial, although Lunt had given the government his name.[37] Lunt, Wilson and Wombell were vindicated by the letters. These showed that arms had been ordered and delivered from London in exactly the way that Wombell had described. For example, Letter 13 is the account of the boxes and porterage of the arms. Paper 11 is an account of those who were to be invited to use them, and it includes Peter Legh of Lyme. Paper 16 is a declaration of loyalty to James signed by those who were arrested.[38]

Some of the documents are in a code, one that is slightly more sophisticated than the Jacobites' early attempts at cipher. It is based on the exchange of letters: two lots of the 26 letters of the alphabet were put on cards and shuffled with letters drawn out from each pile. The pairs made up the code, which then had to be communicated to the receiver. Others of the Standish papers are written in invisible writing, in lemon juice that became visible when warmed. The Standish letters also include ciphers in which whole words have a different meaning:

long cut tobacco = military equipment
estate = kingdom
skins = military recruits
goods in the market = acquisition of arms[39]

The secret army gathering in Lancashire had been surprised by the arrests, and the letters hidden in the wall. The conspirators were lucky that they were not found when Standish Hall was searched, and they lived to plot for another day. Letter 15 is from James to the conspirators, expressing his gratitude:

His majesty approves of what col. Parker brigadier of his army has done in forming of those regiments of horse and dragoon. His Majesty returns his most hearty thanks to all his loyal subjects and to the gentlemen concerned, and desires them to continue in the same disposition and readiness for service.[40]

Many of them would continue, and would come out of the shadows to join the 1715 Rebellion.

One of the aims of the Lancashire plotters was the assassination of William. According to Richard Kingston, a Williamite court scribe, this was to remain uppermost in the minds of Jacobite plotters, and the Lancashire plot was to become a model for others, although the scene was to shift to the south of England.

The assassination plot of 1696

In the two years between the Lancashire plot and the assassination plot the English Jacobites' activities were much more open, revolving around riots centred on Stuart anniversaries. The birthday of the pretended Prince of Wales, 10 June, was a popular Stuart anniversary. On 11 June 1695 Narcissus Luttrell recorded an account of a Jacobite riot that took place at the Dog Tavern in Drury Lane.

Yesterday being the birthday of the Pretended Prince of Wales several Jacobites met in several places, and in particular at the Dog Tavern in Drury Lane, where with kettle drums, trumpets etc., they caroused, and having a bonfire built forced spectators to drink the prince's health, but they refused, which occasioned a tumult upon which the mob entered the tavern and did much damage and put the Jacobites to flight. Some are taken George Porter, Mr Goodman the player, Captain Reginald Chivery, Sir John Fenwick and Mr Roe.[41]

Luttrell noted that the Jacobites were in the taverns again on 14 October to celebrate James II's birthday, but by this time darker designs were afoot, although as in so many Jacobite conspiracies an element of farce creeps in before tragedy takes over. There was not one, but two rival assassination plots planned in 1695–96. The first was discovered on 29 October 1695, thanks to an informer, Chapman of the Southwark Club, who came forward and offered to tell the government about a plan to shoot William as he passed through Southwark on his way back from Flanders.[42] The other plot was better organised, involved more people, and came closer to success. It was managed from France by Sir George Barclay, who was given a commission by James on 27 December 1695.[43] Did this mean that James II was aware of the proposed murder of his rival? It is possible that James was not aware of the nuances of Barclay's plot as the commission creates him brigadier of the first troop of guards, and James may have thought that he sent him to England to raise troops, and that the scheme to assassinate William was dreamt up by Barclay when he realised that troops would not be forthcoming.

Even had they succeeded in assassinating William, there was no guarantee that James would be invited back to take over the throne. The Protestant heir, Princess Anne, was close at hand and would have been proclaimed queen by the Whigs directly William's death became known.

Whatever Barclay's instructions were, he and a companion, Major Holmes crossed secretly to England the evening after he received the commission. Those commuting between England and France used smugglers to transport them. The war with France had created an embargo in England of the export of wool to France, and the import of French wine and brandy to England; the result was a lucrative trade in smuggling these goods to and from secluded ports on the south coast. The Jacobites made use of an operation run by James Hunt, a farmer on Romney Marsh, and a ruffianly boatman Captain Gill, whose boat was a French privateer.[44]

From the coast to London there existed a series of safe houses where the Jacobites could stay, before emerging into the open to take the coach for London from Rochester. Barclay and Holmes were followed into England by 16 to 18 other officers, leaving France in pairs, and making their way to London. They included Piggot, 'a squint-eyed man', Noseworthy, an 'ancient gentleman', and accompanying them was Colonel Parker's wife.[45] Once in London they had to make contact with other conspirators by going to Covent Garden on a Monday or Thursday evening where Sir George Barclay would be waiting in the shadows of the Piazza, with a white handkerchief dangling from his top pocket so they could recognise him.[46]

The conspirators in London were a mixed bunch. They included Caryll Goodman, the ex-actor involved in the Dog Tavern riot, who was the gigolo of the Duchess of Cleveland, the Oxford don Robert Charnock, ex-officers, tradesmen and gentry. Attempts to engage the Earl of Ailesbury and other peers failed when they saw the rashness of the conspirators and their total lack of discretion. The conspirators did succeed in recruiting two elderly knights, Sir William Parkin (1649–96) and Sir John Friend (?–1696). Unlike the Lancashire plotters, they were not Catholics nor were they members of ancient landed families. Parkin was the son of a London merchant who had purchased an estate in Warwickshire. Although he was a Protestant, he had Catholic kin. Friend was a London brewer from Hackney who had been knighted by James II in 1685 and made a colonel of the Artillery Company. He had been very upset by losing the commission in 1689, and his involvement with the assassination plot was probably the result of his pique. His date of birth is not known, but the trial records suggest that he was elderly, hard of hearing and confused. Evidence against Parkin was given by his nephew, Matthew Smith, who demonstrated Parkin's complete involvement with the plot.[47] Friend's involvement is more problematical. He claimed at the trial that he knew nothing about the plot, asserting that 'I am as innocent as the child unborn'.[48] He was probably excluded from the conspirators' meetings because he was 'a great bottle man'.[49]

The main objective of the conspirators was to murder William. This was to be followed by a French invasion, co-ordinated by Barclay, and James's natural son the Duke of Berwick. At first, the conspirators could not decide whether to kill or kidnap William and to shoot him later, claiming he had attempted to escape. Eventually, they decided this plan had too many practical problems, and decided on assassination. But how to do this, where and when? Suggestions included shooting him as he drove through Hyde Park on his way to church at St James. The conspirators would take the gate-keeper of the park prisoner, and once William's coach was through would close the gates and prevent his guard from entering the park. Another plan involved climbing into Kensington Palace by a ladder and overpowering William while he was in bed.

The plan decided upon was based on observation of William's routine. Every Saturday morning he left Kensington Palace in a great coach drawn by six horses to go hunting in Richmond Park. He returned at dusk six hours later. On the way out he was accompanied by the court but they made their own way back to London, leaving William more vulnerable. He was especially vulnerable when the coach, with him inside, was loaded onto the Turnham Green ferry, crossed the Thames and entered a narrow lane leading up from the river. This was the ideal place for an ambush.

The ground was reconnoitred and the final plans made. Forty armed men would take up positions around Turnham Green. Two parties of eight led by George Parker and Robert Charnock would attack the coach from both sides, while a further eight men would make a frontal attack and kill the coach horses and the coachmen. As soon as the king was dead they would ride back to London as fast as they could, send word to France that the affair was concluded, and the invasion could start.

Two observers were posted outside Kensington Palace to send word to Barclay that the advance party of the king's field kitchen had set out; Barclay was to send runners to round up the rest of his men, who had swift horses hidden in various livery stables across London. The date set for the assassination was 15 February. On that morning the field kitchen set out as usual. Barclay was alerted and his runners sent out. Suddenly, the field kitchen returned at full gallop and entered the palace gates which were locked shut behind it. William did not go hunting that day.

This should have alerted the conspirators that William had suspicion that something was wrong, but these were men who did not know the meaning of caution. The assassination would take place on the following Saturday. Once more the observers were posted at Kensington Palace. Once again the field kitchen set out, and once again Barclay sent out his runners, and once again the field kitchen came trundling back. William's coach was returned to the stables, and the palace guard doubled. The conspirators panicked. Barclay and Major Holmes, who had prudently arranged for a boat to be waiting for them off Romney Marsh, left for the continent. The rest had to fend for themselves.

The conspirators had been betrayed. It is not clear who was the first to inform against them, or whether the informer was a double agent. It is clear that William knew of the plot before 22 February and was in full possession of the details when he announced his miraculous delivery to Parliament on 24 February. Both John Evelyn and Narcissus Luttrell wrote about it in their diaries on 25 February, when it had become common knowledge. Luttrell noted that 20 people had already been arrested and that proclamations were out for the apprehension of many more.[50] The comprehensive list of names of those wanted for the conspiracy points to the informer being someone close to the heart of the plot. The main suspicion falls on Richard Fisher of Dartmouth Street, Westminster as being one of the first to inform. His was the first deposition against the conspirators to be taken. He told the Earl of Portland about the plot before 14 February. He was followed by Richard Prendergrasse who went straight to the king on 14 February and later, on 21 February, gave the king a list of those involved. George Porter corroborated their information.[51]

Those arrested in the first round included Robert Charnock, Sir John Friend and Sir William Parkin. All three were found guilty and executed. The person that the government really wanted to get their hands on was Sir John Fenwick, but he did not figure amongst the main conspirators. However, he had been in and out of prison on the suspicion of treason several times since 1689. When the assassination plot was discovered he immediately went into hiding. This suggests that he was guilty, but on the other hand he was described by those who knew him as 'a fearful man'. Fenwick managed to stay free until June 1696 when by a strange coincidence he was recognised by one of the king's messengers who was taking prisoners from Romney Marsh to London. Fenwick, who was in disguise wearing a black periwig and dyed eyebrows, was in the company of a Jacobite lawyer, Mr Webster. Both were well armed and managed to get away. But the messenger summoned help and they were arrested in their beds at New Romney the next morning.[52]

The person who had implicated Fenwick in the conspiracy was Peter Cook. He gave an account of meetings at Leadenhall Street where the details of the French invasion had been discussed with Fenwick present. Cook also gave other names as well: the Earl of Ailesbury, the Lords Montgomery, Russell and Brudenell. They were all arrested and sent to the Tower. In fact Cook would have agreed to anything his questioners wanted in order to save his own neck. He said that he was at a meeting in a tavern in Holborn with Lord Brudenell, Sir Theophilus Oglethorpe and others when they had discussed their part in the plot. He knew Sir John Friend would raise a regiment near the Tower, and Sir John Clarges would recruit MPs to the cause. Cook's efforts paid off. He was sentenced to banishment rather than executed.

Once arrested, Fenwick protested his innocence vehemently. He agreed he had spoken to George Porter, but not about the assassination plot or invasion plans. He pleaded for his trial to be postponed, promising to reveal more details of the plot that he had originally claimed he knew nothing about. He sent the Duke of Devonshire sheets of narrative which named the Duke of Shrewsbury, one of William's loyal ministers, as one of the conspirators, as well as Earl Godolphin, the Duke of Marlborough and Admiral Russell. Godolphin and Marlborough might have been tempted to join the Jacobites but Shrewsbury and Russell were loyal. Shrewsbury wrote to William expressing sorrow and surprise about the accusations, resigned and retired to the country.[53]

Still Fenwick tried to delay proceedings. He went before Parliament and asked to speak to the king personally. Parliament agreed and he was sent to see William, where he offered to withdraw his former accusations but reveal other matters – anything to buy time. Even after he was convicted he managed to delay his execution until January 1697. When it was too late to do anything to save himself he died proclaiming his loyalty to James. He was buried in St Martin in the Fields, and there is a monument to him in York Minster, where his wife is buried. Legend says that the horse Sorrel that stumbled and threw William, eventually causing his death, had once belonged to Fenwick.

Over 300 people were arrested in connection with the assassination plot. Some escaped, for example William Berkenhead, aka Fish, South, East and West, who bribed the Newgate gaolers to let him out, and made his way through safe houses to the collecting point on Romney Marsh where he arrived on 26 October 1696. Here things took an unexpected turn. Hunt, the farmer who had been arranging secret passages for the Jacobites, was suspected of betraying them. On 26 October a party of 20 armed men from a French vessel broke into Hunt's house and carried him and Berkenhead off to France, where they were both imprisoned. They were soon joined in prison by the actor Caryll Goodman who was also suspected of testifying against the plot.[54]

By the end of 1697 most of the conspirators in England had been released from prison. The result of the assassination plot was the reverse of what had been intended. Instead of ridding England of William, popular support for him rose, and it was claimed that divine providence had protected him.[55] The Treaty of Ryswyk in 1697, which made peace between England and France, was a further blow to Jacobite hopes. Morale was low in the secret army. English Jacobites went underground and covered their tracks with coded messages and information fed to them by James's agents from France. As both James II's and William's lives drew to a close the Stuart restoration looked as far away as ever.

Notes

1 E. Cruickshanks, *Ideology and Conspiracy*, Edinburgh: John Donald Ltd, 1982, 3.

2 E.S. De Beer ed., *The Diary of John Evelyn*, Oxford: OUP, 1959, 895–6 (henceforth *Evelyn Diary*).

3 *Evelyn Diary*, 900, 903, 906.

4 W.J. Cameron ed., *Poems on Affairs of State*, Vol. 5, 1688–97, New Haven: Yale University Press, 1971, 277–80.

5 *Evelyn Diary*, 909.

6 M. Goldie, 'The Nonjurors, Episcopacy and the Origins of the Convocation Controversy', in E. Cruickshanks, *Ideology and Conspiracy*, 15.

7 T.B. Howell ed., *A Complete Collection of State Trials*, Vol. XII, AD1687–1697, London: Longman Hurst, 1812, 701.

8 *Evelyn Diary*, 909.

9 W.J. Hardy ed., *Calendar of State Papers Domestic, William and Mary, 1690–October 1691*, London: HMSO, 1898, 219, 224, 228–9, 246, 248.

10 J. Overton, *The Nonjurors*, London: Smith, Elder & Co., 1902, 54–5; *Evelyn Diary*, 1025.

11 *Evelyn Diary*, 940–41.

12 PRO, SP 8/118(2), *List of nonjurors in Newcastle, 1717*; R. Sharp, '100 years of a lost cause: Nonjuroring principles in Newcastle from the Revolution to the death of Prince Charles', *Archaeologia Aeliana*, 5th ser., Vol. III, 1980, 38–55.

13 T. Lathbury, *A History of the Non-Jurors*, London: William Pickering, 1845, 17, 52.

14 H. Broxap, *The Later Non-Jurors*, Cambridge: CUP, 1924, 44–6.

15 Broxap, 89–91.

16 *Evelyn Diary*, 1005; N. Luttrell, *A Brief Historical Relation of State Affairs 1678–1714*, Oxford: OUP, Vol. III, 1857, 34, 44; Howell, *State Trials*, XIII, 1812, 406–8.

17 Broxap, 284.

18 Overton, 238.

19 Overton, 270–71.

20 D. Cherry, 'Sir Nicholas L'Estrange, non-juror', *Norfolk Archaeology* 1968, XXVI, 314–15; *Calendar State Papers Domestic*, 1690–91, 291; G.M. Yould, 'Two nonjurors', *Norfolk Archaeology*, 1972, XXXV, 364–81.

21 W. Beamont, ed., *The Jacobite Trials in Manchester*, Manchester: Chetham Society, 28, 1853, vii–x.

22 Beamont, xvi.

23 Beamont, xiii–xix.

24 Beamont, xxv; E. Estcourt ed., *The English Catholic Non-Jurors of 1715: a register of their estates*, London: Burns and Oates, 1886, 89–154.

25 HMC, *The Manuscripts of Lord Kenyon*, London: HMSO, 1894, 371.

26 Luttrell IV, 224.

27 *Calendar of State Papers Domestic*, 1690–91, 321.

28 P.A. Hopkins, 'The Commission for Superstitious Lands', *Recusant History*, 15, 4, 265–82.

29 *Calendar of State Papers Domestic*, 1694, 262.

30 Beamont, xviii.

31 Beamont, xxxii.

32 Beamont, 27–35.

33 See for example J. Gillow and A. Hewitson eds, *The Tyldesley Diary, 1712–14*, Preston: A. Hewitson, 1873, 35–6.

34 A. Goss ed., *An Account of the Trials at Manchester*, Chetham Society, 61, 1864, 22–7.

35 Cameron/Powers 240.

36 The letters are now in the Wigan Public Library, but they are all transcribed in T.C. Porteous, 'New light on the Lancashire Jacobite Plot, 1692–4', *Lancashire and Cheshire Antiquarian Society Transactions*, 4, 1934–5, 2–62.

37 Porteous, 17.

38 Porteous, 54.

39 Porteous, 4–6.

40 Porteous, 45.

41 Luttrell III, 483–4.

42 Luttrell III, 538, 543, 550.

43 *Stuart Papers* I, 110.

44 Howell XII, 1336–41.

45 Howell XII, 1338–9.

46 Howell XII, 1323–36.

47 M. Smith, *Memoirs of the Secret Service*, London: 1699.

48 M. Howell, *State Trials*, London: 1812, Vol. III, 1.

49 Ailesbury, Earl of, *Memoirs*, London: Roxburgh Club, 1849, Vol. I, 353–4.

50 *Evelyn Diary*, 1003; Luttrell IV, 18–21.

51 Howell XII, 1290–1424.

52 Luttrell IV, 69–71.

53 *Calendar of State Papers Domestic*, 1696, 233–495.

54 Luttrell IV, 104, 123, 135.

55 C. Rose, *England in the 1690s*, Oxford: Blackwell, 1999, 52.

CHAPTER 3

· · · · · · · · · · · · · ·

Spies, ciphers and riots
1702–14

By 1702 the first protagonists of the Jacobite struggle were dead. James II died on 5 September 1701, William III on 8 March 1702. William was succeeded by his sister-in-law Anne, while in France her half-brother was proclaimed as James III, king of England.

Anne, a natural conservative, favoured the Tories over the Whigs and gave them government offices. This helped to defuse the political wing of the English Jacobites. James, whose real parentage was suspect due to rumours that he had been introduced into his mother's bed from outside, via a warming pan, was a sickly boy. He had been brought up as a strict Catholic. Every moment of his day was regulated, and his rightful claim to the British throne firmly implanted in his mind.[1] His father's court had been divided between 'non-compounders' who wanted the restoration of the Stuarts as absolute monarchs, and 'compounders' who advocated a conditional restoration as a constitutional monarchy. James II himself was a compounder.

In an attempt to reassure the English Protestants that if restored James would uphold the Church of England, James's secretary of state, the Catholic Earl of Melfort, was replaced by the Protestant Earl of Middleton. Unfortunately Middleton took to heart the dying James II's assertion that Catholicism was the only true religion, and converted in August 1702.

A little after the Treaty of Ryswyk was signed in 1697, the King of France had suggested to William III that he should name James II's son as his heir to the English throne. William indicated that he would consider this, provided the boy was brought up as a Protestant. James II would not agree to this. The Duke of Berwick, James II's natural son, thought that this 'was a great imprudence to have refused'.[2] It was probably the best chance of a peaceful solution to the Stuart restoration.

The Stuarts' religion was one stumbling block to their restoration. Another was the influence of the Scots and Irish who crammed the court in exile. The English saw this and surmised that it would be the Scots and Irish who would get the best rewards if James was restored, and not his English supporters who had stayed at home. Melfort was aware of this, and had told James that the different groups must be kept apart and managed separately, while the double agent James Semple described the behaviour of the English and Scots towards each other at James's court as 'dogs and cats'.[3] However, Sir Charles Petrie suggests that even at an early stage the English Jacobites were ineffective, depending more on sentiment than action, while the Scots and Irish were active because they nurtured grievances against England that they thought James could redress.[4]

It was in Scotland that the first overtures for rebellion came at the start of the new reign. Scotland was reeling after the failure of the Darien Venture. In 1698 the New East India Company, sponsored by the Company of Scotland, had set up a colony on the Panamanian isthmus. It had to be evacuated in 1700 amidst much bitterness from Scotland, which thought that England had sabotaged the venture. Added to this were four years of failed harvest in Scotland, leading to starvation and massive emigration. By 1703 Scotland was seething with indignation against England, and saw the return of the Stuarts as providing a saving grace.

The impetus behind the new scheme to restore the Stuarts was Simon Fraser, calling himself Lord Lovat, who arrived in France offering to supply 12,000 Scots in arms if France would supply a further 5000. The new king, James III, was delighted with this offer, but his ministers and the French were less sure of Lovat's credentials. Nevertheless, Lovat was sent back to Scotland with John Murray as a chaperone. They carried blank officer commissions, and a paper from James promising to restore all the ancient privileges of Scotland.

Lovat's activities can be traced through the papers of Lieutenant Colonel Macpherson, who based his account on that left by the Jacobite Thomas Carte. Instead of going to Scotland, Lovat went to London and then travelled to Durham where he called an assembly of all good Catholics.

Here a Catholic Irish nobleman promised that the French would send 50,000 armed men. From Durham, Lovat went on to Scotland. The Durham part of Lovat's narrative was false, but he did make contact with the Duke of Queensbury in Edinburgh and other Scottish nobles, and began to set a plot in motion. Then he betrayed it, and fled back to France.[5]

Lovat was playing an intricate game of revenge, intended to implicate his political rivals the Duke of Queensbury, and the Marquess of Atholl who had accused Lovat of raping his sister. Although there were only a few arrests, and no evidence to convict those arrested, it was a lesson to the Jacobites to be wary about those they trusted.

Spies and ciphers

This lack of trust led to an underground movement of spies, counter-agents and coded messages, used by the Jacobites and infiltrated with ease by the British government. The English Jacobite organisation was centred round agents sent across from France, who enlisted others to the cause. The preferred recruits were army officers who could enlist men from their regiments to form a ready-made Jacobite army, and supply information about troop movements.

The agents running the cells tended to be Irish or Scottish. This led to national rivalries between cells, while religious differences led to dis-agreements within cells – a situation that was not conducive for absolute discretion. Money to fund operatives and bribe influential officials was sent from France. Letters in code were sent from England via Rotterdam and forwarded to France by Jacobite merchants. This meant that the correspondence between agent and centre often took a long time and the two sides were out of step, with the agent not being aware of the political situation at the court in exile, and how this might affect planning on the other side of the channel.

Meanwhile the British government infiltrated the Jacobite network with counter-agents, even placing one of these at the Jacobite court. James Ogilvie, who turned up in France in 1710 claiming to have a list of English supporters ready to rise when James needed them, was an English agent planted at the court to spread misleading intelligence that the divisions between the high-church Tories and the low-church

Anglicans meant that many more were favourable to James than he had been led to believe.[6]

The chief Jacobite intelligence-gatherer in England was the French agent Abbé Gaultier. He conducted a two-way correspondence with James and de Torcy, the French minister of state. It was Gaultier's job to find out which English ministers of state might come over to James. In 1712 he wrote to de Torcy that Viscount Bolingbroke was a likely supporter, and in 1713 that the Earl of Oxford was another likely to come over. De Torcy was cynical about these professions of loyalty to James from English ministers, commenting that Bolingbroke always loved a mystery. But James took them at face value and began writing to Oxford in 1713, saying that Oxford's sentiments gave him hope.

Gaultier, on the ground in England, was far more aware of the nuances of English politics and the feelings of the English people than most of the members of the court in exile. On 6 February 1714 Gaultier wrote to James from London telling him it was absolutely necessary to change his religion, and then he would be restored through a lawful succession.[7]

Both the Earls of Melfort and Middleton were suspected of being in the pay of the British government, Melfort because he once put a letter intended for St Germains in the London bag by mistake, where it was intercepted by the government and Middleton because he had had the foresight to place his estates under strict settlement before leaving for France. This meant that he handed them over to trustees to hold for his lifetime so that on his death they would pass to his son as the next heir and life owner of the estate. In the meantime the trustees could pay Middleton the income from the estates, and an Act of Attainder on him would be useless since the estates were no longer his. The Earl of Ailesbury thought that Middleton was run from England by the Earl of Sunderland, and after Middleton's death Richard Rawlinson claimed that Middleton was a pensioner of the British government, and had betrayed all the Stuarts' secrets to them.[8] There is no evidence for this slur.

The problem of identifying Jacobite spies in London is compounded by informers naming people as spies in order to collect the rewards offered for this, or to get themselves out of trouble. For example in 1703 Redmond Joy claimed to have uncovered a nest of spies in Dublin and London, ex-army officers who met at Roehampton to discuss rebellion.

No evidence was found against them, and Joy was anxious to get out of prison at the time of his accusations.[9] However, there were known coffee houses and taverns in London where the Jacobites met to exchange news and correspondence. Those who gathered included George Porter, the grandson of the poet Endymion Porter, renowned for his aggression and gambling. He had once killed a man at a theatre by striking him with his cane. Lionel Walden Esquire of Huntingdon was another coffee house habitué. One of the favourite Jacobite coffee houses in London was Ozinda's, another was Bromfields in Westminster, whilst the Welsh Jacobites met at the Somerset Coffee House, and non-jurors at the Nag's Head. Irish Catholics were to be found at the Highland Man in Queen Street.

Other Jacobite supporters who used these coffee houses included William Fuller, a skinner's apprentice, who managed to get to France and become Mary of Modena's page. He carried letters between France and England rolled up in the buttons of his coat, but on one of his trips he was captured at the Jacobite Half Moon Tavern in Cheapside, and gave evidence against the Jacobites. Another colourful figure was George Flint. He had been a customs officer who had converted to Catholicism and attended the English College in Rome. Somehow he ended up in Newcastle in 1709, and moved to London in 1714. He proposed a scheme costing £1000 by which the Jacobites would seize the Tower of London, the Bank of England, the Treasury, the Royal Family and Whig Ministers. The plan was not taken up, but Flint was back in Newcastle in 1715 with plans for seizing the city for the Jacobites, later claiming that had he not been ill in bed his plans would have secured the 1715 rising for James. Arrested when the rising was suppressed he was sent to Newgate. He was the publisher of a Jacobite newspaper *Robin's Last Shift*, succeeded by *The Shift Shifted*. When he was in prison his wife took over printing the paper. He also produced pamphlets that became an embarrassment to the English Jacobites by drawing too much attention to them. He proposed another scheme whereby he would forge a letter in the hand of the secretary of state Josiah Burdett, and divert the Baltic Fleet from its station. He was told in no uncertain terms by the court in exile to cease his incriminating activities.[10]

Another agent arrested as a spy was Francis Francia, a Christianised Portuguese Jew. As an import/export merchant he was in a good position

Flint
N/castle

to send and receive correspondence, goods and people from the continent. He was arrested in 1717, but was found not guilty. Nevertheless, he felt it was safer to depart to France, where he told the exiled Jacobites that his club had collected £60,000 for the cause, which was deposited in a London bank. However, he refused to say who had given the money, which bank it was in and how the Jacobites could get their hands on it, unless they told him what they would be using it for. A stalemate followed and the money, if it existed, was not recovered.

The English Jacobite gentry preferred agents from among the officer class who could use a network of safe houses across the country, mingle with the family, and behave like gentlemen. But the officers were amateurs and did not understand the concept of secrecy; they were loud and aggressive, and quarrelled among themselves. At times they were impossibly naive. Take for example Colonel Cecil, described by William King as having 'very weak judgement and was very illiterate, and in many other respects was wholly unqualified for such a delicate commission. A man of honour who managed to betray his master.' Cecil was duped by Sir Robert Walpole, the prime minister, into believing that Walpole was a secret Jacobite who wanted to restore the house of Stuart. Accordingly, Cecil handed all his communications from France to Walpole, so that Walpole knew every Jacobite plot in advance. Eventually having got all the information he required, Walpole had Cecil arrested.[11] Later Walpole was to try the same gambit with the non-juror Thomas Carte, but failed. Carte, who had been carrying Jacobite letters backwards and forwards across the channel for years, was not fooled by Walpole's blandishments.[12]

Carte was one of the Jacobites' most valuable agents. He was an Oxford academic with entry to most of the Tory gentry homes in England. He first appears in the Stuart papers sending information to the Duke of Berwick in 1713, but had obviously been in touch before then. He delivered papers and presents to likely supporters in England, and was continually slipping between England and France.[13]

The British government had other methods of finding out what the Jacobites were planning. Probably not one letter sent between the spymasters in England and France got through without being intercepted. This was not revealed to the general public until the *Report of the Secret Committee of the Post Office, 1844*. This showed that 'no reasonable doubt can be entertained that the governments of different monarchs who reigned between 1660 and 1711, had frequently recourse to the practice of opening letters'. Only after a complaint by MPs in 1735 was a warrant needed to open letters, but a warrant could be issued for all suspect letters, so this made no difference.[14] The committee traced only 101 warrants, but admitted that there must have been many more than this, as evidence from many 18th-century state trials depended on seditious letters for which no warrant could be found. In 1745 blanket warrants had been sent to the postmasters to open and inspect all letters and packets going or coming from the continent.

Copied letters were admitted as evidence in the trials of the Jacobites, John Plunket and Bishop Atterbury. Parts of the deciphered and copied letters were underlined, and Atterbury insisted that the post office clerk who had done this be brought into court to swear that these were true copies. This was allowed, but a demand that the clerk produce the key that had decoded the letters was not, and when Atterbury demanded to know how the codes were cracked the clerk was told not to answer as being prejudicial to public safety. When the issue of the deciphered letters came up in the trial of John Plunket, held at the House of Commons, the House was cleared, all doors were locked and the keys were laid on the table while the letters were being read.[15]

The importance of intercepting and decoding the letters can be seen from the salaries paid to the officials involved. John LeFebre, the chief clerk, who had to be present as all the letters were opened and witness the re-sealing and transmission, received £650 a year; his under-clerks received from £200 to £500. These were vast salaries for 18th-century clerks. Eveline Cruickshanks suggests that by the 1740s LeFebre was a Jacobite spy, providing a safe means of correspondence by telling the Jacobites which correspondence would be opened, and sending information about troop numbers. Official British sources in 1745 report that he had been seeing a Jacobite spy, but this was not followed up.[16] It is possible that LeFebre was playing a double-blind set up by the government in order to lull the Jacobites into a sense of false security.

When letters were intercepted everything had to be done with speed so that there was no suspicion that the letter had been tampered with. Once opened an express messenger took the letters on horseback to the decipherers, the Reverend Edward Willes of Oriel College, Oxford and his son, and John Wallis, a mathematician, and John Krill, another Oxford don. Difficult codes could take several days to crack. In the crucial days of autumn 1715 with a Jacobite invasion imminent, John Krill had particular difficulty with a code. He wrote to the government that the monosyllables were all English words, the polysyllables German.[17]

The codes used by the Jacobites had become more complicated since the 1690s. Earlier codes used the substitution of names; for example this is the code used by the Duke of Berwick:

Agincourt = Money
Alencon = England
Enster = Scotch
Horne = Hanover
Jouvelle = Jacobites
La Motte = London
Pery = Protestantism
Prothose = Queen Anne
Tilmond = Tories
Walker = Whigs

Sir Thomas Higgons, one of James's secretaries of state, used a different substitution code:

Anastasia, Andrew, Anna, Anthony = James
Lady Mary = England
The Lawyer = Duke of Marlborough

while James himself used:

The Freeman = England
Mr Storie, Katherine = Scotland.[18]

In 1715 a numerical code was introduced. This was harder to decipher, as described in Krill's letter, written when he had only managed to decipher part of it and there were still many gaps to be filled in. The code was probably compiled randomly with the letters of the alphabet in one pile, and cards with numbers 1–100 in another.

John Menzies, one of the Jacobites' chief agents in England after 1715, used a code based on initials. Thus every Christian name beginning with an H = England, J = James, L = King George. Any surname added to these could be disregarded. He also used word transfers so that Arnot = any, Arthur = England, Brandy = troops, Fish = money. James III, writing to his mother, used a similar code but in their code Kenrick = King George, Arthur = James, Orlando = money.[19]

Viscount Bolingbroke sent James a cipher in October 1717. 'I send your Majesty a block, and a cipher drawn upon it, to fix the pages and section, and to shew the manner of using it. The Duke of Ormonde has the same, and another shall be given to the Queen. No alphabetical cipher is more ready for use, nor more hard to discover. When your Majesty is master of it, you need only remember the pages and sections and keep the book; the cipher you may for greater security burn.'[20]

Official agents in England were sent specific tasks to perform. John Menzies was responsible for liasing with Jacobite MPs. One of his tasks was to instruct Tory Jacobite MPs on how to vote. This was a way for James to keep his finger on the pulse of English politics, and manipulate those he thought would support him. However, this was a two-way process and Whig politicians used Jacobite MPs as a means of staying in power, giving promises of support they had no intention of keeping. Roger Kenyon, who had been the defence counsel for the Lancashire plotters, was the link between France and Lancaster. The Reverend Charles Leslie was the representative of the non-juroring clergy.[21]

One man James could trust was Sir Theophilius Oglethorpe, MP for Haslemere, who came from a committed Catholic Jacobite family and whose daughters were to become important Jacobite agents. Anne Oglethorpe became an agent in England in contact with John Menzies and Lord Oxford, whose mistress she may have become. Her sister Fanny in France was keeping an eye on the English envoy's household there, and their brother became James's envoy to Rome. Other Jacobite women acted as dead letter boxes for Jacobite correspondence. Agents were instructed to go to Mrs Mary Brown's at Mr Mor's a joiner near the Bath in Long Acre in London to collect their letters. Other women sheltered Jacobite agents, and burnt their papers when they were arrested.

These agents were the active wing of the English Jacobites, but there were also a number of 'sleepers'. These were mostly Catholics who were expected to support James in any attempt to regain the throne.

Sleepers

It is easier to trace Catholic sleepers than Protestant Jacobites because the government required Catholics to register their property. By plotting where this property lay it is possible to see where the Jacobites might have expected most support in England for the first two decades of the eighteenth century. In 1716, 3251 estates were registered as owned by Catholics; 21 per cent of these were in Lancashire, 11 per cent in Yorkshire, 4 per cent in Hampshire and Staffordshire, and 3 per cent in Warwickshire and Worcestershire. Regionally 26 per cent came from the north west, 20 per cent from the north east, 10 per cent from the Welsh Marches, 9 per cent from the south west, 8 per cent the West Midlands, 7 per cent London and Middlesex, 5 per cent East Anglia and the Thames and Chilterns, 4 per cent from Wales and 2 per cent from the south east. Clearly most support for the Jacobites was likely to be found in the north or west of England.[22]

Within the regions there were clusters in the same area, usually grouped around a large house, where a priest could say mass, and hide in times of emergencies. These were the safe houses through which agents could be passed, such as at East Hendred in Berkshire, Hathersage in Derbyshire, or Little Crosby in Lancashire where 76 people attended mass on 23 October 1703.[23] In Lancashire the clusters tended to be on the coastal side of the Pennines rather than on the moors and fells, while in Northumberland there were clusters in the remote highlands of Upper Coquetdale and around Hexham.

Not all Catholics were Jacobites, and not all Jacobites were Catholic. A number of high church Tories also supported a Stuart restoration in theory, if not in practice.

Scottish interlude 1708

The attempt to raise a rebellion in Scotland in 1703 came on the back of the Darien Disaster, which created discontent in Scotland against the English government. In 1708 the Scots had another grievance. The 1707 Act of Union had taken away their parliament and had imposed government from Westminster and English taxes upon them, in particular the malt tax, which dealt a blow to Scotland's national drink and to those who drank it. It was thought that the return of the Stuarts would abolish the Act of Union, and give Scotland back its independence.

The French king saw an attempt to restore the Stuarts as an opportunity to engage England's attention away from Europe, and sent his envoy Colonel Nathaniel Hooke to Scotland to enlist men. Hooke was told by the French government that he must be able to raise 25,000–30,000 men and be able to clothe, arm and equip them, and to provide maintenance for them for six months. If these conditions could be fulfilled France would consider helping, after a full report on the situation.[24] The French were being cautious, but James III threw caution to the winds. He gave Hooke a *Declaration to the People of Scotland from James VIII to his good people of his Ancient Kingdom of Scotland*, to take with him. This told the people of Scotland that he expected to be with them soon in order to claim his ancient right. He granted a general pardon to all who joined him. He promised to restore the Scottish parliament, reduce the insupportable burden of taxes, and secure the Protestant religion.[25] What appears to have been in the minds of James and his advisors was a peasants' war of the type current in early 18th-century middle Europe. They envisaged a spontaneous uprising against the English oppressor by the people. Hooke encouraged this by telling James that the Scots demanded the return of 'their' king.

Enthused by accounts of massed peasantry in Scotland waiting for him, James created the Earl of Arran general of his Scottish army, and persuaded France to give him ships to transport him from Dunkirk to Scotland. When James reached Dunkirk he was suffering from measles, and had to be carried on board ship. The fleet consisted of 23 ships and an escort of five men-of-war, carrying about 5000 troops and 12,000 arms. The English were not unaware of what was happening, and the English fleet was lying at Gravelines ready to pursue James through very stormy seas. The French admiral, unused to Scottish waters, sailed past the Firth of Forth where he was meant to land, and had to go through the complicated manoeuvre of turning the fleet. It eventually anchored off the mouth of the Firth on 25 March 1708. Signals were made from the ships to the land. No reply came. James pleaded to be allowed to land. The French admiral refused, and when the sails of the English fleet were seen on the horizon, upped anchor and made a dash for home. Some suggested that the French king never intended James to land, and that the French admiral had orders to that effect.[26]

Such Scots as had gathered to join the uprising melted quietly away. But there had been some panic in England. *Habeas Corpus* was suspended, and known Jacobite sympathisers were arrested. But nothing too dramatic happened. Had James landed, however, a run on the Bank of England would have followed, plunging the country into economic chaos, and he would have been joined by numbers of discontented Scots. Now the Scots felt betrayed.

Nevertheless, James sent them reassurances of his good intent in April 1708, and suggested they should start a civil war in Scotland to create a diversion so that he could land in the south and take the crown. But as Luttrell wrote in his diary on 10 April 1708, the Scots were not so 'hot' for James as he thought they were,[27] and the memories of civil war were still too strong in Scottish minds to start another. Their enemy was England, not other Scots.

Riots

Many of the English Jacobites discussed so far have been members of the landed or officer class. But what of the common people? How did they feel about James, and how can we gauge their feelings? Riots can demonstrate the feelings of the common people through collective action. But crowds can be bribed, incited and guided by agitators. How do we know that those involved in a riot believed in what they were rioting about? In the case of so-called pro-Jacobite riots how do we know what underlying motives there were for a riot that on the surface seemed to be in favour of James? Events in Bristol are a good example of this. The riots in that town in the first decade of the 18th century have been seen as Jacobite riots, because they usually centred around the burning of effigies of the Pretender and the Pope. But Bristol was an intensely political town, with an aggressive division between Whigs and Tories, who quickly manipulated riots to their own ends.

Twentieth-century historians who have deconstructed 18th-century riots have often tried to justify these riots as legitimate protest. George Rudé transformed the mob into a 'disciplined crowd', and denied that they were a mindless mass that could be manipulated.[28] Paul Monod sees

Jacobite riots as evidence of strong Jacobite support among the ordinary people of England; however, he admits that the 'action of Jacobite crowds were not necessarily spontaneous' but 'expressed the sympathies of a large portion of the English population over a long period of time'.[29] However, so-called Jacobite riots were often the result of provocations by the Whigs rather than spontaneous outbursts of Jacobite support.

Riots with obvious Jacobite overtones were usually connected with significant anniversaries: 10 June, James III's birthday; 29 May, the restoration of Charles II; 1 August, George I's accession; 20 October, George I's coronation in 1714. A precursor of what was to come in October 1714 were the quasi-Jacobite Sacheverell riots. Dr Henry Sacheverell, born in 1674, was an argumentative clergyman who despite his high church tendencies took the abjuration oath in 1702. In 1709 Sir Samuel Garrard, the Tory Lord Mayor of London, invited him to preach before the mainly Whig corporation in St Paul's Cathedral. For one and a half hours Sacheverell delivered a frenzied attack on false brethren, and the church in danger. In it he condemned dissenters, Jews and the State.

The sermon was seen as seditious, and Sacheverell was indicted for high treason. He became a popular hero. Thousands accompanied his coach to his trial. The militia was called out to try to keep order, but nights of rioting took place. Dissenting meeting houses were destroyed in London, and across the country. Pro-Sacheverell riots took place in Barnstaple, Cirencester, Salisbury, Shrewsbury and Wrexham. Although Sacheverell denied he was a Jacobite, the riots had strong Jacobite overtones, and the same towns experienced riots on the day of George I's coronation. Geoffey Holmes thinks that the Sacheverell riots were a 'violent demonstration of sympathy for a priest under persecution, of anger and fear for a church in danger, and fury against non-conformity which seemed to prosper, and have tentacles everywhere'. But he points out that economic conditions may have been the background to the riots, which followed two years of disastrous harvests and high prices. Conditions were exacerbated by an influx of 10,000 refugees from Germany. The depositions of the rioters make no mention of these reasons, and Holmes admits that the rioters could have been motivated by any number of factors.[30]

Sacheverell became a key figure for the Jacobites. There is a description of a Coronation Day riot at Bristol that followed a ball held at the customs houses. A set of 'riotous and rebellious persons claimed the Whigs were making an effigy of Dr Sacheverell in order that it could be burnt'. Jacobites ran down the street kicking out the coronation bonfires and crying 'Down with the Roundheads, God Bless Dr Sacheverell'. Windows illuminated for King George were smashed, the house where the effigy of Sacheverell was hidden was wrecked and looted, and Mr Thomas, a Whig, was murdered.[31]

The same story of innocent coronation day revels being broken up by Jacobite mobs can be seen at Abergavenny, Birmingham, Chippenham, Frome, Norwich, Nuneaton and Reading. However, the anonymous author of the accounts appears to have been biased towards the Whigs, and anxious to place the Tories in the worst possible light, and to ally them in people's minds with the banned Jacobites.

It would be possible to read the coronation day riots in terms of customary rites. The illuminations, bonfires and effigies came from a folk tradition, and at Bedford the maypole was draped in black on coronation day.[32] But this may be reading too much into the riots. Drink probably played an important part in proceedings. More riots took place on 5 November 1714, in places that had been peaceful on coronation day. At Axminster, for example, where the effigy of the pope was to be burnt, it was rescued by a rabble armed with clubs and staves.[33]

There was a great disorder at Oxford on 28 May 1715 when Whigs met to celebrate King George's birthday by burning effigies of Dr Sacheverell and the Duke of Ormonde. The local Jacobites hired the room above them in the tavern where they had met, and ordered drinks for the crowd, it being market day. The crowd destroyed the bonfire and guzzled the Jacobites' drink, purchased with money the Jacobites threw out of the window. The mob increased and was joined by students. The university proctors came out and drove the scholars back to their colleges. But the following night an Oriel man shot and wounded a Brasenose Jacobite, and more disturbances followed.[34]

Oxford was known for its Jacobitism, and in the summer of 1715 it was a tinder keg. The king's messenger was sent from London to arrest the Jacobite ringleaders, Mr Boyce and Mrs King, for treason. They were taken to the Star Inn and a considerable mob gathered outside, swearing they would rescue the prisoners and murder the messenger. The messenger came out onto the inn's steps and read the Riot Act. The crowd refused to disperse. They broke all the inn's windows and tore up a fence as ammunition. The messenger went back outside with his pistols, shot them into the air and cried 'God Bless King George and Damn the Pretender'. The crowd replied, 'Hurrah for James III, Ormonde and Bolingbroke'. The messenger called them traitors, and would probably have been lynched had not the proctors and guard from the castle come to assist. A running battle took place through the city streets with many casualties on both sides.[35]

On significant anniversaries in London battles took place between the inhabitants of Jacobite taverns and coffee houses, and the Whig mug houses. These usually started with windows being smashed. The Jacobites utilised the help of the Bridewell boys from the Blue Coat orphan school, and butchers from the city. On 16 November 1714 they attacked the Whig Roebuck Inn, and in July 1716 attacked Reed's Mug House. The landlord fired on the rioters and killed a man. A further riot occurred when the victim was buried, at which point the rioters were arrested and sentenced to death for treason. Reed was acquitted of murder.[36]

Between June and August 1715 there were a series of riots directed at dissenting meeting houses. These were especially fierce in the Black Country, Wolverhampton and the Staffordshire moors, and around Manchester. Monod sees these as part of the Jacobite conspiracy leading up to the 1715 rising. Nicholas Rogers disagrees and suggests that this was not necessarily so. Monod argues that Rogers misses the point, which was that the widespread rioting was to draw troops to an area, leaving other areas clear for the Jacobites. Furthermore, he suggests that the meeting house riots were orchestrated by the local gentry, demonstrating that the whole was a co-ordinated diversionary attempt.[37]

The counties at the centre of the riots, Warwickshire, Worcestershire and Staffordshire, had a considerable number of Catholic estates and there was another cluster of Catholics in and around Wolverhampton. There is evidence that these riots were organised rather than spontaneous. There were reports of people going from place to place in riotous manner threatening Presbyterian meeting houses in Dudley, Oldbury and West Bromwich. When the mob reached West Bromwich Sir Henry Gough brought out the watch and beat off the mob with cudgels and whips, and they promised to keep the peace. But 'like true Jacobites they broke their promise and came the next day in greater numbers, and more desperate weapons such as scythes, reaping hooks set in handles two yards long, large clubs and fire arms. But when they saw the guard they fled, and their arms were picked up by women who came out of their houses.' Thirty-six prisoners were taken. At midnight a mob came from Birmingham to release them and fired on the guard, attacking the house where the prisoners were kept and releasing some of them, but were eventually repelled; the remaining prisoners were sent to Stafford gaol. The next day the mob came again, with increased fury. They fired on the guards, killing a horse, and wounding several men. Some were taken prisoner. The ringleader was found to be the Wolverhampton town crier. All were Catholics. The prisoners said that Mr Vernon and Mr Lane had given 60 guineas to encourage the mob, and pull down the meeting house at Wolverhampton.[38]

The riots continued in 1716; 10 June became known as White Rose Day when the Jacobites wore white roses as buttonholes or in their hats, or decorated local monuments with them.[39] This often led to arguments when the Whigs tried to remove them, and the price of white roses rocketed.

Too much importance can be attached to these disturbances. Were they evidence of popular support for James, or being orchestrated to create a diversion from an invasion? There is no evidence that James and his ministers had suggested this, but agents could have been given verbal instructions. Were the riots spontaneous outbursts of loyalty for the Stuarts? These were more likely to have been spontaneous outbursts against the Whig government and its taxes than loyalty to James. So many factors induced people to riot that it is often impossible to isolate one cause.

Constitutional restoration

As Queen Anne's life drew to a close the Jacobites looked towards the possibility of a constitutional restoration for James. In order to effect this the court in exile began to inform the Jacobite Tory MPs how they should vote, and who they should support. Letters sent via agents from 1711–14 show a change in tone. Intrigues and projected invasion plans disappear and are replaced by political instructions. Agents were told to build up support in parliament and the army, and to tell the 50 Jacobite MPs who held the balance of power to keep the Earl of Oxford in office and the Tory government in control. This suited Oxford whose main aim was to stay in power, and in turn he began to manipulate the Jacobites into supporting any policy he wanted.

The Jacobite MPs represented the country party and were dedicated to maintaining their influence in the countryside. Many of them belonged to the October Club which wanted an investigation against parliament-ary corruption, and voted against any tax which would fund forces for a foreign war.

Overtures were made to Anne by Oxford about altering the succession in favour of James. The Jacobites were convinced she favoured James, giving rise to the question 'Was Queen Anne a Jacobite?'[40] James was encouraged by his advisers to write to her. She never replied. Others spoke to her about the succession; the Earl of Ailesbury and Viscount Bolingbroke sounded her out. She gave no indication she would name James, and anecdotal evidence that she favoured him over Hanoverian George was false. Those who knew Anne knew she would never accept a Catholic heir. On her death, however, the Duke of Ormonde, Bishop Atterbury and Earl Marischal discussed whether they should proclaim James. Atterbury offered to do this, but the College of Heralds forestalled him. George I was proclaimed king at Charing Cross.[41]

Notes

1 HMC, *Calendar of the Stuart Papers at Windsor*, London: HMSO, I, 1902, 114–17.

2 Berwick, Duke of, *Memoirs*, London: 1779, I, 157.

3 E. Gregg, 'The Politics of Paranoia' in E. Cruickshanks and J. Black, eds, *The Jacobite Challenge*, Edinburgh: John Donald Ltd, 1988, 42–3.

4 C. Petrie, *The Jacobite Movement – The First Phase, 1688–1716*, London: Eyre and Spottiswoode, 1948, 105–6.

5 J. Macpherson, *Original Papers Containing the Secret History of England*, London: 1775, I, 630–33.

6 Macpherson, 155.

7 L.G.W. Legg, 'Extracts from Jacobite Correspondence 1712–1714', *English Historical Review* 30, 1915, 501–18.

8 Gregg, 46–7.

9 R.P. Mahaffy ed., *Calendar of State Papers Domestic 1703–4*, London: HMSO, 1924, 24–7.

10 L. Gooch, *The Desperate Faction?*, Hull: University of Hull Press, 1995, 146–8.

11 W. King, *Political and Literary Anecdotes of His Own Time*, London: John Murray, 2nd ed, 1819, 36–9.

12 P.S. Fritz, 'The anti-Jacobite intelligence system of the English ministers, 1715–1745', *Historical Journal*, XIV, 1973, 265–89.

13 *Stuart Papers* I, for example 288, 341, 351, 356, 359.

14 Parliamentary Papers XIV, *Report of the Secret Committee of the House of Lords relative to the Post Office*, Cmnd. 582, 1844.

15 Post Office, 107–8.

16 E. Cruickshanks, *Political Untouchables*, London: Duckworth, 1979, 47, 54, 82, 91.

17 PRO SP 35/4/47.

18 HMC, *Calendar of Stuart Papers at Windsor*, II, 1904, xciv–ci.

19 A full account of these codes can be found in the introduction to the *Calendars of Stuart Papers*, whilst the comments from the decipherers are in PRO SP 35.

20 *Stuart Papers* II, 447.

21 G.V. Bennett, 'English Jacobites, 1710–1715: myth and reality?', *Trans. Royal Historical Society*, 5th ser. 32, 1982, 141–2.

22 E. Estcourt, *The English Catholics, 1716*, London: Burns and Oates, 1886.

23 J. Bagley, ed., *The Great Diurnall of Nicholas Blundell of Little Crosby*, Lancashire and Cheshire Record Society, 110, 1958, 153.

24 Macpherson, 77–84.

25 *Stuart Papers* I, 218–221.

26 Macpherson, 100.

27 N. Luttrell, *A Brief Historical Relation of State Affairs, 1678–1714*, Oxford: OUP, Vol. VI, 1857, 289.

28 G. Rudé, *Hanoverian London*, London: Secker and Warburg, 1971, 205–6.

29 P. Monod, *Jacobites and the English People, 1688–1788*, Cambridge: CUP, 1993, 164.

30 G. Holmes, *The Trial of Dr Sacheverell*, London: Eyre, 1973, 177–80.

31 *An Account of the Riots, Tumults and Other Treasonable Practices since His Majesty's Succession to the Throne*, London: 1716, 4–6.

32 *Riots and Tumults*, 16.

33 *Riots and Tumults*, 12.

34 *St James's Post*, 30 May–1 June 1715; *The Post Boy* 30 May–1 June 1715.

35 PRO SP 35/2/18.

36 Rudé, 206.

37 Monod, 185–6; N. Rogers, 'Riot and popular Jacobitism' in E. Cruickshanks ed., *Ideology and Conspiracy*, Edinburgh: John Donald Ltd, 1988, 72.

38 A. Boyer, *The Political State of Great Britain, X, July–Dec 1715*, London: 1716.

39 PRO SP 35/16/101; The White Rose was the Stuart symbol because James II had been Duke of York before he became king, and the white rose was the symbol of the medieval house of York.

40 E. Gregg, 'Was Queen Anne a Jacobite?', *History*, 57, October 1972, 358–75.

41 Petrie, 152.

CHAPTER 4

High-born traitors:
the court in exile
and supporters at home

A number of high-born supporters were open or closet Jacobites in England and in exile. There were two types of exiles. The first group left England with James II, because of their principles and their religion; they were generally staunch Catholics and had been members of James's government. The second group were mostly discontented Protestant Tories, who went into exile when their activities meant they were likely to be impeached for high treason.

One of the earliest exiles was John Drummond, Earl of Melfort, who had been James's secretary of state for Scotland. He saw that a Protestant revolution against James was inevitable, and prudently departed to France before it happened. On 21 January 1689 when James set up a government in exile, Melfort became the principal secretary of state, and it was Melfort who accompanied James to Ireland in the spring of 1689.

Melfort was deeply unpopular. He was a Catholic convert and had all the fanaticism of a convert. He led the compounders group in France. They believed in the divine right of kings, and that there should be no conditions attached to James's restoration. He was disliked in Scotland, where even committed Jacobites refused to act on his orders, and despised in Ireland. James's Irish general, the Earl of Tyrconnell, loathed him and eventually relations between the two men became so bad that James was forced to send Melfort back to France.[1] Despite the harm he was doing to

James's cause he remained in office as secretary of state. G. Jones suggests that his influence on James was based on 'flattery, officiousness and subservience to the king's exalted conception of prerogative'.[2] Eventually, when it became obvious that no other of his supporters would cooperate with Melfort, James sent him to Rome in 1690, but recalled him in August 1691. It was Melfort who drafted James's declaration that was to be used by Lord Preston, and later by the Lancashire plotters. But Melfort's rigid adherence to restoration without condition and his fanatical Catholicism made it difficult to gain supporters in England. Overtures were made by James's agents to Charles, Earl of Middleton (1650–1719), who had been James's secretary of state in England, and had remained behind in 1689. Middleton was a moderate Protestant and a non-compounder who believed that James's restoration would only be achieved if conditions were attached to this. He sent a paper outlining eight conditions. If James agreed to these he would move to France. James agreed and he arrived in France in April 1693. This was an important move as far as the English Jacobites were concerned; they trusted Middleton's judgement, and were more likely to agree to his plans than they were to Melfort's. It was also an important move for the court in exile, as Middleton was an avenue to a far more illustrious prize, the Duke of Marlborough. Middleton left his wife and children in England, even though he knew that he would never be able to return, unless it was with an invading force. He must have weighed up the possibilities of success carefully before leaving, as he was known by his contemporaries as a man of good understanding.[3]

His first task in France was to rewrite James's declaration to his subjects in terms that were acceptable to the non-compounders. A clause he added on maintaining the Church of England brought him into conflict with James's spiritual advisers and the Earl of Melfort. Melfort resigned as James's secretary of state in 1694. Middleton remained in office until 1703, by which time he too had converted to Catholicism. This made him unpopular with the English Jacobites and, with more exiles arriving from England with promising contacts, life became difficult for Middleton. Although he was recalled to office he resigned for good in 1713. James created him Earl of Monmouth, but this was an empty title with no lands or revenues to go with it. He had left behind his estates and family and thrown in his lot with a lost cause. This was either a matter of high principles or bad judgement.

Other early exiles included James II's natural son, the Duke of Berwick, who was probably the most intelligent and loyal member of the exiles, and the only general the Stuarts had with any experience in the field or any grasp of strategy. Berwick became a naturalised French citizen and served in the French army. When the Stuarts were extradited to Avignon, and then from France altogether, it was Berwick who became their eyes and ears at the French court. The plentiful correspondence between Berwick and James II and III is testament to this.

Berwick, the son of James II and Arabella Churchill, was born in 1670. He was educated in France, and was created Duke of Berwick when James succeeded to the throne in 1685. In his memoirs Berwick claims that he was a reserved man who 'could not say pretty things and trusted only his own judgement'.[4] Berwick sometimes acted as a secret agent in England in 1695, travelling in disguise to contact supporters. In his memoirs he noted that he contacted the English gentry in vain, as they would not rise against William until the French invaded. While in England he found out about the assassination plot, but refused to become part of the conspiracy.[5] The plotters were at pains to make it clear that James knew nothing about the plot, but it is hardly likely that on his return to France Berwick did not tell his father about it, and his refusal to countenance the assassination of a king was written with hindsight, long after the plot had been discovered.

A peer forced into exile because of his association with the assassination plot was Thomas Bruce, Earl of Ailesbury (1655–1741), whose country seat was at Houghton Conquest in Bedfordshire. Ailesbury was one of the peers who persuaded James to return to London in 1688. After William was crowned Ailesbury remained loyal to James and refused to take the oath of allegiance, so was excluded from office until eventually, when it was revealed he would have to pay double taxes if he did not take the oath, he took it as he felt it was his duty to protect the kingdom.

His name came up in connection with the Preston plot, and he went into hiding near Berkeley Street, eventually offering to surrender provided he could be bailed and not sent to the Tower of London in the hot season. He took to going round London in a disguise of a brown periwig and black eyebrows.[6] Ailesbury admitted in his memoirs to be present at meetings of the Earl of Middleton's cabal at the Seven Stars in Covent Garden with others including Lords Dartmouth, Feversham and

Weymouth, Bishop Turner of Ely, the non-juror, and Mr Penn the Quaker. Also present was Ailesbury's cousin, and it may have been him who betrayed the plot.

Ailesbury survived the Preston plot but was seriously worried about the Jacobites' future. He could see that the national differences would be difficult to overcome, and he perceived that Jacobite plotters were hot headed and their plots ill conceived. He wrote that they 'were well pleased with their empty projects as children are of rattles and whistles'.[7] Although he went secretly to France before the assassination plot he was not sanguine about its success, finding Fenwick 'flashy' and 'his head piece not of the best'.[8] He tried to withdraw from the plot as he thought that no restoration was possible without a competent army to back it, and he noted that most of the discussion about the plot was devoted to which offices the plotters would be given after the restoration.

He was arrested when the plot was discovered, and sent to the Tower. He admitted to dining with some of the plotters, but said he had found them so indiscrete that he resolved to have nothing more to do with them. When he was released he was sent into exile. Significantly, he went to Brussels rather than Paris, and although he had some correspondence with the court in exile he refused to become embroiled in any intrigues.

Ailesbury was of a different temperament to the other plotters. He was cautious and sober, they were flamboyant and unable to keep secrets; cavalier temperaments very much at odds with his. He gave the reason for his defection from William as his resentment at the privileges shown by William to his Dutch courtiers.

The second tranche of high-born traitors made more dramatic exits from England. They had been ministers during Anne's reign, but when George I succeeded to the throne and the Tories were excluded from offices they found themselves in a political backwater, and looked towards James to provide them with better rewards. They were traitors through personal aggrandisement rather than strong convictions. The first of these was the great libertine, Henry St John, Viscount Bolingbroke (1678– 1751). He was the son of an old Royalist family, educated at Eton. He first came to public notice when he ran naked through St James's Park, escaping from his mistress's husband. His marriage in 1700 to Frances Winchcombe did little to improve his morals.

He was secretary of state for war for Queen Anne, but was forced to resign when the administration fell in 1704 and retired to the country to write, returning to office in 1710. He was a friend of Dr Sacheverell, and it could have been at the time of the Sacheverell riots that he started to communicate with Jacobite agents. But his degree of commitment to the cause was debatable. G.M. Trevelyan thought this was suspect, but H. Fieldhouse wrote that Bolingbroke 'was more committed than Oxford', but there was nothing to implicate him with the Jacobites until 1713 when he started to meet with Lockhart, one of the Jacobite agents in England.[9]

Bolingbroke may already have had some idea of what would happen when Anne died, and also the way in which he was perceived by the establishment. He had hoped for an earldom but instead was made a viscount in 1712, and was not awarded the coveted garter. He was part of the group that tried to persuade Anne to name James as her successor, and when George I was named instead, Bolingbroke's old friend the Earl of Oxford threatened to expose him as a Jacobite.[10]

George excluded all Tories from office. Impatient and powerless, Bolingbroke slipped away to France in April 1715, but not initially to join James. Instead he waited to see what would happen in England between the Whigs and the Tories, writing to Sir William Wyndham that he was a Tory first and a Jacobite second. When there was no sign of the Tories being given any offices he joined the court in exile.

Bolingbroke was a man who loved and needed power. Soon he gathered the reins of power within the court in exile to himself. It was he who drafted a declaration for James to send to England in 1715, and he advised, correctly as it turned out, that the 1715 rising would not succeed because it was ill prepared. This and his arrogant attitude quickly made him unpopular, and on his return from Scotland in 1715 James dismissed him.

Bolingbroke knew that England would never accept a Catholic king, and that the throne of England could not be won solely through the support of the Scots and Irish. But he warned James against a sudden conversion, and suggested instead that James marry a Protestant princess and have his children brought up as Protestants. James would have none of this, and Bolingbroke's persistence on the religious question made him unpopular with the French government as well as the court in exile. In

1723 he applied for and was given a pardon and returned to England. Part of the condition of his pardon was that he stayed out of politics. He found this impossible to do, and in 1728 tried to organise a coalition between opposition Whigs and Jacobite Tories in the hopes of bringing the government down. His antipathy to Sir Robert Walpole led to his return to France in 1736, from whence he returned shortly before the 1745 rebellion.[11]

Bolingbroke's career shows him to be a man in love with power and prepared to risk everything to get his hands on it. When he fled to France the first time he abandoned his wife and family, and borrowed £20,000 using his estate as security. His actions suggest a man of few principles who acted through self-interest rather than a burning desire to restore the Stuarts. However, perhaps his conscience did eventually begin to trouble him, as he wrote a letter to Sir William Wyndham, the leader of the Tory Jacobites in Parliament, justifying his actions.

Contemporary with Bolingbroke was James Butler, Duke of Ormonde (1665–1745). He was a graduate of Christ Church, Oxford, a place imbued with Jacobitism, and in 1688 he became the Chancellor of Oxford University. In that year he was one of the peers who voted for a regency to govern the country rather than William, but accepted William once he was crowned, and fought on William's side in Ireland in 1691. James II had counted on Ormonde's support, and specifically excluded Ormonde's name from a general pardon he issued in 1692.

Like Ailesbury, Ormonde resented William's Dutch favourites, but unlike Ailesbury he did not enter any conspiracies, and in 1703 became Governor General of Ireland. Ormonde was a soldier rather than a politician, and on resigning from the Governor Generalship entered the Foot-guards and fought in Flanders, for which he was rewarded with the Lord Wardenship of the Cinque Ports and a pension of £5000 a year.

Ormonde's main fault was that he needed someone to lead him. This made him an ideal soldier because he obeyed orders implicitly and unquestioningly. Back in England and re-entering politics he fell under Bolingbroke's spell, and under his influence started a dangerous corres-pondence with the Duke of Berwick in France. Despite this he was one of the peers who signed the proclamation giving George the crown when Queen Anne died, but as a Tory did not reap any rewards from this. Removed from office he continued to write to Berwick, and his meetings with Jacobite agents in London led to him being impeached for high treason. He too fled to France.

Ormonde was a man of action and did not seek political power in the exiled court. Instead he offered his skill as a soldier, and in 1715 sailed to the West Country where his main estates lay, to raise an army there. Unfortunately, signals from his ship were not answered and he returned to France. This and the fact that he steadfastly refused to convert to Catholicism annoyed James, and made his position at James's court difficult. But he could not return to England as he had been named an outlaw and would have been instantly arrested. He was sent to the Baltic and Spain as James's envoy, ending his days on 16 November 1745 in Avignon.

Ormonde remained a popular figure in England, and had he led a Jacobite invasion it might have had some success. His military prowess was remembered and his personal charm revered. The cry of rioters was often 'Ormonde and the High Church', and ballads were written about him. James III was often described as the lost or forlorn lover, but the term was probably applied first to the Duke of Ormonde, as this song found in the state papers shows:

The Forlorn Lover

I am Ormonde the brave, did you never hear of me?
A man lately forced from my own country
They fought for my life and plundered my estate,
For being loyal to Queen Anne, yo ho!

You need not fear Popery, nor such fresh matter
For I think I see forces, I see Derwentwater
You have prov'd me and try'd me. I am Ormonde the brave
I ventured my life my country to save

Though some do upbraid me, I value not a straw
They call me James Butler, I am Ormonde they know
But since it is so, I vow and declare
With a glass of good liquor, my spirit I will cheer.[12]

There were a number of English peers who might be described as Jacobite 'sleepers'. They were wooed by Jacobite agents, but although they showed an interest in the cause they did not commit themselves. Earl Godolphin (1645–1712) was one of the first statesmen approached by the Jacobites. He came from an ancient Cornish family, and had been one of James II's ministers. His correspondence with James and his ministers at St Germains was coy in the extreme, and gave nothing away. At the same time he flattered William, and so remained at the Treasury until Sir John Fenwick implicated him in the assassination plot, whereupon he resigned.

He was back in office with Anne, and was one of the promoters of the 1707 Act of Union, and any contact he might have had with the Jacobites was at an end. He was attacked personally by Dr Sacheverell, and in 1710 after a violent argument with the Duke of Shrewsbury in the presence of the queen he was dismissed. Godolphin is chiefly remembered for his interest in horse racing and breeding with the Godolphin arabs. These activities left him severely in debt, and should have warned the Jacobites that he was unlikely to give them any practical help.

The Jacobites also wooed Robert Harley, Earl of Oxford, and he was to spend long periods in the Tower as a suspected traitor. But the biggest fish of all that the Jacobites angled for was the Duke of Marlborough. If Marlborough defected to them he would bring the army with him. Marlborough wrote in code to the Duke of Berwick on 10 May 1715 about the Hanoverian succession and the dismissal of the Tories.[13] But Berwick was his nephew, being the natural son of Marlborough's sister, and whether Marlborough ever seriously considered joining the Jacobites is a moot point. It was true that he had been in touch with James II from 3 May 1694, but there was no hint that he was going to join him; he had made contact, like others, through resentment against William's Dutch courtiers and he only resumed correspondence whenever he felt threatened by events in England. Marlborough had a lot to lose. A grateful nation had built him Blenheim Palace and fêted him, he was a privy councillor and had risen from being a page in the royal household to one of the foremost aristocrats in England. In 1708 he had organised the country's defence against the Jacobite invasion, and he refused a loan of £100,000 to James III. Perhaps to force his hand Jacobite agents in England spread rumours in 1711 that he was engaged in a plot to kill the Earl of Oxford and murder the queen. Nobody believed this, and in 1712 Marlborough was in touch with Hanover.

Marlborough as a strategist knew where his best interests and those of the country lay. Although he was a high church Tory, he did not want a Catholic king on the throne. But to the Jacobites he was the key to success, and their correspondence is full of hopeful signs that Marlborough and the army were coming to join them. Marlborough never defected.

One young aristocrat who joined James, was Philip, Duke of Wharton (1698–1731). He came from a Whig family, but while on the Grand Tour in August 1716 he evaded his tutors and made his way to James where he 'bowed at James's feet and asked for pardon for the past offences of his family.' He asked for an officer's commission, and promised James he would raise Buckinghamshire for him, as well as getting 14 of his friends elected into Parliament to boost Jacobite political support. As a reward he asked James for the Order of the Garter, which James promised to award him when he was on the throne. Wharton returned to England in December 1716, and for the next six years appeared to support the Hanoverians. However, his lifestyle was out of control. He was the president of the Hell Fire Club, he drank and gambled. When he lost heavily on the South Sea Company his debts were such that in 1726 his estates were sold to the Duke of Marlborough and Sir Robert Lowther, and his pictures to Sir Robert Walpole, and he went into exile renewing his contacts with the Jacobites. He acted as their envoy in Russia, but his dissolute ways led to James banning him from his court, and Wharton died drunk and destitute in 1731.[14]

The court in exile and Jacobite women

As well as the aristocratic members of James's court there were others less exalted who had been in James's service and went into exile with him. They held offices in the royal household – for example Michael Bedingfield, the king's valet, and Charles Booth, groom of the bedchamber, or Charles Leyburn and Joseph Byerley of Belgrave, Leicester; Henry Parry who was the clerk of the kitchen and Henry Conquest, paymaster for the household.[15]

Marriages at the court in exile were usually between other members of the court, or their relatives, and usually the marriages were between those from the same level in the household. Grooms of the bedchamber married their colleagues' daughters, kitchen clerks married daughters of kitchen clerks. This helped to maintain the *status quo* and the hierarchy of the household. This occupational endogamy of marriage between the same groups mirrored the situation in 18th-century England where 'occupation and income helped to define status and a place in society'.[16] Into the equation of class and religion in determining Jacobite marriage partners Paul Monod adds politics. He suggests that politics had a direct influence on the choice of partner, and their relationship after marriage. He argues that Jacobite ideology was permeated with the ideal of 'patriarchal authority'.[17]

This derives from the Jacobite adherence to the idea of the divine right of kings and an absolute monarchy, demanding absolute and unquestioning obedience from its subjects. The family and household became an analogy for the state with their members owing unquestioning allegiance and obedience to the head of the household, (usually male). Questioning this scheme within the family by analogy meant questioning it within the state. Thus Mary and Anne were unnatural daughters to James, and their questioning his authority had brought down the state. Families in flux meant a dysfunctional state. Jacobite marriages were not intended to form households of equals, but of obedience. It is remarkable, therefore, that some strong-minded and independent women emerged, dedicated to the Jacobite cause. Take for example Mary Flint, the wife of George Flint, a printer whose schemes for restoring the Stuarts were to lead him into trouble.

Flint was born in Newcastle but had moved to London. Mary was born Mary Spencer, a gentlewoman. Flint had been too ill to join the 1715 rising, but he was arrested just the same and put into Newgate where he started to publish the Jacobite news-sheet, *Robin's Last Shift*. When this was suppressed Mary took over and produced *The Shift Shifted*, until she too was arrested and put into the Fleet Prison. Hearing her husband was very ill she slipped out of prison with some visitors and went to Newgate, later returning to the Fleet, but eventually being granted permission to move to Newgate. When Flint was sentenced to death it was Mary who engineered his escape, and remained behind to take the consequences. She was released in August 1717 and joined her husband in France. Here they lived in penury while Flint planned fanciful schemes for the restoration of the Stuarts, and was eventually arrested by the French. Mary again showed her initiative and went into the wine business, assuming the identity of the wife of a bankrupt merchant. She purchased good wine, paid the excise duty so that it was imported legally into England, and even though she undercut her rivals she still made a profit. She was helped by her husband's former contacts and sold to both Jacobites and Hanoverians alike. Travelling backwards and forwards from the continent she was able to carry letters and messages until she was discovered.

Equally determined were the Oglethorpe women, daughters of Sir Theophilius Oglethorpe of Westbrook Place, Surrey and Eleanor Wall, an Irish Catholic. This family remained loyal to the Stuarts. It was Eleanor who smuggled Mary of Modena's jewels to France, and carried messages to Stuart supporters in Ireland and Yorkshire. Her daughters, Eleanor, Anne, Frances and Molly were sent to France to be educated, and became Jacobite agents. Anne was arrested on arrival in England in 1703, and placed under house arrest at Westbrook Place. She was to become the Earl of Oxford's mistress, and in this position was able to influence him in favour of the Jacobites. Eleanor junior was to marry a French noble-man, and while living in her household Frances was to become very influential at the court in exile. Bolingbroke complained about them and another Englishwoman, Olive Trant, and was convinced that they had caused his dismissal.[18]

The younger sister Molly took over the job of London correspondent after 1715, but her letters took a long time to arrive, mainly because she spent her time enjoying herself; she ended up in a debtors' prison, from which she escaped to France, eventually ending up at the Spanish court. Meanwhile Anne was continually crossing the channel in the 1720s, negotiating between supporters in England and France. As a gesture of thanks James created her Countess Oglethorpe. The other sister, Eleanor, dominated the plans for the 1745 invasion, and her meddling may have led to the collapse of the first plans and contributed to the diffidence of the French to send aid.[19]

Accounts of the Oglethorpe sisters show them to be overbearing and arrogant, but these accounts were written mainly by men who resented their influence with James and other leading Jacobites. But their bicker-ing with other women such as Mrs Ogilvie did not help the cause, and neither did the strange story of Frances Shaftoe who claimed that she had been abducted by Eleanor and Anne Oglethorpe and placed in a nunnery against her will. Although there was little substance to her accusations she did produce a best-selling pamphlet about her alleged experiences that did not do the Oglethorpes, the Catholics or the Jacobite cause any good.

Women who became actively involved with the Jacobites were of necessity larger than life. The Oglethorpes certainly were, as were better known Jacobite women such as Flora MacDonald and Clementina Walkinshaw, but they are beyond the remit of this book.

Notes

1 G. Jones, *The Main Stream of Jacobitism*, Cambridge, Massachusetts: Harvard University Press, 1954, 10.

2 Jones, 13.

3 Jones, 32.

4 Berwick, Duke of, *Memoirs*, London: 1779, xxx.

5 Berwick, 132.

6 Bruce, T., Earl of Ailesbury, *Memoirs*, London: Roxburgh Club, 1890, I, 259.

7 Bruce, 271.

8 Bruce, 273.

9 H. Fieldhouse, 'Bolingbroke's share in the Jacobite Intrigue of 1710–14', *English Historical Review*, 1937, 52, 443, 449.

10 Fieldhouse, 681.

11 H. Dickinson, *Bolingbroke*, London: Constable, 1970.

12 PRO, SP 35/65/126.

13 HMC, *Calendar of the Stuart Papers at Windsor Castle*, London: HMSO, I, 1902, 365.

14 HMC, *Calendar of the Stuart Papers at Windsor Castle*, London: HMSO, II, 1904, 360–61, 390–91, 470–72; HMC, *Calendar of the Stuart Papers at Windsor Castle*, London: HMSO, III, 1907, 107, 6, 25, 37–8, 69–70, 72, 84–5, 172–3, 198, 268, 279, 306, 312–13, 518.

15 Stuart I, 162, 216, 237; C.E. Last ed., *Jacobite Extracts from the Parish Registers of St Germain-en-Laye*, London: St Catherine's Press, 1910.

16 E. Lord, 'Communities of common interest: the social landscape of S.E. Surrey, 1750–1850', in C. V. Phythian-Adams, *Societies, Culture and Kinship 1580–1850*, Leicester: Leicester University Press, 1993, 130.

17 P. Monod, 'The politics of matrimony: Jacobitism and marriage in eighteenth-century England', in E. Cruickshanks and J. Black eds, *The Jacobite Challenge*, Edinburgh: John Donald Ltd, 1988.

18 HMC, *Calendar of the Stuart Papers at Windsor Castle*, London: HMSO, VI, 1916, 551.

19 P.K. Hill, *The Oglethorpe Ladies and the Jacobite Conspiracies*, Atlanta: Cherokee Publishing Company, 1971.

CHAPTER 5

1715

'One may easily conclude this was not a Day of real Joy to the Jacobites. However, they were all there looking as cheerful as they could, but very peevish with Everybody who spoke to them', wrote Lady Cowper about George I's coronation.[1] Despite the political manoeuvrings of the Tories and the blandishments to Anne by his supporters, James had lost the race towards a constitutional succession to the British throne. Anne had followed her instincts and gone with the Act of Settlement, which decreed that only a Protestant could succeed her. On 29 August 1714 James issued a declaration against this, and a manifesto outlining his hereditary right to the crown.[2] Battle lines were being drawn, and James's supporters in England gleefully sent to France descriptions of riots that took place on George's coronation day.[3]

France

It seemed to the Jacobites in exile that the time was ripe for another attempt at a restoration. On 28 November 1714, the Duke of Berwick wrote to James that Scotland would seem the best option but that 'a little time must be allowed for getting together what is necessary, especially for raising money and taking measures with friends in England without which, little good is to be expected . . . That for the better keeping the secret the King's friends must not expect to know the precise time of his embarquing [sic], but that he will give them sufficient warning, they must keep up their hearts, without giving jealousy to the government and they must give him regularly an account of how things stand'.[4]

Pressure was to be put on eminent waverers in England, such as Marlborough, Bolingbroke and Ormonde, to give practical support instead of paying only lip-service to the cause.[5] In England George I played into the Jacobites' hands by favouring the Whigs, and ousting all Tories from office.

In January 1715 James sent another declaration to his people, warning them he was resolved to recover his right. He wrote that he was most heartily willing to remove all objections, and to give the utmost satisfaction in his power. The first obstacle he had to overcome was religion. He pointed out that he had left England in his cradle, and had been brought up in the religion of his parents. He could not now declare himself a Protestant, as this would be 'mean and dishonourable'. But he would support the Church of England's rights and liberties. The law of the land would be the law of his government, and he would take the advice of Parliament for the security and happiness of the king as well as for the people. He added that he would never give up his right to the crown.[6]

Deconstructing the text of the declaration two centuries later it would be easy to read into it meanings that are not there, and to see hidden hands guiding James's pen; hands that knew what the English people wanted to see. It played on their sympathies for James's vicissitudes, pointing out that he was a cradle Catholic and that his parents, not he, were to blame for this. The final phrases emphasised the injustice of his plight and appealed to the wisdom and Christianity of his English subjects. It asked them to open their eyes 'in cold blood' and recognise his right and how inconsistent it was with natural justice that he should be denied. It was a skilfully put-together document and it was aimed at people like Marlborough and Bolingbroke, who in the early months of 1715 were still unknown quantities, making only vague promises to James while still jockeying for power at the Hanoverian court.

James also needed men, arms and money from France. But the French were lukewarm towards him – they did not want war, and would not venture anything that would threaten the peace with Britain. In England men like Bolingbroke and Ormonde were growing increasingly dissatisfied, and in spring 1715 the filter of high-born traitors across the channel started. In March 1715 Alan Cameron brought assurances to James of Ormonde's support. James replied that 'Nothing could be more welcome', and the Duke of Berwick advised him to send Ormonde a commission making him captain-general of the three kingdoms, but to make sure that the commission was kept at Calais so that Ormonde had to come to collect it.[7] Ormonde was also to be given power to borrow money in James's name.

A reply from James to Berwick on 19 March 1715 shows how little his advisers knew about the day-to-day business of statecraft. Lord Middleton as secretary of state did not know the wording to use for the commission, and there was only one clerk who could write in the legally required secretary hand. They were all ignorant as to what colour wax should be used for the seal.[8] Eventually, the commission was prepared and, disregarding Berwick's advice, taken to England by Mr Pemberton. All the correspondence between the court in exile and England was with Ormonde rather than Bolingbroke, although Bolingbroke was to be the first to break cover and run to France. This may have been the last thing that Berwick and James wanted, as Bolingbroke and especially Ormonde would have been far more useful rallying troops in England.

In June 1715 Berwick began to draw up plans for an invasion, favouring a landing in England rather than Scotland, and still hoping for support from France. He decided eventually that the invasion should take place on two fronts: James and any troops France could supply were to land in the west of England, while a force from Sweden would land at Newcastle.[9]

On 20 August the Earl of Mar, a Jacobite supporter, left London and rode north. On 6 September 1715 he raised James's standard at Braemar. But on 30 August the King of France had died, leaving a boy king to rule, and a Regent who did not favour James. Mar had declared too early, and in the wrong place.

England

The public expressions of distaste for the Hanoverians that erupted on George I's coronation day suggested to the Jacobites that there was considerable public support for them in England. But to counteract this, security was increased. However, in April 1715 a fanatical Irish Catholic proclaimed James as king, and there was continual unrest in the West Country and Midlands on Stuart anniversaries such as James's birthday. These outbursts of popular support helped to convince James that he would be welcomed in Britain as the nation's saviour. But too much significance was being attached to the riots, and not enough to the composition of the mobs. Many of the rioters had been plied with drink by Jacobite gentlemen, and there were other underlying reasons for discontent that had nothing to do with a Stuart restoration. The plight of the weavers in the West Country was dire, their old skills having been supplanted by aggressive new products from the north. High bread prices and bad harvests played another part in the discontent, and religion was the main focus of the Midland riots, where dissenting meeting-houses were attacked.

The more sober Catholic gentry sent money to James, but kept quiet about their intentions should he arrive. In June 1715 Sir John Webb of Canford, Dorset and Hatherthrop in Gloucestershire sent £500 to the cause, but said he could not send more because he had recently married off his daughters, and had to pay their dowries. One of the daughters married the Earl of Derwentwater who was to play a major part in the 1715 rising.

The British government were not unaware of what was going on, not only through intercepted letters, but also through their spies and agents in France. On 21 July 1715 George I made a speech in Parliament saying that he had intelligence that the Pretender was preparing to invade, and asked Parliament to assist him to repel this invasion. They did so by passing the Riot Act, and suspending *Habeas Corpus*.[10] Dudley Ryder, whose diary records the events in London in 1715, was a Whig lawyer who ended up as Attorney General and Master of the Rolls. He had good reason to fear the return of the Stuarts, and his diary shows how the threat of a Jacobite rising preyed on his mind in the summer of 1715:

Sunday July 3rd 1715. Dreamt a disturbing dream about the Pretender, that he was come and got possession of the throne, that I was a very active man against him. The dream made such an impression on me that is not wore off.[11]

On 25 July 1715 a reward of £100,000 was offered for the apprehension of the Pretender.[12] Warrants were issued for the arrest of suspected persons such as Sir William Wyndham.[13]

Not only the Earl of Mar rode northwards in the summer of 1715. Members of parliament from the north east of England also rode home.

In Northumberland the Catholic Lord Widdrington rode across to Lancashire to consult with his friends there. But despite all this activity in the north, it was in the south west that the rising was expected to start.

South-west England

There was an enclave of Jacobites and discontented Tories in the West Country. The Duke of Ormonde had estates there, as did Lord Lansdowne, another Tory, and the ardent Jacobite Sir William Wyndham. In June and July 1715 other Jacobites started to assemble at Bath and to amass an arsenal there.[14] The conspirators planned that James would land at Plymouth, and that Bristol would be seized for the Jacobites. From there they would be able to control the west of England. Ormonde, now in France, would return to co-ordinate events. In August 1715 Ormonde and Bolingbroke sent a memorial to Lord Lansdowne and Sir William Wyndham in the west and the Earl of Mar in Scotland, telling them that had the king of France not died they would have been with them by now, and that 'The Tory exiles on this side of the water are determined to perish or succeed . . .'.[15]

The delay was fatal. Did the government know about the plot and let the western conspirators continue to commit themselves before pouncing, or did they only discover it in September 1715? At the beginning of September the government swooped. Lords Lansdowne and Dupplin were arrested immediately, and warrants sent out for the arrest of six MPs:

Sir William Wyndham, MP for Somerset. Fled but later arrested.
Sir John Packington, MP for Worcestershire. Arrested but released without trial.
Edward Harvey, MP for Clitheroe, Lancashire. Imprisoned.
John Anston, MP for Launceston. Cleared of any implication in the plot.
Corbet Kynaston, MP for Shrewsbury. Fled into exile.
Thomas Forster, MP for Northumberland. Led the 1715 rising. Guilty.

In the West Country, Sir William Wyndham had been fêted as he returned to his home at Orchard Wyndham near Minehead in Somerset. On 21 September the king's messengers and a troop of dragoons arrived to arrest him. They surprised Sir William in bed, and he asked that they would wait until 7 o'clock before taking him so that his wife's rest would not be disturbed. He further requested that he be allowed to travel in his own coach, and that he be allowed to dress, as he was in his night gown. Dragoons were sent to get the coach ready, and Sir William was allowed to go into his bedroom alone to dress. Once in there he bolted the door, jumped out of the window and fled, leaving behind incriminating papers that named others in the plot and gave information about the arsenal secreted at Bath.

Disguised as a clergyman Wyndham made his way towards London, hoping to be lost in its crowds, and eventually to cross to France. But without funds and nowhere to stay he sent a letter to a friend in Surrey asking if he could give him lodgings for a few days. The letter was opened by the friend's wife who promptly told the government agents. Sir William's hiding place was surrounded. He surrendered and was sent to the Tower.[16]

In Bath the Jacobites panicked, and fled on 'a very Rainy and Stormy night'. Those who did not flee were arrested. Most of those arrested were Irish or Scottish, but there were some English among them. The Jacobites arrested at Bath in September 1715 were as follows:

Mr Hart – Bristol merchant
Colonel Lansdowne – Lord Lansdowne's cousin
Sir George Brown
Captain Doyle – Irish
Captain Sinclair – Scots
Mr McCarthey – Irish
Mr Dun – Scots
Mr MacDonald – Scots[17]

Troops were hurried to areas known to be disaffected towards the Hanoverians. General Wade took his regiments to Bath, and Viscount Falmouth to Cornwall, another potential trouble spot. This mopping up operation did not stop the Oxford Dons electing another Jacobite chancellor, the Earl of Arran, in place of the absconded Duke of Ormonde. His election was followed by massive pro-Jacobite demonstrations, joined by Jacobites from London and the east of England who appeared to have been on their way to Bath but had been diverted to Oxford. When the troops moved in to restore order in Oxford, among those arrested were Mr Spelman of

Norfolk and Mr Lloyd who kept a coffee house in Charing Cross.[18] This suggests a fair degree of co-ordinated planning by the Jacobites.

Arrests elsewhere included Lord Scarsdale, Ambrose Crowley the non-juror and iron-master, Francis Francia, a Christianised Jewish merchant and the Portuguese proprietor of Ozinda's Coffee House in the Strand, Joseph Scriven, a militia sergeant and George Dorman, a journalist.[19]

The Jacobites accused William Shippen MP for Newton, Lancashire of betraying them. Shippen, as befitted a Lancashire MP whose seat was in the pocket of the Leghs of Lyme, was a Tory and a constitutional Jacobite who wanted to restore the Stuarts by parliamentary means rather than violence. He denied any involvement in the arrests, and pinned a notice to one of the pillars of the Royal Exchange in London for all to see, stating that the report that he had betrayed the Jacobites was 'utterly, false, scandalous and malicious'.[20] In doing this he cleared his name with the Jacobites but laid himself open to arrest. Perhaps it is evidence that he thought that this time James would succeed, and he did not want to be on the wrong side when this happened. On the other hand the fact that he remained free does suggest that he was involved in some underhand trading with the Hanoverian government, although there is no evidence to verify this.

North-east England

Warrants were also out for Jacobites at the other end of the country – in the north east. Captain John Hunter of North Tyne and Captain Robert Talbot, an Irishman, landed at Newcastle from France, in order to help coordinate affairs with the rest of the country. Further evidence for events in the north east comes from the Reverend Robert Patten's *History of the Late Rebellion*, published in 1717. Patten had joined the rebels, but cleared himself by turning evidence against them. His eyewitness account of events is one of the most factually accurate accounts we have of the English Jacobites' part in the 1715 rising, but we have to remember that Patten had betrayed the trust of his colleagues and was trying to please new masters, in particular General Wills, to whom the book is dedicated. In order to do this, he shows the rebels in as bad a light as possible. So we must keep in mind that this may be a biased account, and remember the circumstances under which it was written.

According to Patten, the plan of the rising 'was laid at London and carried on in the north east by gentlemen riding from place to place as travellers, pretending a curiosity to view the country'. The principal men entrusted with spreading the design were all Irish: Colonel Henry Oxburgh, Charles and Nicholas Wogan, and John Talbot. There was a second class of agents who were English: Mr Clifton, brother of Sir Gervase Clifton, Mr Beaumont of Nottinghamshire, and Mr Buxton a clergyman from Derbyshire. 'They rode like gentlemen with servants and attendants armed with swords and pistols. They kept moving from place to place, until things ripened for action.'[21] Linkage with other records shows that the Irish contingent came from France, and probably brought officers' commissions with them. The north east of England rather than the north west, where there was thought to be a large body of Jacobite supporters, was chosen as a good landing place for James and troops coming from France because it had good harbours such as that on Holy Island, and there was a covey of Catholics and non-jurors in Newcastle and Gateshead and on the remote moorland of Upper Coquetdale, who were expected to declare for James. It was assumed the gates of Newcastle would be opened to the Jacobites, and that the keel men would flock to their support.

Were the English who joined the 1715 rising there solely because of religious reasons, wanting the restoration of a Catholic monarch above all else? G.M. Trevelyan thought that this was the case. He points out that Catholics had no access to Parliament or public office, and he describes the 1715 rebellion as more of a 'gathering of the Catholic gentry' than a public insurrection.[22] It is true that there were only three Protestants among the leaders of the English contingent, John Fenwick of Bywell, George Carr of Eschill and Thomas Forster of Bamburgh, MP for Northumberland. Forster, who had no military experience, was to be appointed commander-in-chief of the Jacobite forces in England. He was probably motivated by politics and the thirst for political power. As a Tory he had been excluded from office in 1714, and saw little likelihood of any profit under the Hanoverians. But in the north east of England there were other, more local elements that helped to determine whether support was given to the Jacobites or the Hanoverians.

The north east around Tyneside, in County Durham and the Hexhamshire moors was heavily industrialised by 1715, producing coal and iron. The owners and exploiters of the mineral resources included a large number of local gentry. For example, the Earl of Derwentwater owned lead mines around Alston, and Lord Widdrington had coal mines on the Tyne. To ship out their coal and lead the owners needed to construct trackways across other people's land running to staithes on the Tyne. This was one area of local dispute. Another was the way in which the price and production of coal was regulated by the Newcastle Hostmen, while shipping the coal and lead depended on the volatile goodwill of the keel men. Thus, there were other theatres of action in the north east where struggles for local control of resources and politics were as important as national considerations.

Squabbles broke out over the rights of way, and which pits should stand idle when the Hostmen decided to limit coal production to send up prices on the London market. It was essential for the coal owners to have their own representatives on the Hostmen. Whigs and Tories squared up to each other in the coal fields, the board room of the Hostmen, and at the election hustings. In this the north east can be seen as at the forefront of modernity. But it also supported an almost feudal system of affinities, or networks of families, related to each other by blood and marriage, and under obligation to help each other. Owing to the complicated family relationships in the area, the family networks or affinities cut across religious and political divisions, and this meant that members had to make difficult personal decisions on which side they would support in 1715.

For example Lady Cowper, wife of the Whig Lord Chancellor at the time, came from the Clavering family, many members of which were Catholic, and joined the Jacobites in 1715; she also happened to be the cousin of Thomas Forster, the Protestant leader of the English Jacobites. The Claverings were also related to Henry Liddell, one of the leading Whig coal merchants of the day, whose affinity included William Cotesworth, their agent and friend, who kept London informed about what was happening in the north east. Henry Liddell's wife was Lady Cowper's sister, so she too had relatives on the other side. Despite being violently anti-Tory and pro-Whig, Henry Liddell could still refer to Thomas Forster as 'honest Tom' because of his fair dealings in the coal trade, but quarrel with the equally committed Jacobite James Clavering over the Stella mines.[23] Honest Tom Forster was the nephew of Nathaniel,

Lord Crewe, Bishop of Durham, so he was well connected in the Church of England.

Further north in Upper Coquetdale was another affinity based around Catholic strongholds. This included the Claverings of Callaley, Selbys of Biddlestone and Fenwicks of Wallington. The area was well known as a nest of Catholics, and in 1714 the Justices of the Peace for Coquetdale listed over 80 heads of households as Catholics.[24]

The principal Catholics in the north east were the Earl of Derwentwater, whose main estate was at Dilston near Hexham, and Lord Widdrington who lived mainly at Stella on the Durham coal measures. Widdrington was known to be of 'careless temper' and Patten suggested it might have been better if he had stayed at home.[25] When warrants were issued for his arrest he went into hiding, as did the young Earl of Derwentwater and his brother Charles.

On 5 October 1715 Derwentwater, Forster and other Jacobites came out of hiding and met at Wideheugh meadow on the Dilston estates. They decided that their role in the forthcoming rising would be to take Newcastle, and hold it until James appeared off the Northumbrian coast. Accordingly, they sent a message to this effect to their friends who were to meet the next day at a place called Greenrigs, a moor near Rothbury and conveniently placed for all supporters from Coquetdale. On the morning of 6 October those who had met at Greenrigs moved to the top of a hill called Water Falls. This lay on Ermine Street, and on the track from Coquetdale. During the morning they were joined by other rebels, and at last the person they had been waiting for, the Earl of Derwentwater, rode up Ermine Street with his tenants and friends, with drawn swords, but mounted on coach horses. The gathering now numbered about 60 horsemen, gentlemen and their tenants. They rode toward the Coquet and stopped at Plainfield. Here they were joined by more supporters, and together they rode into Rothbury to spend the night there. The English part of the 1715 rising had started.

The rising

Although there were officers from France in Northumberland they do not seem to have taken any part in directing affairs. This was left to Forster, 'now styling himself general'[26] and other amateur soldiers. Their lack of professionalism and military experience is demonstrated by the lack of purpose that enters into their actions over the next few days, as they wandered randomly around Northumberland instead of pressing on to Newcastle.

Newcastle, which the Jacobites thought would be overjoyed to see them, had in fact closed its gates. Sir William Blackett, whom the Jacobites thought would open them, had carefully withdrawn to his country estate and instead the Whigs set about strengthening the walls and gates, while low churchmen and dissenting ministers started to organise the militia, and William Cotesworth began to raise troops. The keel men and lead miners appeared to be indifferent to both sides. On 7 October the Jacobites marched from Rothbury to Warkworth.[27] They needed James and his French troops to arrive at this point, while they still controlled the coastal strip, but he did not appear.

Forster sent Mr Buxton, now appointed chaplain to the army, to Mr Ion, the parson of Warkworth, and told him to pray for James. Mr Ion refused. Buxton took the pulpit himself, whilst Ion judiciously slipped away and went as fast as he could to Newcastle to inform the authorities about the numbers involved, and encourage them to hold fast within the city. Buxton prayed for James and then a disguised Forster proclaimed James king, at the market place to the sound of trumpets. That Forster wished to conceal his identity from the townsfolk of Warkworth suggests that he was not entirely confident they would succeed, and that he did not wish to be recognised and accused later. On Monday 10 October the rebels marched to Morpeth; having been joined by 70 border Scots they now numbered 300, and were getting nearer to Newcastle. However, they told the 'common people' not to join them until they had sufficient arms.[28] This was another reason for needing James and his ships to appear as soon as possible. On the same day in Scotland, the southern Scots rose under Lords Kenmure, Nithsdale, Wintoun, Carnwath and Nairne. Their objective was to march south and meet up with the English. But there was also a second Scottish party marching south, Highlanders led by William Mackintosh of Borlum, the only commander with any military experience.

Thus on 10 October 1715, the Jacobites had Mar's army encamped at Perth, Mackintosh in the Lothians marching south to join the southern Scots, and the English and border Scots at Morpeth. This was a

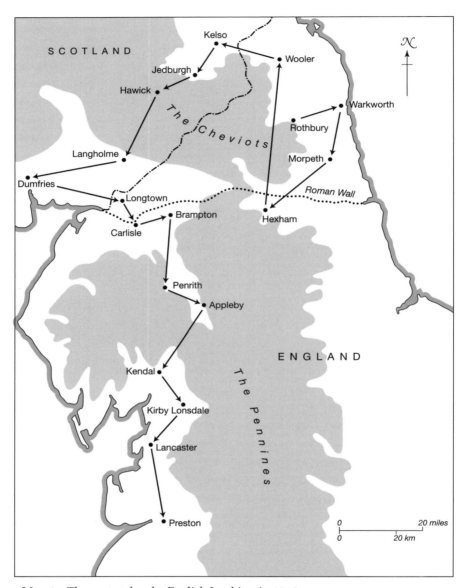

Map 1   The route taken by English Jacobites in 1715

fragmented army that would find it difficult to amalgamate, and it was a force that lacked direction. It was out of the control of James and his ministers who were still in France, and more pertinently it was out of contact with the Duke of Berwick who could have planned its strategy.

While they were at Morpeth the Jacobites learned that Lancelot Errington and his brother had taken Holy Island for the Jacobites. This meant there was now a viable place for James to land. Unfortunately the Erringtons, who had surprised the garrison by swimming to the island at hightide, were themselves surprised the next day by the Governor of Berwick who crossed the sands with 30 men and retook the islands. The Erringtons were put into Berwick gaol, from which they escaped to France.[29]

When it became obvious that Newcastle would not open its gates to them the Jacobites marched west to Hexham, and camped on the Earl of Derwentwater's estates. James was proclaimed king at Hexham market cross. They stayed at Hexham for three days, until news reached them that the southern Scots were close to crossing the border. They marched north to Wooler, and across the border to Kelso. Kelso was barricaded against them, but opened its gates when the Scots arrived. On Kelso moor the men were divided into troops and some semblance of order put into proceedings.

Patten listed the troops, and added comments about some of the commanders. Lord Kenmure was to be commander-in-chief in Scotland and commander of the first troop. He was a grave and serious man. The second troop was the 'merse' troop of borderers raised by James Hume. He was young, but not incapable of command. The third troop was commanded by the Earl of Wintoun, who Patten decided was hot-headed and forward for action. He thwarted the schemes of the Northumberland gentlemen because he wanted to go back into Scotland to take Dumfries and Glasgow, and meet up with Mar. Although the English, including Patten, thought this would have been a foolhardy venture, it was probably their best option. The fourth troop was commanded by James Dalziel, Earl of Carnwath, and the fifth by Captain Lockhart, a half pay officer from the government army, who had changed sides. All of the above were horse; the Scottish foot included Highlanders commanded by Lord Nairne and his son Charles who always marched with the army wearing highland dress, and Lord Charles Murray who also walked with his men, and wore highland dress, without trousers.

The first troop of English horse was the Earl of Derwentwater's troop with his brother Charles in command. Patten is ambivalent about Derwentwater. He found him sweet tempered and generous, but thought his heart was not so much in the enterprise as was expected, or he would have brought along more of his tenants from his mines. The second English horse was Lord Widdrington's, commanded by Thomas Errington of Beaufront, and the third by Captain John Hunter, who was famous for running 'uncustomed goods' from Scotland; in other words he probably smuggled whisky. The fourth troop was led by Robert Douglas and the fifth by Nicholas Wogan, the Irishman from France.[30]

The arrival of the Scots added another dimension to proceedings. When James was proclaimed at Kelso this was not done by someone in disguise, but with trumpets sounding, colours flying and bagpipes playing. The Highlanders made a circle around Seaton Barnes who made the proclamation, and when he had finished there were cries from the Scots of 'No Union', 'No Malt Tax' and 'No Salt Tax'.[31] This injected political and nationalist elements into the rising that had not been there before. The arrival of the old warrior Mackintosh showed the English gentlemen that they were no longer playing at war – this was the real thing. The Scots extracted taxes from the townspeople, and took away all arms and ammunition they found.

The government had not been inactive. Troops commanded by General Carpenter were hurrying north, and the Newcastle militia were stationed on Killingworth Moor, ready to defend the approach to the city. When news reached Kelso that Carpenter and 1000 troops were coming up fast, a heated discussion took place between the commanders which divided on national lines. The Scots wanted to go back into Scotland, the English to go on into England and confront Carpenter whose numbers were inferior to theirs. Eventually, in a state of near panic they left Kelso for Jedburgh. Here it was decided to turn back into England, but the Highlanders refused to cross the border. They marched instead to Hawick. Again the Highlanders refused to go south. They went to the top of a hill, and refused to move unless it was to march into the west of Scotland. Patten thought this was due to Wintoun's evil influence.[32] Thus, from Hawick they went on to Langholme and Dumfries, where another council was held. Should they go on into Scotland and meet up with Mar and defeat the government troops there, or should they go into Lancashire where a further 2000 men might join them? They decided on England.[33]

Again the Highlanders halted and said they would march no further. According to Patten it was only a promise of 6d a day per man that persuaded them to continue. Despite this promise men were beginning to desert.[34] They had seen no action, no help had arrived from France, and now they were being pursued by a government army. From Dumfries they marched to Longtown seven miles from Carlisle, where they learnt that Brigadier Stanwix was on his way with a regiment of horse dragoons. They hurried on through Carlisle to Brampton, and here Forster opened his commission from James and took over command of the army. He had never experienced any military action.

By this time Lord Lonsdale and the Bishop of Carlisle had called out the Cumberland and Westmorland militias, over 14,000 men, and had assembled them on Penrith Fell. Serving in the militia was compulsory for all males aged 16–60, but they were untrained and had only farm implements as weapons. When the Jacobites advanced and took up battle formation, the militia men took one look and fled, to the fury and embarrassment of the redoubtable Bishop. It would seem, however, that the sight of the militia drawn up against them had also panicked the Jacobite army as they entered Penrith in 'general confusion'.[35]

From Penrith they moved to Appleby on 5 November and then to Kendal and Kirby Lonsdale. So far nobody had joined them. This was because Lord Lonsdale and the Bishop of Carlisle had assiduously locked up every known papist they could lay their hands on. However, at Kirby Lonsdale John Dalston of Richmond, Yorkshire and some other gentlemen from that area arrived, and gradually some 'friends from Lancashire' joined the rebels.[36]

Fifty men came from Manchester. They included men recently let out of prison, such as Thomas Sydall who had been in prison for his part in a riot against a dissenting meeting-house. Some Lancashire gentry with their servants appeared. But they were all Catholics, whereas the Jacobites had hoped that High Church Tories would join them as well. Patten ruefully recounted that the Tories 'were Jacobites over a bottle or two, but would not venture any further than the tavern. Having consulted their pillows their force evaporated . . .'.[37]

There was some popular support for the Jacobites shown in Lancashire. In Lancaster, townspeople prevented Colonel Chartres from blowing up the bridge to stop the Jacobites, and welcomed the rebel army. Peter Clark lists the gentlemen who joined the rising in Lancashire:

Sir Francis Anderton of Lostock
Henry Butler of Rawcliffe
Richard and Charles Chorley
John Dalton of Thurnham Hall
Cuthbert and Gabriel Herbert
Mr Hodgson of Leighton Hall
John Tyldesley of the Lodge
Mr Monkcaster, a Protestant attorney
Several poor papists, and a John Cotton of Cambridgeshire also
    joined.[38]

Unfortunately for historians there were two John Cottons who both came from East Anglia, and supported the Jacobites. One Sir John Hynde Cotton of Madingley Hall will be discussed later; however, this particular John Cotton is assumed not to be him but more likely to have been John Cotton, son of Robert Cotton of Huntingdonshire. From Lancaster the Jacobites decided to make for Warrington Bridge over the Mersey, and move on to Manchester where they knew there was support, and then to Liverpool so that they had a seaward escape route. On a rainy day, down muddy roads the tired men marched into Preston, carrying with them six guns taken from ships at Lancaster and brandy seized from the customs house.[39]

It was at Preston that the Jacobites discovered that their intelligence system was at fault. They had been concentrating on the whereabouts of General Carpenter, coming from the east, and still forty miles away. General Wills coming from the south was much closer, at Wigan. Preston was to be their final destination.

The fight at Preston

The town seems to have relished the arrival of so many men. Clark wrote that 'In the afternoon the gentlemen soldiers dressed and trimmed themselves up in their best clothes, for to drink a dish of tea with the

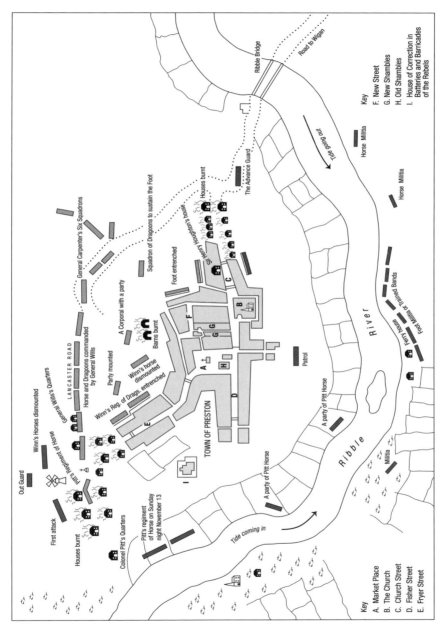

Map 2 The fight at Preston, 1715

ladies of the town, who appeared in their best rigging.' He added 'The ladies of this town, are so very beautiful and so richly attired that the gentlemen soldiers from Wednesday to Saturday minded nothing but courting and feasting.'[40] Patten, who moved in different circles, being a member of Forster's entourage, mentioned nothing about the ladies.

Clark had a poor opinion of Forster's competence as a general. On 11 November, Clark recalled, the Earl of Derwentwater received a letter telling him that Wills was being joined by seven more government regiments, and was on his way to Preston. When Forster was informed of this he became 'dispirited' and Lord Kenmure 'took to his bed'. Nevertheless a council of war was called. It was decided that the most essential thing to do was to guard the Ribble bridges, and to send an advance guard of horse to secure Wigan and a battalion of foot to take Darwen. Clark claims that Forster countermanded these orders, and suggested that Forster might have been suffering from a hangover, 'having taken too much liquor'.[41] But a body of horse went to protect the bridge. Accounts of what happened when they got to the bridge are confused. Clark wrote that on 12 November they found out that Wills was at Walton le Dale, so the Earl of Derwentwater and 300 horsemen went out to defend the bridge. After an hour they withdrew back to the town, and Wills crossed the bridge. Clark defends Derwentwater, explaining the Earl had mistaken Wills's force for a friendly force from Manchester come to join them.[42]

Patten's version is slightly different. He wrote that a body of rebel horse went towards the Ribble bridge, but when they got there they saw the government dragoons advancing and retreated. Patten claimed that he was sent back in all haste to warn the town. Patten blames Derwentwater for allowing the government troops across the bridge because he had not barricaded it. As Wills crossed the bridge he would have been totally exposed to an ambush, as the only road leading from the bridge into town was a narrow lane which would only allow one horse to pass at a time. Patten describes how with drums beating the government troops drew nearer to the bridge. Panic and great activity was taking place in town. Streets were barricaded, and the gentlemen volunteers including the Lords Derwentwater, Kenmure and Wintoun stripped to their waistcoats and dug trenches in the churchyard.[43]

Once the government troops were across the bridge they encountered barricades hastily set up by Brigadier Mackintosh, who was one of the few rebels who knew what he was doing. The houses beside the barricade were set on fire, and there were fatalities on both sides. Peter Farquhson's leg was shattered. He was taken to the White Bull, where he took a glass of brandy and drank to James's health. His leg was amputated by a 'butcher' rather than a surgeon, and he died.[44]

Other casualties started to arrive in the town. At Brigadier Mackintosh's barricade, 300 government troops entered the town at Back Lane, but were repulsed. A second barricade was hastily erected behind this, commanded by Lord Charles Murray. In an act of unspeakable bravery Patten, dressed in his clergyman's robes, was sent over the first barrier to see what was happening. Remarkably firing stopped, he took note of the government forces and coolly returned. Firing restarted.

In the churchyard the Earl of Derwentwater sent an officer to the top of the church steeple to see what was happening. He saw the enemy take Sir Henry Houghton's town house, and march through it to take up position in Broad Lane. This meant they would outflank Lord Charles Murray's barricade. Derwentwater wheeled his men and fired at the enemy. Lord Charles, realising what was happening, joined in and the enemy fled. An officer from the Merse troop suggested they should destroy Houghton's house because it provided cover for the enemy. Forster would not allow this.[45]

Night was drawing in. This was November, and it was dark by four o'clock. General Wills camped outside the town, and burnt several houses and barns at the North End, where the men of the Teviots, Northumberland and Berwick were defending. Wills ordered that all the streets in his hands should be brightly illuminated so that anyone creeping about would be visible. Despite this precaution several rebels made their escape out of Fishergate, and disappeared into the night.[46]

When night fell it looked as if the rebels were safely entrenched in Preston, and that the town would not be taken easily. The next morning the situation had changed. General Carpenter had arrived during the night from Newcastle, with Churchill's and Molesworth's dragoons and a great many gentlemen. The rebels were surrounded, packed into narrow lanes with little chance of fighting their way out, and the escape route through Fishergate onto the marshes blocked by government troops at first light. By 11 o'clock Preston was completely surrounded. The Jacobites held another council of war. The Highlanders wanted to attack the government forces and fight their way out. Forster forbad this, and the talk turned to surrender. The Highlanders were vociferous – they proclaimed they would rather die than surrender. Fighting then broke out among the rebels.[47]

Forster was no soldier. He now relied heavily on Colonel Oxburgh to tell him what to do. Patten ruefully remarks, his Protestant hackles obviously rising, that Forster was named as commander but would always do what Oxburgh told him, and Oxburgh, although a former soldier, was better suited to beads and prayer. Lord Widdrington, who came from the same part of the world as Forster, also had a great influence over him.[48] Oxburgh rode out under a flag of truce to treat with Wills. He took with him the proposition that the rebels would lay down their arms, and surrender as prisoners of war, in anticipation that the king would be merciful. Wills replied that he did not treat with rebels, and all he could guarantee was that he would stop his men from tearing the rebels to pieces if they laid down their arms, but added that the king was clement. Oxburgh was sent back to the rebels who were given an hour to decide what to do. Forster and Widdrington wanted to surrender; the Scots did not.[49] Again we can see the strong national divide in the Jacobite forces. The Scots were fighting mainly for political freedom from England and the right not to pay English taxes; the English were fighting for the right to worship freely and to be able to hold public offices as Tories.

Captain Dalziel was sent across to Wills to represent the Scots. He got the same answer as Oxburgh. Great irritation broke out amongst the Scots and the rebel camp was in confusion; Forster was threatened with lynching. At about 3 o'clock in the afternoon Colonel Cotton arrived from the government forces to get the rebels' answer. The English said they would surrender. The Scots said they would not. Colonel Cotton said he would take this answer back and as he left, six or seven rebels tried to rush him but were intercepted by his bodyguard and cut to pieces before their horrified companions' eyes. In the pocket of one of those killed, Cornet Shuttleworth, was found James III's personal standard. Made of green taffeta it bore the device of a pelican feeding her young with the motto *Tantum valet Amor Regis et Patriae*: 'As this so great is the love for King and Country'.[50]

This action breached the armistice between the two sides, and Wills now demanded hostages from the rebels for their good conduct.

He named the Earl of Derwentwater, and the Lords Kenmure and Widdrington. Dalziel speaking for Kenmure said that he would not agree, but Brigadier Mackintosh might. He went in search of the English lords to see if they would agree. He could not find them, and Mackintosh had retired to bed. At 8 o'clock in the evening General Carpenter sent to say that any English lord and Mackintosh would do. The Earl of Derwentwater, who had reappeared, and Brigadier Mackintosh surrendered themselves to the government army.

Meanwhile the bulk of the Jacobite army, drawn up in the market place, knew nothing about the terms of surrender, and the Scots were still intending to fight their way out. Imagine their surprise as government troops arrived unmolested and disarmed them. Lord Forrester disarmed the gentlemen in the churchyard, and the whole army officially surrendered in the market place; 1088 Scottish prisoners were taken and 462 English; 146 government troops were killed, and 17 rebels.[51]

The fight at Preston was over. The Jacobite rising in England had failed.

Scotland and France

Playing 'what if' is one of contemporary historians' games. What if the Jacobites had held Preston and defeated the government forces and continued south? Would they have succeeded? The answer is probably no. They were rent internally by national differences, and untrained men led by inexperienced officers would have stood little chance against the troops being hurried north from the continent. Besides this, the Jacobites were isolated. Their other army was in Scotland.

On the same day as the fight at Preston, the Earl of Mar's army was involved in the inconclusive battle of Sheriffmuir, which both sides claimed to have won. But Mar's Jacobite army was melting away. Where was James with the French reinforcements he had promised? James was still in France, and still toying with the idea of starting a second front in the West Country. On 8 November 1715 Viscount Bolingbroke advised him that it would be best to land in the west and not Scotland, as his presence was looked for there. On 11 November James despatched Ormonde, who had West Country estates, to set up a base for him. Delayed by wind Ormonde did not sail until 27 November, a fortnight after the surrender at Preston, and time for the news of this to spread across the country. Not surprisingly, when his ship signalled from the sea there was no answering signal from the English coast, and eventually the winds blew him back to Brittany. The idea of a West Country rising was abandoned, and James rode up the coast of France to embark for Scotland from Dunkirk.[52]

He arrived at Peterhead near Aberdeen on 30 December 1715 and rode to Scone Palace near Perth. On 9 January 1716 he made a triumphal entry into Perth, where Mar and the remnants of his army awaited him. He rested at Perth for five days recuperating from an ague. When it was realised that he had not brought French reinforcements with him, enthusiasm for the cause waned; meanwhile the Duke of Argyle was fast approaching with the government army augmented with Dutch and German troops. Talk was made of a honourable surrender.

At this point James and his advisers made a mistake that could have blighted the Stuart cause in Scotland. It was a decision that reflected the fact that James was more used to continental warfare, where it was accepted strategy to destroy resources to keep them from the enemy. James did not realise that issuing such an order on his own territory would not win him friends, and went ahead to issue what became known as 'the Burning Order'. Six villages on Argyle's route to Perth were to be burnt, all their crops destroyed and their animals killed; a scorched earth policy designed to rob Argyle of vital supplies and slow him down.

It was an act of sheer stupidity. Argyle marched with a baggage train of supplies, and each man carried provisions in his haversack. Although James later issued declarations of regret this did not help the inhabitants of Auchterader, Blackford, Crieff, Dubroch, Dunning and Muthill who, in the intense cold of the highland winter, were driven out of their homes on 24–28 January 1716 and had their houses burnt before their eyes. Sixty-five years later the government gave the villagers £4768 in compensation, from which £1000 was deducted as expenses.[53]

On 1 February 1716 the Jacobites withdrew to Dundee, as Argyle's advance guard entered Perth. On 3 February the Jacobites reached Montrose, and on 4 February James embarked to return to France. The 1715 rising was over, a complete failure, and one which was to have wide repercussions throughout the Catholic community of England, and to leave the Highlands under martial law.

The Preston prisoners

Immediately after the surrender at Preston many local men quietly drifted away home, but Wills still had a large number of prisoners to deal with. He started by court-martialling all the army officers who had joined the rebels. They were shot. He then divided the prisoners into groups. The important personages were to be sent to London for trial, the rest were divided between Lancaster and Chester gaols. Those going to London included the Earl of Derwentwater and his brother Charles, Thomas Forster, Lord Widdrington, the Scots lords and Brigadier Mackintosh. They were moved to Wigan, where quarrels broke out as to whose fault it was they had lost at Preston. Mackintosh was hot against Forster and Widdrington, while they blamed him for not defending the river properly.[54]

On 25 November 1715 the Wigan prisoners began to move south. Until they reached the outskirts of London they were allowed to ride on their own horses without fetters, or in coaches. However, the Protestant Forster was singled out for special treatment, and was bound for the whole journey.[55]

Rumours of the rebels' defeat had reached London by 14 November. Ryder wrote in his diary that he had heard at Tom's Coffee House in Westminster the previous evening that Wills had cut the rebels to pieces. However, this was rumour, as London could not have known this by the 13th as the fight was still on. It was not until 15 November that real news came. Ryder writes, 'There is an express today that General Wills had attacked the rebels, had several of his men killed, but had forced the rebels to surrender.' On hearing the news, fights broke out between Tories and Whigs in the streets of London. The Tories burnt an effigy of King William at Cheapside and surrounded the Whig Roebuck Tavern, threatening to pull it down.[56] It is significant that the Tories were careful enough to burn King William and not King George, as the latter would have been an act of treason.

The prisoners from Preston arrived at Highgate on 9 December 1715. Lady Cowper, the wife of the Lord Chancellor, was in an embarrassing position. She belonged to the Protestant branch of the Claverings but the Catholic head of the family was among the rebels, as was her cousin Thomas Forster. She would not go to see the prisoners being brought through London, and would not let her servants or children go.[57] But others did go, and there are a number of eyewitness accounts of the prisoners' entry into London, as well as accounts of what it was like to be one of the prisoners. At Highgate the party was met by 300 foot guards. All the prisoners were tied, and set on horses led by soldiers. Drums beat a triumphal march, and they set out to face the jeering crowds who followed them all the way from Highgate to central London. Cries of 'Down with the rebels', 'No Popish pretender' and 'Long live King George' greeted them. At Holborn they were met by a mob beating warming pans, an allusion to James III's suspect parentage.[58] Overlaying the official procession this added the informal voice of the crowd through the medium of rough music. Forster was the main target for the crowd. Missiles and abuse rained down on him. He was in for a further humiliation. His colleagues were sent to the Tower of London, but he was sent with the common prisoners to Newgate.

Trials and escapes

The winter of 1715/16 was exceptionally cold. On 4 January 1716 the Thames froze over.[59] For the Jacobite prisoners in English gaols there was little comfort. Their fates hung in the balance. They expected the gallows, the axe or transportation to be their only future.

The peers lodged in the Tower of London were examined by secretaries of state on 12 December 1715 at Westminster. The Earl of Derwentwater and Lord Kenmure were regarded as being the most important prisoners, and they were cross-examined frequently. After the re-opening of Parliament on 9 January 1716 a motion was moved to impeach the rebel lords. This was carried by a majority decision. On 10 January they were brought to the bar of the House of Lords and the Articles of Impeachment were read out to them.[60] They were given until 18 January to prepare their defence. As they returned to the Tower they were allowed to break their journey for dinner at the Fountain Tavern in the Strand. This tavern was to play a part in the history of the English Jacobites later in the century.

They were returned to the House of Lords on 19 January. All except Lord Wintoun pleaded guilty. In the eighteenth century the House of Lords was very small, only 70 feet long by 27 broad. It had two rows of benches on the side, and four in the centre arranged in order of precedence. At the north was the Princes' chamber and the throne. The Temporal lords sat on the left of this and there was a stranger's gallery at the south end. There was seating for 125 peers, provided they only took up 18 inches of space on the bench. In 1716 there were 205 peers.[61] All of them tried to squash into the chamber to hear the Jacobite lords admit their guilt.

The rebel lords claimed they acted out of principle with no desire to spill blood. Lord Widdrington said he was too ill with gout of the stomach to plot against the king, so there was no conspiracy. Others explained they had only joined the rebellion when forced, or on impulse with no forward planning. Only Lords Carnwath and Kenmure offered no apology.[62]

They were sentenced on 9 February in Westminster Hall. Unlike today Westminster Hall was divided into legal courts. It was thronged with lawyers, and there were stalls owned by legal stationers, coffee houses and confectioners. The noise in the hall was terrific. Scaffolding had been erected for those wishing to hear the rebel lords sentenced, and tickets were sold. Ryder purchased one of these, but complained afterwards that the hubbub was so great he could not hear what was said.[63] All the rebel lords were sentenced to death, but in the end only the Earl of Derwentwater and Lord Kenmure were executed. Carnwath, Nairne and Widdrington were pardoned, although Widdrington was transported to Carolina, USA. Lords Nithsdale and Wintoun made spectacular escapes from the Tower of London. Nithsdale was smuggled out dressed as a woman, and Wintoun sawed through the bars of his cell with the spring from his watch.[64]

Prison security in London in the early 18th century either left much to be desired, or the authorities wanted to lose embarrassing prisoners whose executions might turn them into martyrs. Forster escaped from Newgate on 14 April 1716, with the help of a key acquired by his sister Dorothy. Drinking late one night with a fellow prisoner, they invited the governor to join them. Forster excused himself to go to the privy, locked the governor in and let himself out, and disappeared. Brigadier Mackintosh and some of his fellow Scots fought their way out of Newgate and later Charles Radcliffe, the Earl of Derwentwater's brother, also escaped and fled to France.[65] Not so lucky was Colonel Oxburgh who was found guilty of treason and executed; 'Mad' Jack Hall of Otterburn,

Northumberland and a non-juror clergyman, the Reverend Paul, were also executed. Oxburgh's petition for mercy said that he had been in London on his private affairs, and being apprehensive about having the oath tendered to him and being committed if he refused to take it, he had taken up an invitation to travel to the north of England with some friends. In Northumberland he had met some of the persons concerned in the rebellion, and they had prevailed upon him to go along with them. Before that he was an absolute stranger to the rebel lords and Mr Forster, and no ways able to give them any assistance. He was deluded at Preston and made an early submission.[66]

The commoners being held in gaols in Lancashire and Cheshire were in the worst condition: 68 prisoners were tried at Liverpool in January 1716, 13 of whom were hanged, 3 died in prison, 7 were acquitted and the rest were sentenced, but there is no record of their executions. Petitions for mercy were sent to London, from John Dalton, Derwentwater's servant, George Gibson, one of the Dilston tenants, and Philip Hodgson, who claimed he had 23 children at home who needed subsistence.[67] In July 1717 there were still 14 Jacobite prisoners in the Marshalsea prison and 147 in Chester. A further 500 had been transported to the West Indies and to South Carolina, Virginia, and Maryland in America. They went defiantly saying they would return and put James on the throne.[68]

Apart from the gentry, who joined the English Jacobite army in 1715? Leo Gooch points out that the lists of prisoners are deficient and selective. Using a correlation of extant lists he estimated that there were 271 Northumbrians out in 1715; 30 per cent were minor gentry or noblemen, 46 per cent of these were Roman Catholics. Two thirds of the Northumbrians were tradesmen, including nine weavers, butchers, wig-makers, a chandler and glove maker. Gooch assumes they joined voluntarily, but others who came from the gentry estates may have been forced. They were the farmers, servants and estate workers.[69] Prisoners listed as being at Liverpool divided into 36 English and 35 Scots. The English divided into one third gentry, one third tradesmen, and one third labourers. Nine of them came from Preston, and six from nearby Walton le Dale.

The English Jacobite army of 1715 was composed of inexperienced men and commanders. This contributed to its failure. Its opponents were trained and experienced soldiers. Furthermore, the Jacobites were isolated from their central organisation, and from each other. The random marches around Northumberland and their failure to take Newcastle shows their lack of direction. They were desperate not only for reinforcements from France, but also orders as to what they should do. Although Forster's inadequacy as a general contributed to the failure, the blame must ultimately lie with James III and his half brother the Duke of Berwick, the only experienced soldier on the Jacobite high command. Some blame must also be attached to the political machinations and national rivalries at the court in exile, and to chance. If the French king had not died French help might have been forthcoming.

National rivalries played a part in the failure of the English part of the campaign. The decision not to march on into the west of Scotland, and eventually to meet up with Mar was probably fatal. When James did arrive it was too late, and the burning order lost him support in the north. James could step on a boat and sail back to the relative safety and comfort of the continent. His supporters were to bear the brunt of the 1715 rising for many years.

The real result of the 1715 rising

The direct result of the rising was the imprisonment, execution or transportation of the prisoners. The estates of landowners were forfeited and their families lost their income. Litigation followed as members of the rebels' families who had charges on the estates left to them in marriage settlements and wills tried to recoup these. Mothers, aunts and uncles of those accused, as well as their wives and children, had claims and emerged to fight for these.

The estates themselves passed into the hands of the Forfeited Estates Commission to be disposed of; some were kept in hand for national investment, others were sold. The net result was a great exchange of owners in the north east, and the chance for up and coming entrepreneurs to buy into land, and increase their grip on the coal industry. William Cotesworth, the Whig agent in the north east, was quick off the mark. In association with his friend Joseph Banks he purchased a life interest in Lord Widdrington's Durham estate. This included the lucrative collieries at Whickham and Stella. However, Widdrington's Catholic agent made it as difficult as possible for them to realise any profit from it. He refused to quit and bullied any tenants that Cotesworth and Banks put onto the estate, thus keeping the 1715 strife alive in Durham for many years, and increasing the bitterness between Whigs and Tories.[70]

The Forfeited Estates Commission pursued their brief vigorously, searching out those whose land was forfeit, not because they had joined the rising but because they had devised some of it to the Catholic Church for superstitious uses. Informers were encouraged by rewards. For example John Mandeville showed the commission that Francis Buck, late of the city of London, had devised lands in his will to his sister Mary, abbess of a convent in Flanders, for superstitious uses. He asked the commissioners for his reward.[71]

Lower down the scale, those transported left families behind who became dependent on poor relief. Treated not as indigent poor, poor through no fault of their own, but as idle poor, they were destined for harsh treatment. To date there has been little research on the families of those transported through Liverpool; they seemed to disappear into the mists of time.

The next group to suffer as a result of the 1715 rising were all deemed to be guilty, whether or not they had joined the rebels. The Catholic population of England were made an example of to deter any further thoughts they might have of a Stuart restoration. In 1716 an Act of Parliament was passed compelling all Catholics to register their estates, and appointing a commission to raise money out of these. Following the discovery of the Atterbury plot in 1723, a composite fine of £100,000 was levied on the Catholic community, and the land tax was doubled for all those who refused to take the oath of allegiance. These actions restored a degree of religious persecution not seen in England for three decades, and it went against the personal inclination of George I who was in favour of religious toleration.[72]

Not only was religious toleration reduced after 1715, but personal liberty was also curtailed. Government troops were stationed at strategic points and their behaviour was aggressive and frightening to the local population. This was designed to show who had the upper hand and quell any future thoughts of a Stuart restoration. Ashbourne in Derbyshire was strategically placed on the road from London to Manchester, and there were pockets of hard-line Catholics in Derbyshire such as the Eyres of Hassop or the Fitzherberts at Norbury. A troop of soldiers from Cotton's and Churchill's Dragoons under a Major Roberts was stationed in the town in 1716. On 27 May 1716 the local squire, Brooke Boothby of Ashbourne Hall, was told by Major Roberts that all those who did not illuminate their windows the next evening in honour of the king's birthday would have them smashed. Hearing this Boothby had the common crier proclaim the threat through the town, and accordingly the next evening every window in the town was lit, Boothby buying candles out of his own pocket for those who could not afford them.

During the evening Boothby and other gentlemen moved about the town declaring their loyalty to King George, and all met up at the common bonfire in the Market Place where wine was drunk to the health of the royal family, all their issue and all their ministers. They stayed out until midnight. The following day there was a service of public thanksgiving, and the houses were illuminated again in the evening. No windows were broken on this occasion, but it shows the tension in the town about the soldiers' presence and what they would do. Boothby tried to alleviate the tension, but it increased.

On 1 August, the anniversary of George's accession, the church bells were supposed to be rung. Ashbourne church stayed silent. Boothby explained to Roberts that this was because the steeple was dangerous and was being repaired. But Roberts went to the churchwarden's house, and he being from home used several violent and threatening words against the warden's wife, telling her if the bells were not rung Lord Cobham would come and sack the town. When the churchwarden arrived, Roberts and Captain Ballantine told him, 'if he did not take care that the bells be rung it was as much as his ears were worth . . .'.

The bells were rung, but the soldiers marched into the market place and fired their rifles, and would only go away when given money to drink the king's health. They continued very merry until 9 o'clock, when they realised there was no bonfire or illumination in the town. Boothby quickly sent for a constable and ordered him to provide a bonfire, but Roberts ordered all windows without lights to be broken. The soldiers ran amok with swords in their hands and, encouraged by their officers, they broke 98 windows.

From then on Boothby suffered intimidation from the soldiers, especially those of Captain Ballantine's troop. His windows were broken and graffiti was smeared on his walls proclaiming 'Long live King George', 'Sudden death to Mr Boothby', and threatening to burn his house down.

Further trouble broke out on 20 October, the anniversary of George I's coronation. On that evening there was a public bonfire in the market place, while Boothby had a private fire with some of his friends. The officers were at the public bonfire, but moved on to Boothby's at 6 o'clock. Mrs Boothby said that when the officers appeared her husband took a bottle and glasses out to them. One of Boothby's guests was Baptist Trott, JP who had taken statements against the officers involved in smashing windows in August. Captain Ballantine challenged him, and Trott 'grinned and shook his fist'. This led to a full-scale fight between the officers and the gentry during which all Boothby's windows were broken, and his parlour wrecked. The fight spilled out into the town. Soldiers with swords drawn hurried to reinforce their officers. A customs and excise officer was assaulted, stones were thrown, and 60 windows were broken.[73]

Law and order had broken down in Ashbourne because it was being flouted by the military imposing themselves in an aggressive manner, and ignoring civil law. They marched through the town at night with corps of drummers, and later claimed it was the noise of the drums that broke the windows. Boothby and Trott as justices of the peace endeavoured to defuse the situation and keep order in the town, doing this through the correct channels, using the town crier and constables. What had been a peaceful market town was turned into a bear garden where the citizens could not sleep peacefully in their beds at night. Was there a Jacobite element in the friction at Ashbourne? Brooke Boothby was a member of the Tory Mock Corporation of Cheadle, and he had Catholic friends, but there is no evidence that he was a Jacobite.

Ashbourne was not alone in suffering at the hands of the troops after 1715, and it is evident that the government's attitude towards social deviants had hardened. Harsh new laws that increased capital offences were to come onto the statute book soon after the rising. The 1715 rising was a Jacobite failure, and it marked a change in English society.

Notes

1   S. Cowper ed., *Diary of Mary, Countess Cowper, 1714–1720*, London: John Murray, 1864, 5.

2   HMC, *Calendar of the Stuart Papers at Windsor*, I, 1902.

3   *Stuart Papers* I, 334–5.

4 *Stuart Papers* I, 336–7.

5 *Stuart Papers* I, 337.

6 *Stuart Papers* I, 343–5.

7 *Stuart Papers* I, 352–3.

8 *Stuart Papers* I, 357.

9 *Stuart Papers* I, 381–2.

10 W. Matthews ed., *The Diary of Dudley Ryder 1715–1716*, London: Methuen, 1939, 48.

11 *Ryder Diary*, 46.

12 A. Boyer, *The Political State of Great Britain*, X, London: 1716, 196.

13 *Ryder Diary*, 58–60.

14 C. Petrie, *The Jacobite Movement – The First Phase, 1688–1716*, London: Eyre and Spottiswoode, 1948, 163.

15 *Stuart Papers* I, 413–14.

16 Boyer, 330–34.

17 Boyer, 333; Petrie, 168.

18 Petrie, 169–70.

19 Petrie, 170.

20 Petrie, 171.

21 R. Patten, *The History of the Late Rebellion*, London: 1717, 24, 26.

22 G.M. Trevelyan, 'The Last Rising in the North, 1715', *The Northern Counties Magazine*, 1, 1901, 293–4.

23 J.M. Ellis ed., *The Letters of Henry Liddell and William Cotesworth*, Leamington Spa: James Hall, Surtees Society, 197, 1987, 89.

24 D. Dixon, 'Notes on the Jacobite Movement in Upper Coquetdale, 1715', *Archaeologia Aeliana*, NS XVI, 1894, 111–12.

25 Patten 125–6.

26 Patten, 29.

27 Patten, 28.

28 Patten, 29–30.

29 Patten, 31.

30 Patten, 49–64.

31 Patten, 41.

32 Patten, 61.

33 Patten, 71.

34 Patten, 74.

35 Patten, 84.

36 Patten, 86.

37 Patten, 93.

38 P. Clark, *The March of the Insurgent Force from Penrith to Preston*, London: 1716, in S.H. Ware, *The Lancashire Memorials of the Rebellion, 1716*, Chetham Society Publications, V, 1865, 89, 94–6. Clark may have been one of the Earl of Derwentwater's servants.

39 Clark, 73.

40 Clark, 96, 107.

41 Clark, 109.

42 Clark, 119.

43 Patten, 97–100.

44 Clark, 124; Patten, 101–4.

45 Patten, 105.

46 Clark, 134.

47 Clark, 139; Patten, 109, 119.

48 Patten, 119.

49 Clark, 141.

50 Clark, 142.

51 Clark, 142–6.

52 *Stuart Papers* I, 433, 456, 461, 467, 471.

53 J. Baynes, *The Jacobite Rising of 1715*, London: Cassell, 1970, 170.

54 Patten, 133–5.

55 Ware, 182.

56 *Ryder Diary*, 138.

57 Cowper, 62.

58 Boyer V, 543; Patten, 136; Ryder, 147; Ware, 181–5.

59 *Ryder Diary*, 156.

60 *Ryder Diary*, 160.

61 C. Jones and G. Holmes eds, *The London Diaries of William Nicolson, 1702–1718*, Oxford: Clarendon Press, 1985, 81–3.

62 There is a full account of the Earl of Derwentwater's trial in the next chapter.

63 *Ryder Diary*, 181.

64 Cowper, 92; *Ryder Diary*, 189, 209.

65 Ware, 214–16.

66 PRO SP 35/7/26.

67 PRO SP 35/7/1–10, 13, 15, 27, 33.

68 PRO SP 35/9/37, 43; E. Hughes, *North Country Life in the 18th Century*, Oxford: OUP, 1952, 349–52.

69 L. Gooch, *The Desperate Faction? The Jacobites of N.E. England, 1688–1745*, Hull: University of Hull Press, 1995, 60–61.

70 L. Gooch, 'Incarnate Rogues and Vile Jacobites; Silvertop versus Cotesworth, 1718–1723', *Recusant History*, 18, 1987, 277–88.

71 J.A. Payne, *Records of English Catholics 1715*, London: Burns and Oates, 1889, 139.

72 C. Haydon, *Anti-Catholicism in 18th century England*, Manchester: Manchester University Press, 1993, 125.

73 PRO SP 35/6/15 (2–8); 42–3; 35/8/3.

CHAPTER 6

＊＊＊＊＊＊＊＊＊＊＊＊＊＊

The Earl of Derwentwater

'Lord Derwentwater was perhaps the most attractive, as well as the most pathetic figure in the Jacobite martyrology.'[1] Aged only 27 when he died, James Radcliffe, Earl of Derwentwater's short life has become embroidered with overtones of historical fiction. The Victorians added myths and legends to it, and in the 21st century websites on Dilston Hall, his Northumberland home, claim that his ghostly figure haunts the ruined tower, and that Dilston Water ran red when he was executed. How near to fact are the stories about the earl? Was he the tragic romantic figure of the 19th-century romance, or merely a disaffected aristo who thought that the Stuarts would serve him better than the Hanoverian Georges? As we shall see, sweep away the romantic additions and we find a rather frightened young man, caught up in events over which he had no control or experience in handling. We shall also see that there was indeed a heroic streak in him as he faced death rather than renounce his religion, and that although others might support the Stuarts through self-seeking motives, he genuinely believed that James was his rightful king.

The earl's early death illustrates the sacrifices made in the 1715 rising, and although he had responded to the call to arms of his own volition, he and others like him would have preferred to live quietly and unobtrusively on their country estates, worshipping in the Catholic faith with like-minded neighbours, hunting and dining with them, attending race meetings and the assizes, and managing their estates. For many Northumbrian families this way of life was cut short in 1715. Let the Earl of Derwentwater stand as their representative.

The Radcliffes and the Derwentwater estate

The Radcliffes were a powerful northern family with property in Cumberland and Northumberland. Their obstinate recusancy barred them from lucrative court offices in the 16th century but enabled them to keep a finger on the pulse of local affairs, especially when it came to the purchase of land. Their original estate was at Derwentwater in Cumberland, on an area once known as Lord's Island. This was a proper island in the lake, but had been joined to the shore by a bridge. They also owned all the shores of the lake. They acquired Dilston in Northumberland in the 15th century when Sir Edward Radcliffe married Anne Cartington, the heiress of Dilston, on the south bank of the river Tyne, and this became their main residence.[2]

Another Sir Edward increased the family fortunes further in the early 17th century when he purchased lead mines on Alston Moor. He was granted the tolls of Keswick market by Charles I, and by the end of the 17th century the Radcliffe estates included the barony of Langley in Northumberland, encompassing the manors of Aydon, Elrington, Newlands and Whittengstall. They also owned the manors of Dilston, Throckley and East Thornton, and other pockets of land in Northumberland. In Cumberland they owned the manors of Derwentwater alias Keswick and Thornthwaite, and the manor of Scremerton in County Durham. Their income was increased by tithes from Broxfield, Lurbitte and Whinnethy. The whole was worth at least £11,500 a year, with timber on their estates bringing in a further £4500.[3]

James Radcliffe was a very wealthy young man and also a young man with royal connections. The speed with which the transition was made from northern country gentry to peers of the realm, related to royalty, can be judged from the fact that the family did not even acquire a baronetcy until 1619, when Francis Radcliffe purchased one for £700.

As recusants their fortunes took a tumble in the Civil War; their estates were sequestered by Parliament and the life interest in them sold. The house on Lord's Island at Derwentwater was wrecked, but apart from that they emerged from the interregnum relatively unscathed. As the estates had been legally settled so that the head of the family held them for his life from trustees, they only had to buy this back at the Restoration, and not the actual land.

Sir Francis Radcliffe, who succeeded to the title in 1663, could look forward to a long and prosperous life. Charles II favoured Catholics and his brother James, Duke of York, was one. There was a minor setback when Catholics were blamed for the Great Fire of London in 1666 and anti-Catholic hysteria spread across the county. While following the false accusations of Titus Oates that there was going to be a Catholic invasion Sir Francis was briefly imprisoned, but with the accession of James II in 1685 everything looked rosy again for the Radcliffes.

Sir Francis Radcliffe II was ambitious and had his eye on the earldom of Sussex. This had been in the hands of a Lancashire branch of the Radcliffe family who had become extinct in 1641. Although there was no blood relationship between the Northumberland Radcliffes and the Lancastrian Radcliffes, if Sir Francis became Earl of Sussex at least he would be carrying on the right name. He set out to win himself an earldom. One way of advancement in the late 17th century was marriage to one of the illegitimate progeny of the monarch or his brother. Although Charles II and his brother were short on legitimate male heirs they had produced a large clutch of illegitimate children. The boys were given peerages, and the girls advantageous marriages.

Charles II had at least seven mistresses who between them produced at least sixteen children. The dukedoms of Monmouth, Leeds, Cleveland, Grafton, Northumberland, St Albans and Richmond all owed their origin to the illegitimate progeny of Charles II. Sir Francis Radcliffe perceived that those who married the illegitimate daughters of the king were also elevated to the peerage. He began to angle for a marriage between his eldest son Edward and Lady Charlotte Fitzroy, the daughter of Charles and Barbara Villiers. The negotiations fell through, and Lady Charlotte married the Earl of Lichfield. Undaunted, Sir Francis kept his eldest son unmarried to wait until another of Charles's daughters became available.

There has been considerable debate on the attitude towards marriage in the early modern period. Were marriages made from affection, or were marriages arranged by parents who demanded absolute obedience from their children? In *The Family, Sex and Marriage in England, 1500–1800*, Lawrence Stone created a model on marriage choice and relationships within marriage that historians have been testing ever since.[4] Between 1550–1700 the family was seen as an analogy for the state. Children were expected to obey their parents without question, just as subjects were expected to be obedient to the king. Stone suggests that in upper-class families relationships were distant, based on obligation, and marriages were arranged by the parents rather than made for love. This generation of the Radcliffes bears this out. Edward, the eldest son, was not allowed to marry until his father had identified a suitable bride, and his four brothers were to remain unmarried.

The next candidate as a bride for Edward Radcliffe was another of Charles II's illegitimate daughters, Lady Mary Tudor, the daughter of Moll Davis, an actress. This time the negotiations were successful. Francis Radcliffe won his prize of an earldom and became the Earl of Derwentwater, and Edward Radcliffe a bride. This meant that Edward and Lady Mary's children were the grandchildren of a king, and first cousin to half the nobility of England. Their eldest son James was born in 1689. He came from a seriously dysfunctional family. Lady Mary was a Protestant and wayward; her taste was the social whirl of London whereas Edward, 20 years her senior, was set in his bachelor ways, writing verse and reading the classics. Lady Mary was only 16 when James was born, and after the birth of two more sons and a daughter it was clear that the marriage had irrevocably broken down. In February 1700 a deed of separation was drawn up. Edward agreed to pay his wife's debts and to give her an allowance of £1000 a year. He got custody of the children. Lady Mary's debts included £36 to 'The Indian Queen', and £12 to 'The Naked Boy' as well as money owing to clothes, her stay-makers and perfumerer.[5]

Lady Mary left to live with Henry Grahme, MP for Westmorland, whom she married after her husband's death. There was no modification in her lifestyle. Shortly before her second husband died she wrote to her father-in-law complaining that they were being dunned by creditors as her husband lay on his death bed. Grahme died shortly afterwards, and within a few months she was remarried to James Rooke. History has not dealt kindly with Lady Mary. She had abandoned her children and departed to live in sin but, as we shall see, her eldest son bore her no malice.

Edward Radcliffe died in 1705, and James Radcliffe became the third Earl of Derwentwater at the age of 16. Three years earlier he had been sent abroad with his brother Charles to be educated in France. Tradition says that they were educated with their cousin, the son of James II. However, they do not appear on James's household list. Undoubtedly they would have met their cousin, but there is no documentary evidence to support this. Similarly, accounts of the idyllic life led by the children at St Germains are not borne out by the poverty experienced by the court in exile.[6] The Earl of Derwentwater, unlike other Jacobites in France, was a voluntary exile. His father had not been attainted for treason, and he still received the income from his estates. It is clear that the stay in France was temporary as when Derwentwater came of age in 1709 he applied for a licence to allow him to return to England and take up his inheritance. Thus, in December 1709 he travelled to Holland with his brother and fellow Northumbrian Roger Fenwick and was back in England by January 1710.[7]

At first they went to London and stayed with Derwentwater's distant relative Dr John Radcliffe, who financed the Radcliffe Camera, the Infirmary and the Observatory in Oxford. Radcliffe may have obtained the licence for Derwentwater's return as he had been corresponding with him in France. It was John Radcliffe who wrote to Derwentwater's Northumbrian neighbours to tell them that he was back, and would be with them shortly.

Dr Radcliffe had another connection with Derwentwater. He was the physician to Derwentwater's uncle Thomas who was suffering from what today would be identified as schizophrenia, hearing voices and thinking he was being followed by something he could only escape by travelling by sea.[8] Derwentwater was in Northumberland by 10 February 1710 when Lady Swinburne wrote to Dr Radcliffe that 'My Lord is well pleased with Dilston and says it answers all he has heard of it; but he is resolved to build a new house, although Roger Fenwick told him he need not alter another stone of it.'

Dilston Hall

Dilston Hall was built around a bastle (or pele tower, as these used to be known). This was a strongly fortified tower in which the family and their cattle could hide when border raiders came. When the Radcliffes took up residence in the 16th century they began to enlarge the building. In 1621 a three-storied stone house was added to the tower. This was rebuilt in 1663 with a brick extension added to the north of the tower, and a chapel linked to the tower by a gallery.[9] The site itself was in an excellent position, on a bluff overlooking the stream known as Devils Water and surrounded by parkland. The third earl decided to rebuild the house yet again, this time in the French style. It was to be re-orientated to face a forecourt to the south with the mansion flanking it on three sides. There may have been a fountain in the middle of the courtyard. A grand entrance hall paved with marble led to the family's apartments. The tower was to remain, but would be made to look less warlike by adding a flower garden around it.

Over the years after Derwentwater's execution the hall built by him was demolished, although the tower remained. In 1731, following the death of Derwentwater's son, an inventory of the hall was taken. If the inventory follows the usual pattern in which the appraisers walked from room to room we can see that the New Building, presumably the earl's addition, contained a parlour with a nursery directly above it, and opening off the passage the Plad (sic) room, with the servants' hall and cellars beneath it. In the south-east wing of the old building was a room belonging to one of Derwentwater's aunts and known as Lady Ann's room, and below more servants' rooms, a kitchen and bakehouse, and above garrets. Outside there was a brew house. In all, ten living rooms are mentioned, exclusive of the kitchen. The goods remaining in the rooms in 1731 are sparse, but show that building stopped suddenly and the fittings were incomplete when Derwentwater joined the 1715 uprising. There were loose timbers, wainscoting, and an unfixed stone chimney piece stored in the house.[10]

Prints of Dilston Hall show a square house, lacking in charm, on an eminence above the stream. Items remaining in the inventory, and other sources give some idea of how it looked when Derwentwater rode out to war on an autumn morning in 1715. There were silver candlesticks, a silver coffee pot, a silver shaving basin, salvers, sugar castors, salt-cellars and a child's saucepan. These were sold in 1715 to settle the earl's debts; remaining unsold were other silver coffee pots, a tea kettle, more salvers, silver sconces for the wall, and a silver snuff box called the philosopher's stone with a rim of gold, another snuff box made of mother of pearl within a rim of gold with gold hinges, and a gold toothpick case.

Other goods offered for sale in 1715 included a scarlet cloth saddle cover, a crimson velvet cradle saddle, copper drinking pots, dressing glasses, beds, china, pewter and a turkey work carpet worth together £38. Unsold items included prints and pictures, curtains, bed linen, and tapestries valued at £246. Derwentwater's personal possessions were valued at £86.[11]

From these we can get a good idea of what a young nobleman wore. This included a gold hilted sword and gold watch. He carried a silver wand and dressed in suits of cinnamon, brown and black with waistcoats of brocade, crimson satin, as well as flannel and calico waistcoats. He had two summer suits, two nightgowns and hats with silver braid. He possessed 42 calico shirts, some trimmed with lace, 12 handkerchiefs, 10 stocks, 18 pairs of stockings, 4 periwigs, and a scarlet riding coat with gold buttons, shoes, slippers and a muff. His travelling equipment consisted of a trunk and two leather cases, in which there were three pairs of sheets, two old towels, two gowns, a knife and fork in a case, and a case of instruments for the teeth. He also had a wash bag and screen.[12]

The inventory gives some idea of what the interior of the house looked like. In the parlour there was a cabinet inlaid with gold, and cane chairs. Cane chairs were to be found in many rooms. The plaid room was presumably named after the dominant design of its furnishings. Perhaps to balance the colour of the plaid the cane chairs in there were painted black. Many of the items were described as old in 1731. Undoubtedly, had James Radcliffe lived, Dilston Hall would have been furnished in the height of fashion.

As well as replanning Dilston Hall, Derwentwater was getting to know his Northumbrian neighbours. He went hunting with the Swinburnes at Capheaton in March 1710. With him was a Yorkshire Jacobite, Sir Marmaduke Constable. Derwentwater's contribution to the bag was a squirrel, but he was hampered by a bad leg. He also visited Whitton and Widdrington.[13]

Having inspected his Northumbrian estates Derwentwater left for a tour of his Cumbrian lands. While in the north west he attended a meeting of the mock corporation of Walton-le-Dale, which had been founded in 1701, with Derwentwater's father as one of its founder members. Walton-le-Dale was one of several 'mock corporations' found in the north west, and the West Country. One theory for their origin is that they grew out of the traditional custom of a lord of misrule elected on Twelfth

Night. The mayor of the mock corporation, it is suggested, was one of the village clowns.[14] Given the identity and status of some of the mayors this does not seem likely.

Another theory is that they were formed when James II issued a *mandamus* that called in the charters of all incorporated boroughs. Robbed of their mayor and corporation, places such as Cheadle elected a mock mayor and aldermen who re-enacted all the civic panoply of the mayor's feast. At Cheadle local gentry and nobility belonged to the mock corporation, including the Leveson-Gowers, the Grosvenors, and Brooke Boothby from Ashbourne, who had such trouble with the soldiers, was mayor from 1718–19.[15]

Were these Jacobite secret societies? There was no secret about these organisations. Everything was in the open. Minutes of meetings were kept, corporation officials elected, and processions taken through the village or town with official regalia worn by the officers. The regalia of Walton-le-Dale mock corporation included two staves covered with silver hoops, and one covered entirely in silver given to the corporation by James Radcliffe when he visited it in 1710. A further staff had the names of the mayors and officers engraved on it.[16] The mock corporation of Walton-le-Dale met at the Unicorn Inn, and as well as having officers that one would expect to find in any corporation such as a mayor, recorder and mace bearer, it included a master of hounds, poet laureate, house groper and custard eater – all of which points to it being a social drinking club, although Ralph Arnold suggests that 'it maybe presumed, the corporation plotted rather vaguely in the Jacobite interest.'[17]

Arnold writes that Derwentwater was elected mayor in 1711, but Coupe disagrees with this, and the minute book leaves 1711 blank. This suggests that it might have been written up after the events, and that the Earl of Derwentwater's name is omitted from fear of government reprisals.[18]

Following his tour of his north-western estates Derwentwater spent the next eighteen months at Dilston, enjoying the company of his neighbours, overseeing the management of his estates, and planning the rebuilding of Dilston Hall. But a young gentleman with a landed estate needed an heir, and a wife to provide him with one. The Earl of Derwentwater not only needed a wife, but he needed a Catholic wife so that his children could be brought up in his religion.

The Earl of Derwentwater's marriage

Unlike his father James Radcliffe had no parents to arrange his marriage. He could marry whom he chose, for love. His marriage illustrates the next phase of Lawrence Stone's model, the affectionate marriage in which the marriage was made by mutual attraction, and relationships within the marriage were warm and loving, with wife and husband more equal partners, and children valued as individuals.[19] The Earl of Derwentwater's marriage stood on the cusp of the transition between the patriarchal model and the affectionate model, with the additional constraint of religion.

The Catholic gentry were a close-knit group with a country-wide network of contacts. Probably during one of his periodic visits to London, Derwentwater met Anna Maria Webb, the daughter of Sir John Webb, one of the most important West Country Catholic landowners with property in Dorset, Somerset and Gloucestershire. His wife, the daughter of Lord Belasye, came from a Catholic and royalist family.

According to tradition Derwentwater fell in love with Anna, and his courtship was undertaken while he was a house guest with her parents at Canford in Dorset. Much of the tradition about the wooing of Anna Maria is Victorian embroidery. According to this one of the other young men at the house plucked a moss rose and gave it to Anna, who placed it in her bosom. When Derwentwater asked if he could have it she refused, and a lovers' tiff followed. After she had retired to bed Derwentwater stood on the terrace beneath her window, and serenaded her so sweetly that she accepted his proposal of marriage. There is no evidence for any of this, but subsequent events showed that there was a strong bond between the couple, and even if they did not marry for love, a deep affection later developed.

Anna Maria had been educated in a Paris convent. She came from a good Catholic family, and her parents should have been delighted at the match, but they were circumspect when it came to arranging her future. The marriage settlement drawn up on 24 June 1712 shows that she had a marriage portion or dowry of £12,000. This was to be paid in instalments: £5000 when the marriage took place, £5000 after five years and £2000 in the year following her father's death. So in effect Derwentwater would only get £5000 as a down payment. In the event of her surviving him she was to have a widow's jointure of £1000 a year, with a further £100 added if her parents were already dead. She was to get pin money of £300 a year. Any daughters born to the marriage would get marriage portions of £12,000 each, rising to £20,000 each if there was no male heir. An unusual condition was that after the marriage the couple were to remain at the Webbs' house at Hathethrop in Gloucestershire.[20]

Why was this condition added? A number of reasons have been suggested. Dilston Hall was still being rebuilt so was not fit to live in, or Anna Maria was too young to leave home. The reason could have been connected to Derwentwater's own family. His mother, Lady Mary Tudor, was not only a Protestant but was known as a libertine and a spendthrift. The Webbs may have wanted to protect their daughter from Derwentwater should he show similar tendencies. However, the real reason can probably be deduced from Derwentwater's own words. He writes that his mother-in-law was reluctant to part with her daughter and was not of a steady temper.[21] It is also clear that the young couple did not know each other well before the marriage. On 7 August 1712 Derwentwater wrote from Hathethrop to Lady Swinburne in Northumberland that 'My Lady Derwentwater's great merit and agreeable temper makes me think I have all the prospect imaginable of being entirely happy.'[22]

Derwentwater's letters to Lady Swinburne show that he was eager to return to the north. At last in April 1714 they began their trip back. In May they were at York races, and with their infant son John born in 1713, were back at Dilston by the summer of 1714. Here they spent what must have been the happiest period of their marriage, furnishing the new hall and entertaining their neighbours.

1715

This northern idyll was to end in the summer of 1715. The Earl of Mar raised the Stuart standard, and Derwentwater had to decide whether he would join the rebellion and help to restore his cousin to the throne. Tradition has it that in the summer of 1715 Derwentwater and other gentlemen, dressed as travellers, met at Fourstones, a Roman altar west of Hexham, to discuss their plans. Derwentwater was later to claim that he was not involved in any planning for the rebellion. Locally, Fourstones was known as the Fairy stone and during the rising, letters were left there to be collected and passed on.

The government was keeping a close eye on the Catholic community in the north east. No Catholic was allowed to keep a horse worth more than £5. Derwentwater prudently sent his best horses to be looked after elsewhere.[23] In September 1715 warrants were issued for the arrest of prominent Catholics, and Derwentwater went into hiding with his brother Charles. What he did and where he hid is the matter of legend. One tradition is that he went to the local justices of the peace and demanded that his warrant be made public so that he and everyone else knew what charges were levelled against him; another has it that he went to Sir Marmaduke Constable's house in Yorkshire, and when Sir Marmaduke was arrested went into hiding in a cottage at Newbiggin on Sea; a third that he hid at Shafto's crags, a spot only accessible by climbing down a cliff face.[24] In reality he probably lodged with some of his tenants, and kept moving to avoid discovery.

He obviously stayed in Northumberland as he returned to Dilston when he heard about the rebels meeting on Greenrigs, still undecided what to do. Again tradition intercedes. One story tells us that his wife chided him for a coward and forced him to join the rising; another that she clung to him and beseeched him not to go. The sober reality was that he rode to Errington, the home of the Claverings, to get advice. They were for the rising, and on 6 October 1715 he collected together his servants, mounted them on carriage horses and rode out to join the rebels.

He was to argue later that he had not been party to the plot, and he was by inclination peaceful. In a letter to Lady Swinburne he admitted he was lazy by nature, and Robert Patten wrote that Derwentwater was not enthusiastic about the rising, and had made no effort to recruit his lead miners from Alston Moor. It would seem that he joined the rising because he felt it his duty rather than from intense commitment.[25]

As he left Dilston Hall a phantom nun or monk was supposed to have appeared and given him a cross which would render bullets and swords harmless. The dogs howled as he left, and his horse stumbled, reluctant to take him any further, and as he rode out of the park he lost a ring from his finger.[26] All of these traditions are adaptations of folk tales. Derwentwater was accompanied by his brother Charles, and together with Thomas Forster the little troop crossed the Tyne and joined the rest of the Jacobites. The wanderings of the English Jacobite army around Northumberland have been described in the previous chapter.

On 15 October they were back in the Dilston area. Here they learnt that Lord Kenmure had crossed the border, and they moved northwards again, marching into Scotland and then to Preston.

Neither Derwentwater nor his brother had any experience of war, but as young gentlemen they would have had instruction in using arms, sword play and target practice. Derwentwater's part at Preston is confused. What happened at the Ribble bridge which he was meant to be guarding? Arnold suggests that Derwentwater thought that Wills' force was friendly, and this is why he failed to challenge them. He reinforces this theory by quoting from a letter written in 1716 to William Cotesworth from his sons who were on holiday in Lancashire. They write that from what they can learn Derwentwater was exercising his men on the marsh when the government troops arrived. He shouted to his men that 'they were all for them', and rode to meet them, but as they approached the bridge he saw they came with drawn swords, and shouting 'We are undone. They are against us', fled back into town.[27]

This blunder surely comes from the youthful commander's lack of experience. His inexperience is further seen when he sent 300 horsemen to the bridge, but withdrew when in sight of the government troops. However, it should be realised that the terrain made the troops on the town-side of the river very vulnerable. The town was only accessible up a steep incline and narrow alleys, and it would have been easy for them to have become trapped and cut to pieces.

The description of the fight at Preston can be found in the previous chapter. When it came to the surrender Gibson suggests that Derwentwater argued against this.[28] But as Derwentwater pointed out at his trial he was one of the first to lay down his sword. Before being taken he directed his huntsman to ride to Dilston and take the family papers to the Swinburnes at Capheaton for safe keeping, and to prepare his pregnant countess for the worst – that he was a prisoner of the Hanoverians and could face execution.

The prisoner

Derwentwater and his brother began their journey to London on 25 November 1715, Derwentwater riding in a carriage until Highgate, when in common with the other prisoners he was pinioned and placed on a horse, to be subjected to the insults of the crowd. At the end of his journey he was taken to lodge at the Tower, where his wife who had travelled from the north, joined him. They remained together until February 1716 when an outbreak of small pox in the Tower meant the Countess had to leave.

When Parliament returned after its Christmas recess in January 1716 the first item on its agenda was the impeachment of the rebel lords. The Commons passed the impeachment bill with speed, and on 10 January 1716 the rebel lords appeared at Westminster for the first time to hear the articles of impeachment. They arrived from the Tower with the executioner's axe borne before them, but its edge turned away.[29]

The articles stated 'that for many years a most wicked design and contrivance had been carried on, to subvert the ancient kingdom and established government; extirpate the Protestant religion, and introduce and settle horrid Popery . . .'. There had been plots to encompass the death of the king, and raise levies in a warlike manner in order to raise tumults, and that they unlawfully took up arms, had the Pretender proclaimed and seized the town of Preston.[30]

On 19 January 1716 Derwentwater knelt before the House of Lords to answer the accusations against him. He said he had no desire to spill blood, and asked for mercy. He acknowledged with real sorrow that he was in arms and did march through the kingdom; and confessed he was thereby guilty. He pointed out that he was one of the first to lay down his arms at Preston, and to offer himself as a hostage. In mitigation he pleaded his youth and inexperience, and that he had gone without any purpose to meet the rebels. Once more he was asked if he was guilty. He answered 'yes', and was taken away.[31]

Judgement was to be pronounced on 9 February. Unfortunately, by this time the situation was exacerbated because James had landed in Scotland, raising a further spectre of rebellion. On 9 February Derwentwater came back to the House of Lords and appealed for mercy, if not for himself then for his wife and children who would be deprived of their estates. Again he pleaded his youth and inexperience as extenuating circumstances, and that he went into the rising unprepared. He was sentenced to be hung, drawn and quartered.

Lady Derwentwater made a desperate bid to gain mercy for her husband. With Derwentwater's cousins, the Duchess of Cleveland and the Dukes of Richmond and St Albans, she forced her way into the king's presence and handed him a petition for mercy. The king is supposed to have been moved by the countess's entreaty but adamant that unless the earl acknowledged the Hanoverians' right to the throne and renounced the Catholic religion he would die. A Protestant minister was sent to him in the Tower to put this offer to him, and it was at this point that Derwentwater summoned up a vein of heroism, and proclaimed that he would never renounce his faith.

The account of Derwentwater's last days come from a letter sent to the countess by Father Pippard, a Catholic priest. Pippard was concerned with creating a hagiography for Derwentwater that might lead to his being made a saint, and his portrait of the earl may have been embellished. Lady Derwentwater and her supporters, and Derwentwater's mother, continued their efforts to get a reprieve, exploring all avenues.[32] They even offered £60,000 to save his life. Lady Cowper records in her diary some of the efforts they went to. 'On 21st February the ladies of the condemned lords brought a petition to the House of Lords for a reprieve. The Archbishop of Canterbury opposed the court in rejecting the petition which is seen as a ploy to bring down the ministry, and the Princess of Wales chided the Duchess of Bolton for bringing Lady Derwentwater into the King's presence.' In Dudley Ryder's version of events, Lady Derwentwater fell on her knees and presented a petition to the king in French. The king said he was sorry for her misfortune.[33]

Derwentwater saw his wife for the last time on 23 February 1716. She gave him a letter from the Vicar Apostolic of London, the Reverend Bonaventure Giffard, which told him to say 'Jesus, Jesus, Jesus' with his last breath. Derwentwater spent some of his last hours writing letters. To his father-in-law Sir John Webb he wrote asking that he would look after his wife and children, and thanking him for giving him his daughter. He wrote to his mother telling her he loved her and sending his best wishes to his stepfather, and to his brother Charles, telling him that he wished to be buried at Dilston. He named the Protestant Earl of Scarborough and Lord Lumley as his son's trustees, but stipulated that he should be brought up a Catholic. Then he spent the rest of the time reading the New Testament, St Augustine, and making his confession.[34]

The execution

The execution was 'the final act in the Jacobite theatre of death'.[35] It was a chance to address the crowd and for the last speech to be written down, printed and distributed as propaganda. Sorrow could be expressed for the crimes committed, and the victim's beliefs reiterated. Szechi suggests that there is a common theme and style in Jacobite scaffold speeches that may have been suggested by their spiritual mentors. The texts centred on their belief in the rightness of the cause, stating that James was the rightful king and would make the country happy, returning it to the true religion. To die bravely was to become a martyr for the cause.

The drama of the occasion was heightened by the black draped scaffold, the lines of soldiers, and the hooded executioner. Accounts of Derwentwater's execution show that he played up to the occasion. Derwentwater was to die on the same day as Lord Kenmure, the Scottish peer, and his fellow Northumbrian Lord Widdrington. Lord Widdrington was reprieved on the day of execution so only Kenmure and Derwent-water travelled to Tower Hill in two hackney carriages. The scaffold had been built out from the upper room of the Transport Office, so it stood above the heads of the crowd, who were kept back by a ring of soldiers. Derwentwater was taken into the Transport Office and allowed to pray for half an hour before going out onto the scaffold. There he was once more offered his life and freedom if he would acknowledge George as king and renounce the Catholic religion. Once more he refused.

He was dressed in a black velvet suit with a flaxen wig and beaver hat with a feather, a suit still preserved at Ingatestone Hall. On the scaffold he read out from a paper, probably written by Pippard, admitting his guilt, but refusing to acknowledge he was wrong as James was his rightful sovereign, and he preferred death to dishonour. He would die a Roman Catholic and commend his soul to God. Then he prayed again before taking off his hat, coat and wig. He forgave the executioner, and gave him money for his pains, asking him not to strike until he had said 'Lord Jesus, receive my soul' three times. The executioner waited until this had been said and then struck off Derwentwater's head with one blow.[36]

Abel Boyer wrote that when Derwentwater had first seen the scaf-fold he had turned very pale and staggered, but then became steady and resolute. So confident had his friends been of a reprieve they had provided no coffin or hearse, and the body had to be taken away in the carriage he had come in.[37] Dudley Ryder's diary shows that the common people also expected a reprieve. On the morning of the execution his maid told him that the lords were reprieved, but he did not believe her and set out early to Tower Hill to get a good place to see the execution.

'The whole hill was full of people that I never saw such a large collection of people in all my life, and a vast circle was made by the horse guards around the scaffold, and a great many foot guards in the middle. At length the Lords Derwentwater and Kenmure came in two hackney coaches from the Tower to the Transport office. I saw them both. Lord Derwentwater looked with a melancholy aspect, but Lord Kenmure looked very bold and unconcerned.

'Lord Derwentwater was executed first. After he was brought upon the stage and was saluted by several officers and others that were there, he prayed and spoke to them, I am informed that as he was about to die he said he was sorry he had pleaded guilty, for he was an innocent man who knew no other king but James III. He seemed to behave himself well, and made his exit decently enough . . .

'The executioner struck off his head with one blow, and then held it in his hand and showed it to the people and said "Here is the head of a traitor. God Bless King George!" His head and body were covered with black cloth and put in the coach in which he had come, and carried away.'[38]

Ryder added that after Kenmure's execution there was no disturbance, the mob were as quiet as lambs but there did not seem to be any face of sorrow amongst them. Ryder brooded on what it felt like to imagine one's certain death, and although he found the idea of executing men in the prime of health repugnant, he added that it had to be done.[39]

Lady Cowper mentioned Kenmure's resolution, but commented that Derwentwater was very young and bred in softness and care. The scaffold dismayed him at first, but he recovered. She suggests that there was no coffin provided because it was intended that his body be allowed to lie on display.[40] This would have enabled the crowd to dip their handkerchiefs and rags in the blood as relics, in the same way as had happened after the execution of Derwentwater's maternal great-grandfather.

Burial and exhumation – the northern lights

Derwentwater's body was taken to an embalmer, the heart was removed and the head and body placed in a lead-lined coffin, and taken to Dagenham Park where Lady Derwentwater had rented a house. After suitable obsequies, in recognition of the Earl's last wish it was conveyed northward. As it reached Sunderland Bridge there was a spectacular display of the northern lights that could be seen as far south as London.

On 6 March 1716 Dudley Ryder found his household in great terror on account of the strange appearance in the air. 'It was indeed very strange: all towards the north a pale light like smoke mixed with flame shot up and down through the air in great sheets. It was in perpetual motion, sometimes here and sometimes there . . .'[41] Lady Cowper saw it as well. She described it first appearing 'as a black cloud, from whence smoke and light issued forth, at once on every side, and then the Cloud opened, and there was a great Body of pale Fire, that rolled up and down and sent forth all sorts of colours like the Rainbow on every side. . . . After that it was like a pale elementary Fire issuing out on all sides of the Horizon.'[42]

Very soon these strange lights were seen as a portent and were being used for political purposes. 'Both Parties turned it on their Enemies', wrote Lady Cowper, 'The Whigs said it was God's Judgement on the horrid Rebellion, and the Tories said it came for the Whigs taking off the two Lords who were executed.'[43] The coincidence of the northern lights with the arrival of Derwentwater's body in Northumberland was seen as a special portent. It was claimed that at the same time Devils Water at Dilston ran red, and a shower of meteors greeted his return.[44] The mythologising of the Earl of Derwentwater had started.

More prosaically, we know how much Derwentwater's funeral at Dilston cost: £10 went to the priest, £10 was distributed to the poor, and £40 was sent to the Poor Clares of Dunkirk to pay for perpetual masses for his soul. In all the expense of moving the body, the funeral expenses and obsequies came to £252. Lady Derwentwater also paid £126 to his servants, and debts owed by him of £11. It appears from the accounts that Lady Derwentwater and her infant son accompanied the earl north, as £45 was paid for 'my son during his stay at Lumley Castle and at Dilston after my Dear Lord's decease . . .'.[45]

Derwentwater was laid to rest in the chapel at Dilston Hall. Very soon miraculous cures were being reported from the tomb, and from the earl's heart that had remained in London. Northumbrian children were taken to the tomb to be cured of the King's Evil or scrofula. The touch of a divine king could cure this, and English monarchs had touched for this up to 1688 when William discontinued the practice. Anne had revived it reluctantly, but James II, III and Prince Charles Edward all touched. By implication some of the royal divinity had rubbed off on Derwentwater, the grandson of a king.

The coffin was opened in 1805 by the Commissioners of the Royal Hospital for Seamen at Greenwich, who by then owned Dilston. The body was found in a good state of preservation, but the local blacksmith drew out teeth to sell. The tomb was reopened after a fall of masonry in 1838, and after Greenwich Hospital sold the estate in 1874 other arrangements had to be made. Derwentwater's daughter, Anna Barbara, had married Lord Petre, head of an Essex recusant family and already related to the Radcliffes through the marriage of Derwentwater's aunt Mary to William Petre. The 19th-century Lord Petre offered to find a final resting place for Derwentwater in the chapel of Thorndon Hall. The body was exhumed on 9 October 1874 and taken south by train; the reinterment took place on 16 October 1874 with a solemn office and mass.[46]

After Derwentwater's execution the unfortunate countess stayed with her parents for a while, but in 1721 left for the continent with her two children because their grandmother, the redoubtable Lady Mary Tudor, had tried to convert them to Protestantism, and was petitioning Parliament for their guardianship. The countess died of small pox at the convent of Louvain where her aunts were nuns, in August 1723.[47]

The story does not stop there. The earl had been attainted, therefore his title and his estates were forfeit. Lengthy litigation was to follow as the estate was subject to a number of charges on it, including the Countess's jointure of £1000 a year, and annuities to Derwentwater's brothers, aunts and uncles, which amounted to £3015 per annum.[48]

John Radcliffe's grandfather, Sir John Webb, set about trying to retrieve his grandson's fortune. He had to prove that the estate had been settled on trustees before Derwentwater's death, and that the earl was only the life tenant and not the owner. If that was the case the estate was not forfeit to the crown. The Forfeited Estates Commission assumed there was no settlement, and took over the estate, even though Derwentwater's father had set up an entail, and this was reinforced by Derwentwater and Anna Maria's marriage settlement.[49]

The estates were restored to John Radcliffe in 1720. If he were to reach a majority he could bar the entail on the estate, and settle it on his own heirs. If he died without an heir, the next male heir, his uncle Charles, was already barred from inheriting it because he too was attainted for high treason. John Radcliffe was to come of age in 1734 but he died in 1731, and the estates were sold to a Mr Smith for a paltry £1000, before being transferred to the Greenwich Hospital. In the 19th century a claimant appeared known as Amelia who said that John Radcliffe had married, and she was the descendant of the match, and therefore Dilston was hers. This was never proved.

Derwentwater and the Jacobite cause

There is no evidence that Derwentwater was involved in any prior planning of the 1715 rising. As he said at his trial he joined it on the spur of the moment because of his duty to James. News of his execution reached Bolingbroke in France from a Mr O'Neil on 10 March. On the same day the Earl of Mar who had fled with James to France received the news from a Captain Straton. Straton wrote that Derwentwater had made 'a gentlemanly and most Catholic speech or so the Jacobites say'.[50]

James had the news by 21 March when he wrote to his ally the Duke of Lorraine that Derwentwater was a Christian hero.[51] By April the Jacobites realised that Derwentwater's martyrdom could be used to their advantage. Hugh Thomas in London wrote to David Nairne in Paris that the Duke of Argyle, the commander of the government forces in Scotland, was displaying great generosity to the remaining prisoners, and had manoeuvred a defeat of the bill which would seize two thirds of the Roman Catholic's estates. 'All this goodness, it's thought, proceeds entirely from Argyle who met Lord Derwentwater's body on the road, and heard and saw the great numbers of the people, what honours they paid his dead body, and what vast concourses went out to meet it in all towns it was carried through and what wonders they reported of him . . .'. Thomas thought that the execution had caught the imagination of the people, and that the Jacobites should use this quickly as the people 'have nothing but the Pretender in their brains, and their common cry is they shall never forgive Lord Derwentwater's death.'[52]

The majority of English people had known nothing of Derwentwater before his execution. He was young and had spent most of his life in France, or away from public view in Gloucestershire or Northumberland. But it was his youth that caught the imagination and made him into a hero. The display of the northern lights at exactly the right time added to his mystique, and he and the lights became a symbol for all that was romantic and glamorous about the Jacobites. Thus James Radcliffe, Earl of Derwentwater, passed seamlessly into myth, legend and song:

Derwentwater's Farewell

And when the head that wears the crown
Shall be laid low like mine
Some honest hearers may then lament
For Radcliffe's fallen line
Farewell to pleasant Dilston Hall,
My father's ancient seat
A stranger now must call thee thine
Which gives my heart to griet.[53]

Notes

1 C. Petrie, *The Jacobite Movement – the First Phase, 1688–1716,* London: Eyre and Spottiswoode, 1948.

2 W. Gibson, *Dilston Hall*, London: Longman, 1850, 8–9.

3 PRO ADM 76/70; House of Commons, *Report from the Committee to whom the books, instruments and papers relating to the sale of the estate of James, Late Earl of Derwentwater were given*, London: 1723.

4 L. Stone, *The Family, Sex and Marriage in England, 1500–1800*, Harmondsworth: Penguin, 1982.

5 Gibson, 30.

6 See for example R. Arnold, *Northern Light*, London: Constable, 1959, 46; Arnold appears to take his information from Gibson, page 32.

7 Gibson, 38.

8 Gibson, 38.

9 Gibson, 17.

10 PRO ADM 76/59/56.

11 Society of Antiquaries, Newcastle upon Tyne, *Proceedings*, 3rd ser., Vol. VI, 1914, 97, 135–6.

12 Society of Antiquaries, *Proceedings*, 135–6.

13 J. Hodgson, *The History of Northumberland*, Newcastle upon Tyne: 1827, Vol. I, pt ii, 225.

14 G. Martin and S. McIntyre, *A Bibliography of British and Irish Municipal History*, Leicester: Leicester University Press, 1972, 263–5.

15 T. Pope, 'The Ancient Corporation of Cheadle', *Transactions North Staffordshire Field Club*, Vol. LXIV, 1929–30, 52–88.

16 These artefacts can be seen in the Harris Museum, Preston; F. Coupe, *Walton-le-Dale. A history of the village*, Preston: Guardian Press, 1954, 142–9.

17 Arnold, 53–4.

18 Arnold, 54; Coupe, 146; Gibson, 40.

19 Stone, 217–53.

20 PRO ADM 76/59.

21 Quoted in Gibson, 44.

22 Hodgson, 226.

23 Gibson, 48.

24 Gibson, 49.

25 R. Patten, *The History of the Late Rebellion*, London: 1717, 125.

26 Gibson, 51–2, 54.

27 Arnold, 111–12.

28 Gibson, 79.

29 House of Lords, *The Whole Proceedings upon the Articles of Impeachment of High Treason against the Earl of Derwentwater*, London: 1716, 3–4.

30 *Whole Proceedings*, 4–6.

31 *Whole Proceedings*, 7–8.

32 PRO SP 35/7/14.

33 W. Cowper ed., *Diary of Mary, Countess Cowper 1714–1720*, London: John Murray, 1864, 85–7; W. Matthews ed., *The Diary of Dudley Ryder, 1715–1716*, London: Methuen, 1939, 180.

34 Gibson, 95, 110.

35 D. Szechi, 'The Jacobite Theatre of Death', in E. Cruickshanks ed., *The Jacobite Challenge*, Edinburgh: John Duckworth, 1988, 57–73.

36 Pippard quoted in Gibson, 110–12.

37 A. Boyer, *The Political State of Great Britain*, London: 1716, XI, 237–8.

38 *Ryder Diary*, 186–8.

39 *Ryder Diary*, 188.

40 Cowper, 87.

41 *Ryder Diary*, 191.

42 Cowper, 90.

43 Cowper, 91.

44 Gibson, 111.

45 Society of Antiquaries, Newcastle upon Tyne, *Proceedings*, 1914, 3rd ser., Vol. VI, 18, 207.

46 S. Forster, 'The Earl of Derwentwater: A note on his last resting place', *Northern Catholic History*, 20, 1984, 15–7.

47 S. Forster, 'The Countess of Derwentwater: A note on her fate', *Northern Catholic History*, 18, 1983, 32–6.

48 Society of Antiquaries, *Proceedings*, 148.

49 Society of Antiquaries, *Proceedings*, 180.

50 HMC, *Calendar of the Stuart Papers preserved at Windsor Castle*, London: HMSO, Vol. II, 1904, 2, 7, 10.

51 *Stuart Papers* II, 35.

52 *Stuart Papers* II, 84.

53 Petrie, 201–2. This is the last verse of what is probably a 19th-century ballad.

CHAPTER 7

Sweden, smugglers, the bishop and the Black Acts, 1716–35

France 1716

When James returned to France in March 1716, after the failure of the 1715 rising, recriminations followed. Bolingbroke was dismissed, and the French blamed for not supporting the rising: 'That enterprise, for want of being timely succoured failed', wrote William Dicconson to Captain David George on 2 March 1716.[1] But James was still optimistic of being restored to the English throne, and immediately started plotting again. However, to start planning another invasion with so many English Jacobite supporters still in prison awaiting their trials seems from the 21st-century point of view extremely insensitive. But James and his supporters were driven not only by the desire to restore the House of Stuart, but also by their belief that James was the king of England by divine right, and that God was on their side. Their desires and beliefs were fed by news from England of discontent with the Whig government leading to riots in the towns, and near mutiny in the fleet. Correspondents told the court in exile that the majority of the people would flock to James should he arrive in England.[2]

The court in exile tried to increase their political influence in England by wooing individuals dismissed from office by George I because they were Tories. On 16 April 1716 the Earl of Mar wrote to James

Gibb the architect, 'Let us hope still there are more polite days coming', telling him to contact Mr Bromley at the House of Commons for a
commission.[3]

The panic in England of 1715 had not entirely subsided by the spring
of 1716. William Cotesworth sent information from the north east to
London about new Jacobite conspiracies. Cotesworth, who was hated by
the Jacobites, was continually harassed by them, and warned that his life
was in danger.[4]

Survivors from the 1715 rising and escapees from gaol ended up at the
court in exile, offering their services, and giving first-hand information
about the situation in England. In July 1716, Lancelot Errington from
Northumberland gave the Earl of Mar a description of all the harbours
on the north-east coast from the Humber to the Tweed.[5] His compatriot,
Lancelot Ord, took on a number of aliases and under the name of George
Blackwell travelled back to England in May 1716 to meet with the chief
Jacobite agent in London, John Menzies. He was not welcome, and after
he had returned to France in July 1716 Menzies wrote to his masters in
France that Ord was obnoxious and dangerous to his friends, and asking
that he should not be sent back. Again in August 1716 Menzies wrote on
hearing Ord might well be returning that, 'several friends are extremely
alarmed at hearing Blackwell is returning'. Mar thought Menzies was
being peevish.[6]

Was Ord really a loose cannon who would endanger other agents in
England, or was Menzies jealous of Ord's wide range of contacts? Ord
came from a northern gentry family and would have had a large acquaintance among the gentry, legal profession and the church. His zeal for the
Jacobite cause was not in question, but he was impatient for a restoration.
In August 1716 he addressed James about his life-long devotion to the
cause and that he found the north 'wonderfully inclined to us . . .';
he suggested that they land a force at 'Errington's citadel' (Newcastle)
while King George was overseas. His offer to go personally to the north
to organise this led Menzies to write to him directly, begging him not to
return. Ord was not dismissed so easily. He persisted, writing again to
James on 23 August 1716 that Lancelot Errington had said there were
5000 good men to be raised.[7]

The exiles were innovative with their ideas for a restoration. Thomas
Southcott, known as an honest man in London, wrote to Mar in July 1716

about a plan he had thought out whereby coal was ordered for Paris from Newcastle, to be unloaded at Rouen. The boats would not raise suspicion as Newcastle colliers could be used as cover to transport men and arms. This would cost, he estimated, between £12–13,000. In August 1716 a Mr Douglas suggested a similar scheme. He would buy a cargo of wine, take it to Scotland and set up as a wine merchant so as not to arouse suspicion. He claimed to know a hundred horse guards in London whom he would contact, beside foot and other men in the army. He offered to transmit letters and instructions to the north of England and the south of Scotland, and asked for money to set up his business.[8]

Money was something that was not in ready supply at the court in exile, and furthermore the misguided enthusiasm of the English exiles was endangering far more serious plans afoot with Sweden.

The Swedish enterprise

Just as William III's accession to the throne had precipitated Britain into continental territorial wars, so the Hanoverians also involved Britain in European politics. This brought the Jacobites onto the international stage, giving them a political and strategic importance. If a Jacobite invasion of Britain could be mounted at the same time as British troops were occupied abroad so James could be restored, and opposition to Britain and Hanover triumph. Once James was on the throne he would become, in effect, a puppet king of whichever foreign power had placed him there. Furthermore, the Stuarts had no European territory, so that Britain would be safely removed from the continent for the future.

Sweden was at war with a coalition that included Hanover, Denmark and Prussia, over Bremen, which Sweden controlled to the detriment of the other states' Baltic trade. Sweden was anxious to engage Hanover on two fronts, and it was an attractive ally for the Jacobites because it was a Protestant state. An invasion with the help of a Protestant power would remove the stigma of popery from the Jacobite cause.

Sweden was mooted as a possible ally for the Jacobites as early as 15 March 1716 when James had only just returned to France.[9] But despite being described as the madman of the north, Charles XII of Sweden was no fool. His Baltic wars had left his coffers empty. He would not move to assist James until he had received a down payment of £60,000.

The English Jacobites were called upon to raise this sum, and Bishop Atterbury of Rochester was to be the collector.

Throughout the summer of 1716 negotiations took place between Jacobite agents in London and Count Gyllenberg the Swedish ambassador. Sweden would undertake to raise 10,000 men and arms for a further 20,000, and suggested that March 1717 would be the best time to invade.[10]

In England other contingency plans were also being made. Sir Redman Everard was sent from France to contact Bishop Atterbury, Sir Henry Goring and Sir Constantine Phipps, a Jacobite lawyer. Their discussions centred on how many troops would be needed to 'beat all the forces which could of a sudden be brought together in England.' They fixed on the number as no less than 6000, and that if they were led by the Duke of Ormonde their chance of success would be better. They suggested a landing place near London, in Essex or Suffolk. From there they could be in London within twelve hours and 'blow up the credit of George and his Parliament'. The ensuing panic would bring down the Bank of England, while they optimistically expected that in 'every part of England there were common people and farmers who would cheerfully join them, as well as half pay officers in and around London'. Eventually, the plan was altered; 12,000 troops were required of which 6000 would go to the West Country and land near Exeter where there was an abundance of good horse.[11]

These grandiose plans came to nothing, and it is remarkable that not two months after the execution of the Earl of Derwentwater and Lord Kenmure there were still those willing to commit themselves. Although Bishop Atterbury was loath to make any firm promises, by the summer of 1716 he was more inclined to give practical help to the cause and to assist in the collection of money to be sent to Sweden. Despite Ezekiel Hamilton's assertion that there was money enough in England and persons ready to part with it, Atterbury found it difficult to extort any. He managed to raise only £18,000 of the £60,000 demanded by Sweden. Of this, £5000 came from his funds, £5000 from Charles Caesar MP, and the rest from English Catholics.[12] Without the money Sweden would not move, and it transpired later that despite Count Gyllenberg's assurances Charles XII had made no firm promises to act. There was an additional complication: what Charles really wanted the money for was to buy corn as the Swedish harvest had failed, and pursue war against Russia.[13] Peter

II, Czar of Russia, was one of Mar's cousins and he too hated George I, but an alliance between Sweden and Russia to restore James was impossible; nevertheless James contacted Peter with a view to this end. This upset Sweden.

Gyllenberg on the ground in England had a clearer view of the support likely to be available to James than the court in exile. He saw that for the present time the nation was inflamed with Jacobitism and a longing for the return of the man they believed to be their lawful sovereign, but they would not declare openly for him. On the contrary perceiving that it was only a foreign quarrel that drew the King of Sweden in, they expected to see his expedition frustrated.[14]

Meanwhile Atterbury packed up the money he had collected into small amounts and sent it to Mary of Modena. The British government were well aware of the plot, and despite his diplomatic immunity had been systematically intercepting Gyllenberg's mail. In January 1717 they pounced. Gyllenberg and Charles Caesar MP were arrested. Atterbury, who had been extremely discreet, was not.[15] Had the Jacobites but known, Gyllenberg had already started a correspondence with Whigs on behalf of his master.[16] Sweden had little intention of helping James. The plotters in England were lucky to escape lightly, and agents such as John Menzies remained free.

Spain and the 1719 rising

By October 1716 the Jacobites had given up on Sweden, and were courting Spain instead, both for military aid and as a residence for James.[17] As far as the English Jacobites were concerned this would have been a disaster. Spain was not only a Catholic country, but it was an old enemy and major European power with British troops camped on its doorstep in Gibraltar. War was to break out between Britain and Spain in 1717. A second front in Britain or Gibraltar would greatly help the Spanish war effort.

Perhaps we should consider the effect of war on the public psyche in general, and the English Jacobites in particular. An all-out war needed manpower and goods. Employment and trade benefited, while the country when faced by a common enemy from outside got behind the government even if it did not agree with its domestic policies. This left the English

Jacobites in a peculiar position. Could they invite an invasion by a foreign power that was at war with their country? Was the likelihood of having the Stuarts restored worth the risks of being overrun from outside? It would seem that most who weighed up the two decided it was not.

Still expecting support in England, a plan was drawn up in 1719 whereby Spain would invade the West Country, and send a small Spanish force to aid a Scottish rising in the Highlands. The West Country invasion force was scattered by storms, but the smaller flotilla bound for Scotland got through and landed in Scotland. This was the perfect opportunity for a surprise rebellion, as it appears that the government in London was, or at least gave the impression of being, taken by surprise. But the putative commander of the Scots Earl Marischal fell out not only with the Spanish commander, but also with other Scots who questioned his commission and refused to take his orders.

By this time the government had assembled enough forces to defeat the Jacobites at Glenshiel. The 1719 rising was over before it started, and the speed with which it was mopped up by the government troops suggests that although the government appeared to be taken by surprise this was not the case. The government knew which areas to watch, and the West Country was already suspect because it was the home of known English Jacobites like Sir William Wyndham, Lord Lansdowne and the Duke of Beaufort, while the Highlands of Scotland were still infested with troops left there after 1715. The Jacobites needed a new approach.

Jacobites and smugglers

One new approach could have been to unite the disparate social deviants such as poachers, highwaymen and smugglers into a coherent body. The Jacobites had contacts with these groups, and were already using the owlers or smugglers to bring propaganda over from France for them, and to transport agents.[18]

It has been argued that there was a close relationship between the smugglers and the Jacobites, and that smugglers were part of a Jacobite guerrilla movement, paid verbal allegiance to the Pretender, and openly drank his health.[19] Winslow suggests that this was one of the reasons that the government took the smugglers seriously and posted troops of dragoons all along the south coast.[20] In the 20th century smugglers became folk heroes, celebrated by Rudyard Kipling's

> *Five and twenty ponies trotting through the dark*
> *Brandy for the parson, baccy for the clerk*

and through fictional characters such as Russell Thorndike's 'Dr Syn'. Smugglers were flouting tax laws, and this was seen as legitimising their illegal activities.

Smugglers specialised in running spirits, wine and tea into the country. This was not the social service as suggested by Kipling and others, bringing in the odd cask for the local gentry, but a highly organised business dedicated to profit. Owlers specialised in exporting wool to countries where there was a trade embargo with Britain, and bringing back luxury goods for sale. They had no compunction about threatening, maiming or killing anyone who stood against them. They were the mobsters and gangsters of the 18th century. In 1721 a particularly notorious group known as the Mayfield Gang roamed around Sussex, pursued by the dragoons. Forced out of Mayfield on the Sussex/Kent border they took refuge in St Leonard's Forest, a densely wooded part of the Sussex weald. Their prohibited goods were landed at Ferring, Goring or Beachy Head, stored in a tavern in the forest, and distributed through an outlet in the market town of Horsham.

Witnesses told of intimidation if they got in the gang's way. On 21 August 1721 William Cook of Horsham said he had been threatened by the gang, who told him they would shoot him. Thomas Garrett of Rotherfield said that he and his father had been returning from St James' Fair on Midsummer Day driving sheep when eight men with pistols fell upon them and abused them for not making way quickly enough. They recognised the men as the Mayfield gang, and reported them to Humphrey Fowle, a justice of the peace, who gave them a warrant against the gang, but said they had to execute it themselves. They tried to do this at a bare-knuckle fight at Woodgate in Kent, where the landlord of the inn was a constable. They gave him the warrant and he handed it to a justice, who was drinking with a papist. The papist warned the gang, and they came out of the inn with blacked faces and their pistols firing and escaped. The soldiers came and the smugglers fired at them too.[21]

There are interesting hints in this account of complicity between the law and the smugglers, and between the smugglers and the Catholics, if not the smugglers and the Jacobites. Undoubtedly, the Jacobites did use the smugglers' services to land agents and packets in isolated places, and the Duke of Richmond whose estate was at Goodwood in Sussex was convinced that the smugglers needed to be rooted out.[22]

The smugglers themselves probably had no political motives; provided a passenger could pay that would have been enough. They were in it for the money, and smuggling needed a financial incentive to make it worthwhile.

Christopher Layer

In 1722–23 two parallel Jacobite plots unfolded. How far these were connected is not clear. Eveline Cruickshanks suggests that there was only one plot, under the direction of Bishop Atterbury. She criticises Sir John Plumb and G.V. Bennett for interpreting the sources as indicating two separate plots.[23] It is true that Bishop Atterbury appeared in the Layer correspondence. But Layer's schemes would have been anathema to a man of Atterbury's standing, especially as Layer wanted to place the Earl of Oxford at the head of the Protestant interest in England, a man that Atterbury had fallen out with.[24] Even contemporaries were not sure whether there were one or two plots. Thomas Stackhouse, writing in 1723, asked rhetorically whether Atterbury was mixed up with Layer, or was Layer acting on his own?[25]

As the same personnel appear in both plots they would have been aware of developments. Both plots (if there were two) were capitalising on the financial crash of 1720 known as the South Sea Bubble, which had made thousands bankrupt, paralysed the economic life of the country and threatened to bring down the government. The main blame for this was levelled at the Earl of Sunderland who was threatened with impeachment, and to save his skin had made contact with the Tories, using Bishop Atterbury and Lord Orrery as his go-betweens. Orrery was definitely involved with Layer.

Christopher Layer was born and brought up near Aylsham in Norfolk. He came from a non-juror family, and was the heir of his uncle, a modest country squire. He was educated at his uncle's expense at Norwich

Grammar School and, destined for a legal career, was placed with Henry Rippingell of Aylsham, an attorney, to learn his trade. After Layer's death it was suggested by his detractors that he had seduced Mrs Rippingell and had led a dissolute life, but the truth of these accusations cannot be verified. However, Layer did fall out with Rippingell, and moved to London to be called to the Bar. About the same time he managed to acquire his uncle's estate whilst his uncle was still living, taking it over in return for paying his uncle an annuity. Detractors claimed this was never paid. In 1709 Layer married Elizabeth Elwin.[26] In 1715 Layer was back in London practising the law; one of his clients was Lord North and Grey, although at his trial Layer was to claim he had no acquaintance with North and Grey until 1722, when he went with Stephen Lynch to see his lordship at his house in Epping Forest.[27] Undoubtedly, Layer was in contact with the Jacobites before this as in 1721 he left England with John Plunket, an agent of Lord Orrery, and travelled with him to the court in exile in Rome. They carried with them a list of sergeants and men dismissed from the army, and serving army officers who might rise in favour of James. Cruickshanks suggests that what became known as 'the list' was an extremely important document. It divided the country into county groups, and named a nobleman to command each group. James asked Layer in particular about Jacobite support in Norfolk, and Layer drew up another list for him. Layer's papers were to reveal lists of alleged Jacobite supporters in Norfolk and Suffolk, as well as in the army and the city of London.[28] James rated Layer highly and agreed with his queen to become proxy godparents to Layer's daughter Mary Clementina.[29]

During the spring and summer of 1722 Layer perfected his plans. His scheme was to take the Tower of London through Sergeant George Wilson, who would bribe the other soldiers and officers, and open the Tower gates to allow in a body of supporters at exactly 9 o'clock in the morning. At the same time James would be proclaimed at the Exchange. The gates of the city would be shut and artillery drawn up on Tower Hill. Soldiers would march down Ludgate to Newgate. One detachment would cross the Thames to Southwark and make a bonfire, and another go to Whitehall and proclaim James there. A third would enter St James' Park, and a fourth march onto Westminster to rouse a mob. Eventually they would all reassemble in two groups, on Tower Hill and St James' Park. A captain would take the Thames watermen to break into the royal arsenal at Greenwich and bring powder. Horsemen would ride into the counties to proclaim James, and thousands would flock to his standard.[30] Arms were to be stockpiled and buried, to be dug up as the rising started. The narrow streets of the city were to be barricaded, and bricks and stones were to be stored in upper rooms to be thrown down onto the heads of government troops by women and those unfit to bear arms.[31]

This was a grandiose and impractical plan that depended on synchronised action. Undoubtedly there were Jacobite supporters amongst London aldermen, but probably not as many as the Jacobites hoped. Once London was taken the Duke of Ormonde would come in a single ship from France, bringing officers to take command.[32] Lord North and Grey was sent a commission appointing him as commander-in-chief of London and Westminster, and he was the key of the early stages of the plan. The rising was to be timed for when George I was in Hanover, in April or May 1722. It had to be delayed for two reasons. George delayed his trip, probably because he knew about the plot, and the Earl of Sunderland died. Cruickshanks suggests that Sunderland knew about the plot, and had made no attempt to report it or stop it, and that for once Walpole was not aware of what was happening through his spies, until he was informed of this by France. Walpole immediately seized Sunderland's papers that confirmed the plot. Walpole brought troops back from Holland and Ireland and stationed them in Hyde Park.[33]

Hard evidence about the plot came from Philip Neynoe, an impecunious Irish clergyman who sold Walpole information, but at the same time told the Jacobites what he was telling Walpole; a dangerous double game that did not endear him to either side. Neynoe's contacts included Lord Orrery, Rev. George Kelly, Atterbury's secretary, Sir Henry Goring and Lord North and Grey. When he was arrested, while attempting to flee to France, he named all of them as conspirators. But he did not name Christopher Layer. This is one reason for thinking that there were two plots, one centred around Atterbury and the other around Layer, with figures such as Orrery and North and Grey providing links between the two.

In a panic, as he was now *persona non grata* with both sides, Neynoe attempted to escape. He got out of the room where he was imprisoned in the palace of Westminster, into a walled garden where the only exit was the river Thames. In desperation he threw himself in and was drowned.[34]

The only evidence against Atterbury were the depositions made before Neynoe was drowned, and intercepted and deciphered letters. At this point there was little to incriminate Layer and his group of conspirators, apart from his professional relationship with Lord North and Grey, and that he was known to have visited Rome.

It was probably the latter that led to his arrest on 18 September 1722, while he was still in bed at his lodgings in Southampton Row, Holborn. The warrant against him was for attempting to enlist non-commissioned officers for the Pretender. But on searching his room two bundles of letters were found which contained the plans of his scheme. Mr Doyley, an attorney to whom Layer had once been clerk, attested that the handwriting was Layer's. At the trial Layer's attorney claimed this was not legal proof as it was 14 years since Doyley had seen Layer's handwriting, and the letters could have been forged.

The day after his arrest Layer made an attempt to escape. This led to him being put in chains and being badly treated by his gaolers. When he appeared before the select committee called to arraign him of high treason, he was dragged through the streets still in chains, and appeared in the dock in fetters. Before proceedings started there was a long discussion as to whether he should be released from the chains for his trial. This was refused.[35]

Layer was accused of treason. Two of those accused with him, Steven Lynch and James Plunkett, turned king's evidence against him in return for their freedom and a reward of £40.[36] Evidence brought at the trial suggests that Layer was not the sole instigator of the plot, but this had been the idea of Orrery, Goring and North and Gray, who plotted at the Burford Club that 'they were going to do a rash thing for the pretender'. The evidence also connected Atterbury and Layer, by suggesting that Atterbury was the financial manager of the scheme.[37]

Layer was found guilty, and hung, drawn and quartered on 17 May 1723. His head was set on the Temple Bar in London. Lord North and Grey was bailed from the Tower and went into exile in Spain, converting to Catholicism. Sir Henry Goring boarded his private yacht and sailed away; Lord Orrery, also released from the Tower, returned to politics.

Layer would seem to have been made a scapegoat for his more illustrious colleagues.

Bishop Atterbury and his plot

Francis Atterbury was born in 1662 into a clerical family. He was educated at Westminster School and Christ Church, Oxford, becoming dean of that college and a member and patron of a group of neo-Latinist, quasi-Jacobite poets and academics.[38] One of Atterbury's students was Charles Boyle, Lord Orrery's son, another Jacobite, but at this point there was no hard evidence of Atterbury's Jacobite leanings, and indeed his background was Parliamentarian and Whig rather than Royalist and Tory.[39] But there was evidence of his argumentative and litigious character, which came to light in a pamphlet he wrote questioning the legal rights of the university visitor. In 1693 he left Oxford to become the minister of the Bridewell and Bethlehem Hospitals, and the St Bride's lecturer. Bridewell Hospital was already known for its Jacobite leanings, and Bridewell boys, as they were called, were involved in anti-Whig riots.

Atterbury became a noted preacher, much in demand. He also became a rallying point for high church Tories within the Church of England convocation, challenging the crown's right to ignore its orders. Convocation was to become a battleground for high and low churchmen, with Atterbury the principal spokesman for the high church parish priests. Fearing an attack on the low church moderates which might alter the character of the Church of England, the Archbishop of Canterbury suspended the convocation. By this time Atterbury had become an influential political figure, advising both Queen Anne and the Earl of Oxford on church matters. In 1704 he was made Dean of Carlisle, an appointment that appalled William Nicolson the Bishop, who was a moderate. Soon Dean and Bishop were at loggerheads, a disagreement that at times descended into childishness. It started when two minor canons came to blows in a chapter meeting in Carlisle cathedral. They were suspended, but returned to office after they apologised to the vice-dean and chapter. Atterbury objected to this.[40] Animosity grew and in January 1705 Nicolson tried to get Atterbury's appointment suppressed by raising doubts about the legality of the letters patent. The date on these was 15 July 1704, whereas the former dean did not die until 31 July 1704.[41] The matter went to the ecclesiastical court.

On his one visit to Carlisle, not only was Atterbury annoyed because there was no civic reception waiting to meet him, but he managed to alienate the whole chapter except one, Dr Hugh Todd, whom he left in Carlisle to fight his place. A dispute broke out between the Dean and the chapter after the appointment of Christopher Whittingdale to the living of Castle Sowerby. On 13 November 1705 Nicolson wrote that 'Mr Dean of Carlisle, is half in a passion about the vice-dean and chapter presenting the Sowerby living'. But Atterbury had returned to London to live in Chelsea 'in a pretty Box, with good Gardens', and on 4 January 1706 Secretary Harley, Atterbury's friend, granted him permission to live away from Carlisle.[42] Efforts were made to dislodge him from the deanery but he remained in place and when Nicolson proposed a visitation to the diocese, Atterbury protested that Carlisle was a royal foundation and only the queen could act as visitor.

Personal animosity was at the bottom of these disputes, but all the time Queen Anne lived and the Tories were in power Atterbury could get away with outrageous behaviour. He argued with Nicolson in public, and undertook historical research to prove that the only legal charter for Carlisle cathedral was dated 1541, and this charter gave him, as dean, supreme power of making appointments. A petition was given to the queen on this, but the Archbishop of Canterbury told the queen to have nothing to do with it, and to Nicolson's great relief Atterbury was moved from Carlisle back to Christ Church, Oxford in December 1710. This was just as well because Atterbury naturally supported Dr Sacheverell, and Nicolson was against him.[43] When Godolphin's ministry fell, Atterbury looked to the Earl of Oxford for advancement. When this did not come he allied himself to Bolingbroke. His presence in Oxford caused more public friction. At first the university had been glad to see him back, until he started to search for legal loopholes by which he could change the government of the colleges and the university as a whole, and by this get rid of elderly resident canons. It was Carlisle all over again. Atterbury, suffering badly from gout, was seen hopping from meeting to meeting, making accusations of conspiracy and theft against those he wanted to get rid of, trembling with rage and shaking his cane at his protagonists.[44] In 1713 to the relief of his colleagues in Oxford he was created Bishop of Rochester.

Atterbury clearly had strong Jacobite tendencies. Many of his friends were known Jacobites, and as a high churchman he naturally allied with the cause. But he had taken the oath of allegiance, and as Queen Anne's life drew to a close he was faced with a decision as to whether he should remain in office and support the Hanoverian succession, or throw himself openly into the Jacobite cause and lose his bishopric. As Anne lay dying, rumours circulated that he had offered to proclaim James at Charing Cross, and when Anne died he immediately got in touch with the French agent Abbé Gaultier.[45]

Probably, he did not seriously consider aiding the Jacobites until George I dismissed the Tories, and George's low church Lutheran principles became more widely known. Nevertheless, in his capacity as Dean of Westminster Atterbury helped to officiate at George's coronation. Even then he managed to take umbrage over a misunderstanding with George. The Dean of Westminster's rightful perquisite for attending the coronation was the canopy under which the monarch progressed through the abbey. Atterbury refused this and offered it to George out of politeness. Also out of politeness George refused it; Atterbury took this as a personal affront. In 1715 Atterbury was recorded as dining with known Jacobites such as the Duke of Ormonde and Sir William Wyndham.[46] But he was not involved in the rising, although his old protagonist Bishop Nicolson was one of the leaders of the Cumberland and Westmorland militia.

Following the rising, Atterbury refused to sign a declaration of loyalty to George, and by 7 April 1716 was noted by the Jacobites as being some- one who could be trusted. During the planning of the Swedish plot it was concluded that 'The Bishop will do his part in animating the clergy and warning the city of London from the pulpit the Sunday before the inva- sion'.[47] Atterbury was not keen to get too involved, but he agreed to raise money for the Swedish expedition. He escaped arrest after the Swedish plot was revealed, and must have been rather annoyed when in January 1717 James asked him to raise a further £70,000. Atterbury did not reply to this request.[48] His lack of real enthusiasm for a rising must have been obvious, but he was a valuable contact in England and Jacobite agents continually pestered him. But there was a difference of aims between the court in exile and its agents, and Atterbury. Atterbury wanted to bring the government down first, and to follow this with an invasion. The court in exile saw things happening the other way around.

A new plan was circumvented by the failure of the Spanish expedition but, optimistic as ever, the Jacobites returned to planning in 1720, once more using Atterbury as their main contact – a part he did not seek. He was not impressed by the new agents sent across to him, or the plans they brought with them. He advised waiting until 1722 when the country might be destabilised during the general election. Agent George Kelly brought other plans. There was to be a surprise invasion on two fronts: in the Highlands, and in the West Country. Its success would depend on the materialisation in arms of the English Jacobites. Atterbury was to rally them, and to collect funds.[49] This was a different type of plot to that proposed by Christopher Layer. It came from the exiles rather than the English Jacobites, but it is possible that Layer's plan for taking London became attached to this plan. Bennett suggests that Strafford and other English aristocrats wanted action rather than tedious conspiracy, whereas Atterbury was a politician first and foremost.[50]

Atterbury and his contacts amended the plan. Arran was to be in command in Scotland. Ormonde was to sail secretly to the Thames with Irish officers and foreign troops, and Lord Lansdowne would raise the West Country. They dictated the revised plans to George Kelly, and asked that he acquire commissions and letters of authority for them. The plans were accepted and the commissions sent. Parliament was dissolved on 10 March 1722 and the machinery of the plan went into action. Another element linking Atterbury and Layer emerges here; the impecunious and treacherous Irish cleric Philip Neynoe. It was Neynoe who was taken into Atterbury's household to copy his letters.

Atterbury still had grave doubts about the plan. Little money had been collected, and nothing had been done on the ground to organise men and arms. He said that Ormonde must be told about this, but the rest of his war council showed no concern, so he wrote to France himself describing the plan as 'wild and impracticable'. He said he would have nothing more to do with any conspiracies and wished to be allowed to retire to the country and live quietly.

George Kelly, who delivered this message, was told that Atterbury must not be allowed to slip through the Jacobites' fingers. He was their link to the Church of England, and if they lost his support the Protestants in the plan would become suspicious. He was also their link with the

Tory party; he was a great orator and the Jacobites might need his skills to get the country to accept James. Not only that, but he was their fund manager and essential to their economics. In order to soften up Atterbury a present was sent to him – a small dog called Harlequin. This ridiculous gift was to bring down Atterbury, and is surely evidence that the Jacobites in exile had little grasp on real affairs. What would a bishop with a dying wife want with a small dog?

Boyer, using intercepted correspondence, shows that Kelly took the Bishop's letter to France on 2 April 1722, and left it at Boulogne to be collected by a 'tall black man called Crow', in reality John Talbot, an Irish papist. On 1 May General Dillon in Paris wrote to Kelly, who had returned to London, that there were sufficient barrels ready for wine, in other words troops ready for arms. The invasion was imminent.[51]

The British government had been tipped off by the French, and were opening all Atterbury's correspondence. Information from government agents was that Irish officers were being withdrawn from service with the French army, and gathering at channel ports. In London all known Jacobite coffee houses were kept under observation.

On 19 May, Kelly was arrested, threw off his captors and started to burn his papers.[52] It was his landlady, a Mrs Barnes, who implicated Atterbury, as she was in possession of the dog sent from France for him. The unfortunate animal had broken its leg during its journey from France, but she had taken a liking to it. She told the government that Kelly had said he would get it from Atterbury for her, and that it had been a gift from King James.

Throughout the summer of 1722 other conspirators were arrested, and key figures such as Thomas Carte went into hiding. Atterbury's arrest was withheld until after he had helped to perform the rites at the Duke of Marlborough's funeral. He was arrested on 24 August 1722, still in his nightclothes and hardly able to walk through gout, and was taken to the Tower. Every scrap of paper in his house, including the toilet paper, was confiscated.[53]

Walpole had to be very sure of his evidence, as arresting a bishop was politically sensitive. The main evidence against Atterbury was the copies of decoded intercepted letters and the evidence of Philip Neynoe, a dead man. Atterbury declared his innocence. However, the Commission on the Conspiracy were satisfied that there was enough evidence to try him as being part of a conspiracy to solicit a foreign power to invade, to raise a rebellion, and incite an insurrection in London and other parts of the kingdom.[54]

Atterbury was taken from the Tower to be tried on 6 May 1723. In his opening speech he complained about his ill-treatment at the Tower, and the want of evidence against him. His defence was that the intercepted letters could be forgeries, and the whole construction of the case against him based upon the suspect testimonies of post office clerks.[55] He demanded that the post office clerks be called to give sworn evidence and claimed that the letters carried no treason.[56]

Atterbury was found guilty, stripped of his bishopric and sent into exile. James wanted him to join him in Rome, and become one of his ministers. Atterbury was reluctant to do this, and ended his days in the south of France, acting as pastor to Protestant exiles. Others arrested at the same time as him were released. Was there one plot or two? Evidence suggests that there were two plots to start with, but these merged. Layer's was the product of his enthusiasm and a vivid imagination that led him to exaggerate the extent of the support for the Stuarts in England. He took his ideas to James in Rome. Meanwhile in France a more moderate plan was forming. The key to this was an invasion led by the Duke of Ormonde, with the help of Spanish or other foreign forces. Money was needed for this, and was to be raised and managed by Atterbury. This led to the two plots coinciding.

State papers show that the government were collecting information about possible plots from 1718 onwards. In 1719 they were concentrating on the West Country and arms being sent there, but later their attention switched to Yorkshire and the Humber Estuary. All likely Jacobite correspondence was being intercepted from February 1721.[57]

The Black Acts and the Jacobites

It has been argued that one of the results of the clean-up after the Atterbury plot was discovered was the Black Acts.[58] The Black Acts were so called because they were brought in to deal with gangs of poachers who blacked their faces to prevent identification. Their main spheres of activity were Windsor Forest, the Hampshire forests and woods, especially those belonging to the Bishop of Winchester, the Midlands and Enfield Chase. In the spring of 1723 the Waltham gang who poached in Enfield Chase shot a keeper through the head, and open warfare was declared between poachers and keepers. Royal proclamations failed to stop the poachers, and the result was a series of repressive legislation that lasted until the 19th century, and put 50 new capital offences onto the statute book.

Just as the owlers are seen as part of a legitimate form of protest, so the Blacks are seen 'not as aggressors but victims'.[59] Like the owlers they are also seen as being on the periphery of the Jacobite cause. Evidence for this was sometimes hearsay. Parson Power told the king's messengers that three Blacks were engaged in high treason. On Cannock Chase, an area known for its Jacobite sympathies, the Whig Earl of Uxbridge's estates were attacked and poachers were reported as mocking the keepers with Jacobite songs.[60] Julian Hoppitt suggests that the Black Acts were passed because 'there were fears that the Blacks might be recruited to do the work of Jacobite gentlemen'.[61]

Was it merely coincidence that the Black Acts coincided with the discovery of the Atterbury plot? Seen in their long-term context the Black Acts are part of a series of repressive measures that started in the late 17th century, and are probably as much connected with a rising population and scarce resources as with any political sentiment, and were an attempt by the government to control social rebels and protect property. English Jacobites tended to come from the social class which owned the property, rather than the under-class which was given to stealing it, and although the under-class might borrow Jacobite songs and symbols, their needs were far removed from the aims and objectives of most English Jacobites.

The Cornbury plot

As Atterbury left for exile Bolingbroke returned. He found the Tory party in shreds and himself banned from politics. The only way he could assert himself again was as a puppet master, and to this end he made overtures to Henry Hyde, Lord Cornbury, a great-grandson of the Earl of Clarendon and a cousin of James III. His pedigree and education at the heart of intellectual Jacobitism, Christ Church, Oxford, made him a suitable candidate as a Jacobite saviour.

In 1730 Cornbury went to Rome to meet secretly with James and to plan an invasion, with the help of France. Cornbury was sent home and told to win supporters in England by offering peerages to Whigs and Tories alike. On his return, Walpole offered him a pension of £400 p.a. for his loyalty. He refused and became MP for the University of Oxford instead, and continued to scheme with the Jacobites. He proposed a plan similar to that of Christopher Layer that included seizing the Tower of London and the Bank of England. All his correspondence was intercepted by the government, and France, which was going to back the plans with an invasion, lost interest. The plot died a natural death.

The English Jacobites had achieved very little in the 1720s and 1730s, but they had acquired a bright new hope – Prince Charles Edward Stuart.

Notes

1 HMC, *Calendar of Stuart Papers in the Possession of HM the King at Windsor Castle*, London: HMSO, Vol. II, 1904, 1–2.

2 *Stuart Papers* II, 89–90, 246–7, 267–8.

3 *Stuart Papers* II, 92–3.

4 L. Gooch, *The Desperate Faction?*, Hull: Hull University Press, 1995, 126–7.

5 *Stuart Papers* II, 249.

6 *Stuart Papers* II, 151–2, 308, 344, 382.

7 *Stuart Papers* II, 352–3, 364–5.

8 *Stuart Papers* II, 271, 325.

9 *Stuart Papers* II, 41–2.

10 *Letters which passed between Count Gyllenberg and others relating to the design and raising a rebellion in H.M. Dominions to be supported by a force from Sweden*, London: 1717, 4.

11 *Stuart Papers* II, 67–70.

12 G.V. Bennett, *The Tory Crisis in Church and State, 1688–1720: The career of Francis Atterbury, Bishop of Rochester*, Oxford: Clarendon Press, 1975, 203–5, 209.

13 *Gyllenberg Letters*, 17.

14 *Gyllenberg Letters*, 17–18.

15 HMC, *Calendar of the Stuart Papers at Windsor Castle*, London: HMSO, Vol. III, 1907, 538–9; Bennett, 210.

Plate 1 James II
By courtesy of the National Portrait Gallery, London

J. Rily pinxit.

John Ashton Gent:

Plate 2 John Ashton
By courtesy of the National Portrait Gallery, London

Plate 3 Jacobite plotters: victims of the assassination plot
Ashmolean Museum, Oxford

Plate 4   Prince James Francis Stuart
By courtesy of the National Portrait Gallery, London

Plate 5 Henry, Viscount Bolingbroke
By courtesy of the National Portrait Gallery, London

Plate 6   James, Duke of Ormonde
Ashmolean Museum, Oxford

Plate 7 Sir William Wyndham
By courtesy of the National Portrait Gallery, London

Plate 8 James Radcliffe, Earl of Derwentwater

Lord Petre's Estate

Could Wisdom, Learning, Piety, & all
The gifts ÿ Crowns to their assistance call
Protect the Worthy in an impious Age,
From party Spleen & vile Fanatick Rage;

Then some ÿ are Confin'd had been reverd
And this unhappy Scene had ne'er appear'd,
But now! you may behold a second Laud,
Whose Christian Courage nothing fears but
God.

Plate 9   Bishop Atterbury
Ashmolean Museum, Oxford

Plate 10 Jacobite watch paper
The Drambuie Collection

Plate 11   Jacobite drinking glass
The Drambuie Collection

Plate 12   Madingley Hall, Cambridgeshire
© *University of Cambridge Institute of Continuing Education*

Plate 13 Sir John Hynde Cotton II
Courtesy of Richard Elliott

Plate 14 Sir John Hynde Cotton's tartan suit
© *The Trustees of the National Museums of Scotland*

Plate 15 Prince Charles Edward Stuart
By courtesy of the National Portrait Gallery, London

Plate 16   Sir William Watkins Wynn
Ashmolean Museum, Oxford

Plate 17   Swarkestone Bridge, Derbyshire
Author's photograph

16 *Gyllenberg Letters*, 26.

17 *Stuart Papers* III, 11, 19.

18 *Stuart Papers* III, 183.

19 E. Cruickshanks, *Political Untouchables*, London: Duckworth, 1979, 15;
    C. Winslow, 'Sussex Smugglers', in D. Hay et al. eds, *Albion's Fatal Tree*,
    London: Penguin, 1977, 156.

20 Winslow, 119–20.

21 PRO SP 35/28/37; SP 35/28/39.

22 Winslow, 140, 156.

23 E. Cruickshanks, 'Lord North, Christopher Layer and the Atterbury plot:
    1720–23', in E. Cruickshanks ed., *The Jacobite Challenge*, Edinburgh: John
    Duckworth, 1988.

24 A. Boyer, *The Political State of Great Britain*, London: 1722, Vol. XXV, 235;
    H.C. Beeching, *Francis Atterbury*, London: Pitman & Son, 1909, 276.

25 T. Stackhouse, *Memoirs of the Life & Conduct of Dr Francis Atterbury*,
    London: 1723, 85.

26 R.W. Ketton-Cremer, *A Norfolk Gallery*, London: Faber, 1948, 125–9.

27 Boyer, 70; Cruickshanks, 92; Ketton-Cremer, 131.

28 Boyer, 267, 272; Cruickshanks, 94, Ketton-Cremer, 134.

29 Cruickshanks, 95; Ketton-Cremer, 136.

30 Boyer, 65–9.

31 Parliamentary Papers, House of Commons, Select Committee upon
    Christopher Layer, Report, quoted in Boyer, 248–52.

32 Boyer, 70–72.

33 Cruickshanks, 100–101.

34 Bennett, 261.

35 Boyer, 47–65.

36 Boyer, 75.

37 Boyer, 252, 260.

38 D. Money, *The English Horace*, Oxford: OUP, 1998, 59.

39 Bennett, 23.

40 C. Jones and G. Holmes eds, *The London Diaries of William Nicolson,
    Bishop of Carlisle, 1702–18*, Oxford: Clarendon Press, 1985, 240.

41 *Nicolson Diaries*, 271.

42 *Nicolson Diaries*, 303, 331, 347.

43 *Nicolson Diaries*, 505; Bennett, 99.

44 Bennett, 144–7, 159.

45 Bennett, 181.

46 W. King, *Political and Literary Anecdotes*, 2nd edn, London: John Murray, 1819, 7–9.

47 *Stuart Papers* II, 67, 69–70.

48 Bennett, 211.

49 Bennett, 233.

50 Bennett, 234.

51 Boyer, 369–71.

52 Bennett, 249.

53 Bennett, 256, Boyer, 380–93, Stackhouse, 86–95.

54 Boyer, 472.

55 Stackhouse, 108–112.

56 A Speech in the House of Lords upon the Third Reading of the Bill for Inflicting Pains and Penalties against Francis, Late Bishop of Rochester, London: 1723, 9.

57 PRO, SP 35/15/73, 81, 87, 101, 116, 123; SP 35/16/2, 3, 90; SP 35/17/14, 16, 33; SP 35/22/10; SP 35/61/9.

58 E.P. Thompson, *Whigs and Hunters*, London: Allan Lane, 1975, 68.

59 Thompson, 111.

60 D. Hay, 'Poaching and the Game Laws on Cannock Chase', in D. Hay et al. eds, *Albion's Fatal Tree*, London: Penguin, 1977, 189–253.

61 J. Hoppitt, *A Land of Liberty? England, 1689–1727*, Oxford: OUP, 2002, 473.

CHAPTER 8

The trappings of Jacobitism

The trappings of Jacobitism were the objects, poems, ballads, broad-sheets, pictures, prints and organisations that gave the English Jacobites a corporate identity. Replete with symbols, these proclaimed an allegiance, either openly through the representation of a member of the Stuart family in exile, or secretly through hidden meaning such as the rose with two buds (James III and his two sons).

The abundance of these trappings illustrates changes in the way in which both formal and popular culture was being used in the 18th century. Professor Blanning argues in *The Culture of Power and the Power of Culture* that prior to the 18th century, culture had been based on the court and wielded by those who exercised power in order to show their status. In the 18th century it became used for the communication of information, ideas and propaganda, attracting a wider audience than before. More cultural objects were produced, and more escaped from the control of the censors.[1] A good example of the latter are the numerous portraits and prints of Prince Charles which escaped the censor and are still in existence today.

Some historians have divided Jacobite cultural objects into the high culture of the courts, represented by classically inspired odes, expensive objects and sermons, and the low culture or 'folkways' of the people, the latter being represented by the popular ballads, music and broadsheets, which are the 'coded and explicit cries of the mob'.[2] Popular symbols used by the mob representing Jacobite sympathies were, for example, the white rose or the oak leaf. These were readily understood by all who saw them, and wearing these marked out the bias of the mob.

Murray Pittock claims that in Jacobite culture, high and low culture, the court and the country converged. Both were derived from 'common dynastic, religious or national aims'. Both were opposed to the financial revolution, enclosure and other social developments which threatened communities.[3] It could be argued, however, that the English Jacobites were strong on culture and symbols, but weak on action. Drinking the health of the king across the water in a glass engraved with a thistle, or sporting a plaid waistcoat was not the same as buckling on a sword and riding out to fight for the restoration of the Stuarts. Much Jacobite culture was rhetoric or propaganda,[4] and much of the rhetoric was ambiguous. Alexander Pope's poem *Windsor Forest* was written in 1713 and dedicated to George Granville, Lord Lansdowne, one of the West Country Jacobite conspirators. It conveys a picture of peace brought out of chaos:

Here hills and vales, the woodland and the plain
Here earth and water seem to strive again
Not chaos-like together crushed and bruised,
But, as the world, harmoniously confused

Here 'blushing Flora paints the enamelled ground', there 'Ceres gifts in waving prospects stand'. Who has brought about this peace and plenty?

Rich Industry sits smiling on the plains
And peace and plenty tell, a Stuart reigns[5]

But which Stuart monarch? Anne who is monarch *de facto*, or James who is monarch *de jure*?

Windsor Forest takes Virgil as its model, and the allusions and images in it would be readily understood by 18th-century intelligentsia and at court; understood but, of course, interpreted differently as to whether it was a poem in praise of Queen Anne or a promise of things to come with James. Similarly, Pope's epic *The Dunciad* has been interpreted by some critics as being a study in 'emotional Jacobitism'.[6] Although it is difficult to decipher it has been suggested that Jacobitism is its key. Order will not be restored until 'Genial Jacob' returns.[7]

Pope undoubtedly had Jacobite leanings, and testified on behalf of Bishop Atterbury. Dr Money shows that there was a circle of neo-Latinists centred on Oxford, whose Latin poetry was using parallels from Horace, Catullus and other classical writers and who displayed strong

Jacobite leanings. For example Archibald Pitcairne's *Ad Carolum II* is an open invitation to Anne to bequeath the crown to her brother James, while Anthony Alsop heaped invective on the Dutch who came over with William III.[8]

Augustan poets and popular ballads

There are hints of Jacobitism in John Dryden's later verse.[9] Dryden too takes his models from classical texts such as *The Aeneid*, Juvenal and Lucretius. But what appeal outside the court and universities did the Augustan poets have? The Augustan influence, if not the Latin poem, spread out into the Jacobite gentry in the provinces. A collection of poems found in the manuscripts of the Townley family shows this. The Townleys were Jacobites and Catholics, and Colonel Francis Townley was executed after the 1745 rebellion. The collection of poems and songs includes popular Jacobite songs and ballads that will be discussed later, but also imitations of Horatian odes. For example:

> *The 5th Ode from the 4th Book of Horace Imitated*
>
> *O Prince from English princes Sprung*
> *Why does thou stay from us so long?*
> *Thy Absence, James, thy subjects moan*
> *And longing sigh for thy return*

It continues by comparing James to the spring, and England the mother and James the son who will restore justice and free England from the fetters of taxes. The last verse gets firmly to the point:

> *What e're we do what e're we are*
> *To Heaven we dayly send our prayer*
> *Restore our Monarch to his throne*
> *And send the Booby Germans home*[10]

The anonymous author of the poems translated the classical idiom into a popular and political mode. He/she shows us George II as Nero fiddling while Rome burns, and referring to the failure of the 1715 rising has Cato's ghost addressing Britain demanding the country rise again.[11]

Augustan poetry was read and collected in the houses of the gentry and it was also sold on the streets, as this fragment, picked up in London and sent to the secretary of state, shows. It uses the same Horatian poetry as its model:

> *A land tired of oppression, land of liberty*
> *Let Royal James adorn his Native Isle*
> *Then will all things Jocund Smile*
> *And James will be a bright north Star*[12]

There are other good examples of crossovers between high and low culture, so that placing these in discrete boxes may be a mistake. Popular culture borrowed from formal poets, and courtly poets in turn used popular ballads and songs. There was considerable seepage between the two, as Money shows in the case of the Duke of Wharton's parody using the well-known ballad *Chevy Chase* as a model, with Lord Witherington, alias Widdrington of the '15, as one of its central characters.[13] Of course the tune of *Chevy Chase* was well known everywhere, and it was one that lent itself to social and political satires of all kings.[14]

The importance of using ballads as propaganda was realised by the government and the Jacobites. In June 1712 Abel Boyer recorded that ballad singers had been stopped from wandering about singing and selling ballads that encouraged sedition and riot.[15] In March 1718 John Menzies, a Jacobite agent in London, wrote to J. Inese in France that he was frightened to send him any new ballads, 'although these swarm everywhere. One to the tune of Chevy Chase is reckoned extraordinary humour and wit. There must be some very industrious enemies who undertake to promote that engine against the government'.[16]

These ballads were selling at 2d each, and were beyond the reach of the labouring population.[17] But ballads could be easily learnt by heart and taught to others, and so they proved a good medium for communication. But the versions sold by the ballad singers were often forwarded by well-meaning citizens to the secretary of state. In January 1725 William Preston, a tailor, purchased this ballad and sent it to the secretary of state:

> *Potatoes is a dainty dish, and turnips is a springing*
> *And when Jemmy does come o'er, we'll set bells a ringing*
> *We'll take the cuckold by the horns and lead him unto Dover*
> *And put him in a leather boat and send him to Hanover*[18]

It has to be remembered that many of the so-called Jacobite ballads were not written until the 1820s, well after the events they commemorated were over. In particular Lady Nairne and Sir Walter Scott created 'the historical narrative of the Jacobites' and 'made Charles Edward Stuart into a Romantic figure'.[19] The best-known Jacobite song of all, *The Skye Boat Song*, was not written until 1908. James Hogg's *Border Ballads* that celebrate the English Jacobites of the 1715 rising are also a 19th-century construction, although W. Donaldson claims that Hogg passed his ballads off as antiques.[20]

We have to beware of the provenance of all Jacobite ballads, such as this on the Earl of Derwentwater quoted in Gibson's *Dilston Hall*:

> *Oh Derwentwaters a bonny lad*
> *And golden is his hair*
> *And glinting is his hawking eye*
> *With kind love dwelling there*
> *Yester'een he came to our Lord's gate*
> *And loud, loud did he call*
> *Rise up, rise up for good King James*
> *Buckle and come awa*[21]

Perhaps more authentic is an *Acrostic On the Right Honourable James, Earl of Derwentwater* found in the Townley Manuscripts, in which the first letter of each line spells out 'Derwentwater'.[22] In the contemporary poems and ballads about the Stuarts they become the bringers of Spring and new life, or the lost or forlorn lover. There is another genre of Jacobite verse that owes its origin to courtly poetry. Odes celebrating royal birthdays, marriages and deaths, or on seeing a picture of one of the exiled Stuarts for the first time were popular both in the court in England and the court in exile. For example:

> *An Ode on Seeing the Picture of Prince Charles for the First Time*
>
> *The Christian hero's looks here shine*
> *Most with sweetness of the Stewart's line*
> *Courage with mercy, wit with virtue joined*
> *A beauteous person with a beauteous mind*[23]

Or

Verses written by a Lady on seeing the Picture of the Prince

What Briton can survey that heavenly face
And doubt it being of the Martyred race
Every feature does his birth declare
The Monarch and the Saint are shining there
His face would the boldest Whig convince
He peaks at once, the Stuart and the Prince.[24]

Or from the Townley manuscripts:

A Birthday Ode on the Prince, 20th December 1747

Forget scenes of woe and the axe
'Tis Charles that bids us crown the day
And end the night in joy . . .[25]

The Townley manuscripts also include verses about James II, such as *The Departure of James II*, referring to him as the 'great good man'.[26]

Another genre of Jacobite verse either pillories the Whigs or Hanoverians, or uses their songs and verses for their own ends. The victor of Culloden, the Duke of Cumberland, comes in for especial opprobrium.

Verses Addressed to the Duke of Cumberland

Go Monster, raised to Gold the monument
And near the base place Treachery
Veiled in a mantle of eternal shame[27]

The promotion of Britannia as a national element, the inclusion of *Rule Britannia* in Thomas Arne's masque *Alfred* in 1745, and the development of the national anthem *God Save the King*, were seized on by the Jacobites as vehicles to parody and imitate. Entitled *A Song*, these verses can be sung to the tune of *God Save the King*:

Church, King and Liberty
Honour and property
Are betrayed
By the foreigners
That rule the land
Will be restored again
By James our king

Down with Dutch politics
Whigs, Knaves and Fanatics
The Old King's cause
Recall your Injured Prince
Drive Hanoverians hence
Such do rule here again
All English laws

Borne on the wings of Fame
Charles that heroic name
All his foes dread
He from his father's throne
Shall pull the Tyrant down
Glorious success shall claim
His sacred land[28]

Jacobite verse also pilloried those who had betrayed them. John Murray of Broughton, who turned King's evidence after the '45 rebellion, received this rebuke.

To all virtues holy ties can boast
To truth, to Honour and to Manhood lost
How hast thou wandered from the sacred host
The Path of Honesty, the pole to God
O further! O further! For the high degree
Of spotless fame and poor integrity[29]

In the papers belonging to Sir John Hynde Cotton of Madingley Hall in Cambridgeshire is a manuscript poem entitled *Lichfield Races*. This goes through a list of English Jacobites who have defaulted on the old cause. Lord Gower becomes 'corruptions slave' with his son Lord Trentham and the Duke of Bedford. 'Degenerate Wrottesley and the poisonous viper Wyerley' also appear.[30] Poetry and verse was, therefore, a valuable tool by which the English Jacobites could express their views and put out propaganda. Another medium for propaganda was the newspaper and the pamphlet.

Pamphlets and newspapers

The Jacobites were well aware of the power of propaganda through the printed word. On 6 November 1716, Mary of Modena wrote to the Countess of Bute that Thomas Willis has written some very good pamphlets and if the King approves she will encourage him to write more and set up a printing press at St Omer. With the letter she enclosed a note from Willis suggesting that it was books and pamphlets that had deceived the public and led to the ruin of Charles I, and then undeceived them and led to the restoration of Charles II. By pamphlets the Whigs had gained both the army and the people and deposed the late king, and by continued writing they confirmed the people's prejudice against him.

Willis wanted to fight them on equal terms by setting up a press at St Omer and sending the pamphlets back to England at night by owlers 'who run goods secretly between both nations and will assist in getting stuff to London', and from there across the country to a list of sympathisers given to Willis by a friend.[31]

A number of pro-Jacobite news sheets were printed in England. One ran in different guises for over 21 years. Robert Mason's *Weekly Journal* or *Saturday Post* became Nathaniel Mist's *Mists Weekly Journal* in 1716, then *Fogs Weekly Journal* eventually ceased publication in 1737. George Flint's *The Shift Shifted* started publication in 1714.

These newspapers had a wide circulation. Between 1700–1712 it has been estimated that 70,000 copies of these newspapers were sold each week. This number was curtailed by the Stamp Act that sent up the price, but there was still a large number in circulation. Attempts at censorship by the state, local authorities and institutions such as the University of Cambridge did not deter the clandestine printer, who was running a great risk in publishing what were deemed to be seditious items.[32] Daniel Defoe claimed that he could show that the contents of the Jacobite journals were high treason, and copies of Jacobite journals are appended as evidence of treason in 18th-century state papers.[33]

Examples of other journals include *The Champion or Evening Advertiser* edited by Captain 'Hercules Vinegar' of Pall Mall. This cost 3d a week, and campaigned for the restoration of the Stuarts and against the 'dirty policy of corruption'. *Old England or The Constitutional Journal*, edited by 'Jeffrey Broadbottom', was more openly Jacobite. On Saturday

31 August 1745 it compared Prince Charles Edward with Henry Boling-broke arriving back in England from exile to wrest the crown from Richard II. George II was equated with Richard and his ministers were described as 'nasty drivelling tittle tattle fellows'. The issue includes extracts from the *Caledonian Mercury* on the progress of the Jacobites in Scotland, and reports a general press on seamen to defend the country.[34]

Provincial newspapers such as the *Norwich Gazette* were covertly Jacobite, printing articles on tyranny to coincide with Hanoverian anniversaries, while John Byrom and Robert Thayer collected together all the articles in *Chester Courant* and *Manchester Magazine* about Manchester's part in the 1745 rebellion and published these in one volume called *Manchester Vindicated*.[35]

Jacobite and Tory journals and anti-Jacobite Whig magazines had a wide circulation by the mid-18th century. More people had access to information and understood the political issues of the day, and the nexus of power.

Music

The Hanoverians had Handel to celebrate their victories. His oratorio *Judas Macabees* was written to celebrate the Duke of Cumberland's victory at Culloden. But the court in exile had its own musicians and was a centre for musical excellence.[36] In England folk songs and traditional tunes were borrowed to provide accompaniment for Jacobite songs and ballads, and at least one dance tune became synonymous with the Jacobites. John Byrom's journal records that at a ball in Manchester in 1750 Sir Watkins Jig was announced. A government officer in the crowd cried out that this was an anti-government and treasonable action as it was written for Sir Watkin Williams Wynn, a well-known Jacobite. This led to a heated argument between Byrom and the officer, which developed into a brawl. Later Byrom saw the funny side of this and wrote an epigram on it:

> *To Her Majesty's presence a Barker advanced*
> *Says he 'lets jig of Sir Watkins be danced'*
> *But as in our bosoms it raised a pain*
> *Pray let it be called by some other name*
> *No by its true name we call it says Dolly*
> *You may if you like call it Warriner's Folly*[37]

Paintings and prints

A great number of Jacobite portraits and prints have survived in national, local and private collections; for example the National Portrait Gallery in London has 15 portraits and prints of James III and 16 of Prince Charles, with equally numerous collections in galleries such as the Ashmolean Collection in Oxford. The finest collection of Jacobite portraits, prints and artefacts is that owned by the Drambuie Corporation in Edinburgh. Famous artists such as Sir Godfrey Kneller or Nicholas de Largillière painted portraits of the Stuarts, as did less well-known artists.[38]

These illustrate three 18th-century trends. One was the development of the consumer-led art market, with demand especially high for the cheaper prints and engravings, and copies of paintings. It became normal for the houses of the gentry, the professional classes and tradesmen to adorn their walls with representational art. Inventories of possessions taken after the owner's death show that there were an increasing number of pictures appraised.

The second trend is the English Jacobite's desire to have artefacts that represented the cause. These could be an original portrait of a member of the Stuart family, or a print taken from a portrait. As there is little evidence of anyone being prosecuted for possessing such an article we must assume that these were purchased openly and overtly hung in the English Jacobites' houses.

The third reason for the popularity of paintings and prints was the necessity to have something by which the Stuart family and their adherents could be recognised in the street or battlefield. The government needed to be able to identify the faces of its enemies, while many English Jacobites would never have met James III, or Prince Charles and his brother. It would have been easy to foist an imposter onto them; they needed a portrait to match to the original, and as the 18th century was before the age of the instant image, the changes over time of the Stuart royal family needed to be recorded through series of prints, portraits and medals that traced them from childhood through adulthood to old age. For example, in 1691 Nicholas de Largillière shows the future James III as a naked chubby child sitting on a cushion and clutching a King Charles spaniel to emphasise his antecedents. In 1694 Pierre Mignard painted a family group of the Stuarts in exile with James II wearing the garter robes, and his son wearing a scarlet cloak held up by a Negro slave, an armour breastplate, over which is the garter sash.[39] The garter sash is an emblem of royalty found on most of the Jacobite portraits.

James III's growth to adulthood was recorded in a series of portraits. There is a fine example of him as a youth wearing a grey and silver coat in the Scottish National Portrait Gallery. In this portrait he gazes directly out at the observer, whereas a 1714 portrait shows him in profile indicating the strong features and large nose by which he would become recognisable in later life, and seen in a portrait of him in old age by Louis-Gabriel Blanchet.

Each representation is more than an identity card. They contained symbolic elements of kingship and conquest. Robin Nicholson, curator of the Drambuie collection, has traced and dated the development of the romantic image of Prince Charles Edward, and is the foremost expert on this.[40] The garter figures heavily in portraits of the Prince as a child, for example aged six he appears in a portrait by A. David with one hand on his hip wearing the garter sash, and flanked by a table with the Prince of Wales feathers on it. In 1729 in twin portraits of Prince Charles and his brother Henry they both wear the garter. The garter also appears in a 1737 portrait.[41] A portrait by J.E. Liotard painted a year later shows Prince Charles armed ready for action, his armour covered with an ermine-trimmed gown, and the Prince of Wales feathers on his helm.[42] After 1745 Scottish themes appear in his portraits. The plaid is either thrown over his shoulder or worn as a tartan suit with trews. Representations of the prince wearing tartan led to a fashion of tartan waistcoats worn by English Jacobites.

Portraits of the Stuarts were given to their supporters in England. In August 1717 Anne Oglethorpe, a Jacobite agent in England, delivered a picture of James III from France to Charles Caesar and his wife. This was not an up-to-date portrait but had been drawn ten years earlier, and it would seem that the Stuarts kept a stock of portraits to be sent out to their admirers. Although Mrs Caesar was delighted with it – 'She shows it to everybody and cannot be a moment without looking at it' – what she really wanted was a more recent portrait. In April 1718 Anne Oglethorpe wrote to the Earl of Mar to remind him 'to send a picture of the King as he is now, that you promised I should have for Mrs Caesar'.[43]

Other prints were sent from the continent to be distributed generally. L. Inese in London, writing to the Earl of Mar in France, reported that he had received the bundles of prints and would distribute these as fast as he could. He found people were well pleased with them, and clamoured to possess them.[44]

Oil paintings were expensive. Prints of paintings or original prints of engravings were cheaper and easy to transport. In his book *The Engraved Record of the Jacobite Movement* Richard Sharp has identified 757 different prints connected with the Jacobite cause, with many versions of some of these still extant.[45] The prints can be divided into portraits of the Stuart royal family, portraits of known Jacobites and political prints. Like the paintings the prints of the royal family follow them from childhood to old age. Like the paintings they are embellished with symbols of legitimacy such as the garter, ermine robes or a crown, as well as Jacobite symbols such as the white rose or the oak tree. Some had obviously been reworked to include up-to-date symbols. For example, an engraving of Prince Charles as a child made by Edelenck after David had a Scottish bonnet in honour of the Scottish campaign of 1745.[46] Prints of the Prince in Highland dress became popular after the '45. Some prints were allegories: a mezzotint by Borderach of Prince Charles in the Scottish National Portrait Gallery frames the Prince with the figures of Hope and her anchor and Time with his sickle.

The second type of Jacobite print was of famous Jacobite figures such as Viscount Bolingbroke or the Duke of Ormonde, and of those who had sacrificed their lives for the cause like John Ashton or the assassination plotters. These prints were sold openly in the streets of London, and were often used as illustrations to broadsides that recorded the victim's 'gallows' speech. Coupled with harrowing details of the execution these went some way towards creating a Jacobite hagiography. There were also narrative prints showing exciting events such as the fight at Preston.

The third group of prints was political and often satirical. A good example of this genre is the *Agreeable Contrast* print that shows Prince Charles with a greyhound and a corpulent Cumberland with an elephant. With heavy *double entrendre* a country wench, said to be Flora Macdonald, indicates the greyhound and says 'Oh! The Agreeable Creature, what a long tail he has'. Coming out of the Prince's mouth are the words 'Mercy, Love, Peace & etc'.[47]

The Jacobites satirised the Hanoverians and the Whigs, similarly the Whigs produced satirical prints of the Jacobites and their supporters. Notorious among these are the prints produced during the Broadbottom Administration in 1744. This was a coalition between the Whigs and Jacobite Tories, and was called Broadbottom both because it represented a broad church of ideology, but also from the girth of one of its members, Sir John Hynde Cotton. The prints tend to concentrate on his substantial haunches, and are anal in the extreme.

Jacobite images also appear on less formal objects such as watch papers that were hidden inside the timepiece, on snuff boxes and ladies' fans. On the domestic front mugs and teapots were decorated with transfer prints of Prince Charles, ladies embroidered handkerchiefs with his head, and a pincushion was made with the names of 72 victims of the Jacobite Cause on it.[48]

The prints were produced in London or on the continent and distributed to the provinces to be sold in print shops or at gatherings such as the assizes or race meetings. Usually, the transactions went undisturbed by the authorities. Purchasers included Dr William King, an Oxford academic, and Sir Robert Cotton, a Huntingdonshire gentleman.

The Great Seal, coins and medals

Before he went into exile in 1688 James II destroyed the Great Seal. He explained that he had done this to prevent it falling into the hands of the Prince of Orange.[49] When he reached France and set up his court in exile he regretted this rash action as he needed the seal to authorise his orders. In 1689 he asked the Roettier brothers to make another one for him to take to Ireland, but this was made in haste and was imperfect. In January 1691 a new version was ordered, and the 1689 seal was broken in James's presence, whilst another version was produced on the accession of James III.[50] Two more seals were produced for James III in 1716. One was to be the signet for Scotland showing the Arms of Britain and Scotland with the Thistle and the Saltire and the words *Jacobus VIII.D.G. Mag. Brit. Fran et Hib.Fi. Def.* The other was to be a pocket seal for use in England.

This was to be made of steel set in gold rather than the softer silver. To prevent any mistakes the Roettiers were to send the Earl of Mar a design of each before starting work.[51] Prince Charles took one of his father's seals with him in 1745.

In 1708 when James was planning an expedition to Scotland he realised he would need money to cover expenses and to pay the Swedish troops who were supposed to be helping him. In May 1708 a warrant was issued to Norbert Roettier, engraver-general of the mint, to direct punshions and dies to be produced for coining £5 pieces, 40s pieces, golden guineas, half guineas, silver crowns, half crowns and sixpences.[52] Medals were also struck in great numbers. These commemorated Jacobite events such as the birth of Prince Charles, or portraits of the royal family. Prince Charles had medals struck to take to Scotland in 1745. Medals were small and could easily be slipped into a pocket or sporran and carried with the army. The 1745 medals bore the legend *Carolus Walliae Princeps 1745 Amor et Spes* (Charles Prince of Wales, Love and Hope). The reverse showed Britannia standing on a rock by the seashore, resting upon her shield and spear, awaiting the arrival of Prince Charles's fleet. Behind her on a globe was a map of Britain.[53]

Other metal pieces made by the Stuarts had a specific function. Touch pieces were sent by the Stuart kings in exile to those who had King's Evil or scrofula. The touch of an anointed king was believed to cure this, and kings of England had special touching days. James II touched regularly, but William and Mary refused to have anything to do with such a superstitious practice. Queen Anne touched reluctantly, using a lode stone rather than her fingers. James III's first touch pieces were struck in 1708 and were given to members of the Scottish expedition to take with them. Prince Charles touched while he was in Edinburgh in 1745. A painting records this as happening in the picture gallery of Holyrood house. Charles, surrounded by priests, touches the sores of a kneeling child, saying 'I touch but God heals'.[54]

Another series of medals was struck for Jacobite clubs such as the Oak medal, struck in 1750, showing an old oak tree leafless and hollow with a young sapling springing from it; this was for the Jacobite society that met at the *Crown and Anchor* in The Strand. Members paid one guinea for a copper version of the medal.[55]

Jacobite clubs and societies

'Clubs and societies were an increasingly common and pervasive feature of British social life from the seventeenth century on'.[56] Each club had its own special identity and many were Jacobite organisations which met in coffee houses and taverns across London and the provinces (see also Chapter 3 for a discussion of the coffee houses). Notable amongst these was the Cocoa Tree Chocolate House in Pall Mall which opened in 1698 and was converted into a private Jacobite club in 1745–46. The Half Moon Tavern and Coffee House in Cheapside was another well-known Jacobite haunt, as was Ozinda's Chocolate House in St James Street and the St Albans Tavern and Coffee House in Pall Mall.[57] There were also Tory clubs which although not openly Jacobite had a number of Jacobite members, such as the October Club or the Board of the Loyal Brotherhood which was established in 1709 with the Duke of Beaufort as its first President.

F.P. Lole, who has produced a *Digest of Jacobite Clubs*, has identified 223 Jacobite clubs.[58] However, there are some problems with Lole's figures as he includes places where Jacobite glasses were found, and these were not necessarily clubs but private houses. He includes mock corporations and True Blue Hunts, and the relationship between these and English Jacobites cannot always be proved. Twenty-three Jacobite clubs have been identified in Wales and it is from Wales that some of the best evidence about Jacobite clubs comes. The Cycle Club of the White Rose was founded on June 10 1710 by Sir Watkin Williams Wynn. Its badge was the white rose of the Dukes of York, James II's badge before he became king. It was called the cycle club because it met on a three-week cycle at different members' houses. This was not to preserve its secrecy but to give members from all directions a chance of attending at least some of the meetings. This was not an unusual way of organising a society. The Lunar Society of the Midlands, an organisation dedicated to science and the discussion of philosophy, was so called because it rotated round members' houses at each full moon. The Cycle Club drew up a formal rota of meeting places and laid down its rules in 1723.[59] As these rules show, club meetings were formal affairs. Societies had a full tier of officers, presidents, chaplains and treasurers, and intending members had to serve a term as probationers. The clubs possessed their own regalia, buttons and badges, and commissioned paintings showing the officers wearing the regalia.[60] They met to dine, discuss politics and the restoration of the Stuarts, and to drink the health of the king over the water.

As well as being the age of clubs and societies, the 18th century saw the foundation of the Freemasons. Unlike the Jacobite clubs the Freemasons were a really secret society, and would have been an ideal medium through which to create a network of Jacobites, except for one problem. In August 1737 Pope Clement XII published a severe edict against Masonry and forbade Catholics from becoming Masons. The edict also resulted in the expulsion of the Jacobite Roman Lodge of Masons from Rome.[61] Members of this lodge included well-known English Jacobites such as Sir Marmaduke Constable of Yorkshire, Thomas Dashwood, and a Mr John Cotton of Cambridgeshire who was lodge master in 1735. The infamous John Murray of Broughton, who was to turn King's evidence in 1745, joined the lodge in 1737. His name was struck from the register.[62]

Hughan speculates as to whether Prince Charles was a member of the lodge, but admits there is no documentary evidence for this, and suggests instead that he was connected with the Order of the Temple through his contact with the Earl of Mar, a member of that order. In 1843 Dr George Beyermann wrote that Prince Charles had been created Grand Master of the Scottish Templars during his stay at Holyrood House, but Hughan points out that no evidence for this can be found.[63] Baigent and Leigh admit that 18th-century Masonic lodges could be of any political persuasion but 'There is no question but that the Jacobites had a crucial influence on the development of Freemasonry'. They show that the Duke of Wharton was a Mason, and that many of the leading Jacobites in exile were members, including Charles Radcliffe.[64] Noel Paton suggests that both Charles Radcliffe and his brother James, Earl of Derwentwater, 'had been Freemasons in Lodges around Hexham'.[65] No evidence for this has been found.

One figure who does link the Stuarts to the Masons is Andrew Ramsay, a Scot who became tutor to Prince Charles and his brother. It was Ramsay who claimed that there was an unbroken relationship between the Masons and the medieval Order of the Knights Templar. Other historians accept that there was a link between the Masons and the Jacobites.

Frank McLynn writes that it was 'to such an extent that later witnesses were to describe Freemasonry as a gigantic Jacobite conspiracy'.[66] In Wales the Freemasons were seen as part of a Jacobite network linking clubs and societies, with members in common including Sir Watkin Williams Wynn and a number of non-juror clergy. J.P. Jenkins thinks that this network helped to play a part in creating a Welsh Tory opposition to the Whig government.[67] In England, however, the Grand Lodge had members that included crypto-Jacobites such as John Byrom as well as anti-Jacobite Whigs such as the Duke of Richmond.[68] It is probable that in England Freemasonry transcended political and ideological boundaries.

Freemasons were a secret society in all senses. Their membership, rituals and beliefs were hidden from public gaze, but the Jacobite clubs and societies wore their badges and insignia with pride. They also purchased what are surely some of the best-known Jacobite artefacts, drinking glasses.

Jacobite glass

Many of the extant Jacobite glasses came from Jacobite clubs, and bear the club insignia as well as Jacobite symbols. Other glasses were used in private households such as Oxburgh Hall in Norfolk. The full corpus of surviving Jacobite glass has been recorded and photographed by Geoffrey Seddon. He has identified 472 drinking glasses, as well as decanters, tumblers and other glass objects. Seddon bids us beware of fakes as Jacobite glasses are much coveted objects and expert guidance is needed that a glass was made in the 18th century and is not a modern forgery.[69]

Seddon identified nine separate glass engravers, five of whom were working in London. He dates the majority of glassware to the mid-1740s and 50s. Greatest demand for these glasses was between 1744–45, which he suggests is evidence of the government's complacency about the Jacobite threat.[70]

The glasses were made to order, engraved with specific images chosen by the purchaser. The images included the white rose, the oak and thistle, and portraits of Prince Charles sometimes crowned, the garter star, and the Prince of Wales feathers. Words were often included such as 'Amen', 'God Save the King; and '*Fiat*'. The rose was the most popular emblem.

Tracing the original owners of the glasses is difficult as these have changed hands many times. However, when a collection of Jacobite glass is found in a country house it was probably purchased by a member of the family. Examples of this are the collection found at Chastleton Manor in Oxfordshire, or Oxburgh Hall, Norfolk.

Splendidly engraved glass was expensive and Jacobite glass was top of the range. Most glass was purchased for clubs or societies and held in common amongst the members.

Women purchased less expensive items to show their allegiance to the Jacobite cause. Elizabeth Byrom of Manchester, who was introduced to Prince Charles in 1745, purchased a blue and white gown in his honour in that year, and in 1768 after James III had died she purchased a blue-glazed teapot with CRIII and a white rose on it.[71] Thus the trappings of Jacobitism could be found in the domestic setting, the country house, the coffee house and tavern. In the 18th century the symbols would have been instantly recognisable and would have marked out the owner as a supporter of the House of Stuart.

Notes

1 T. Blanning, *The Culture of Power and the Power of Culture*, Oxford: OUP, 2002, 2–6.

2 M. Pittock, 'Inventing and resisting Britain', in *Cultural Identities*, Basingstoke: Macmillan, 1997, 110–11.

3 Pittock, 110.

4 P. Monod, *Jacobitism and the English People, 1688–1788*, Cambridge: CUP, 1993, 45.

5 D. Brooks-Davies ed., *Alexander Pope. A Collection of Poetry*, London: Dent, 1996, 3–13.

6 D. Brooks-Davies, *Pope's Dunciad and the Queen of the Night*, Manchester: Manchester University Press, 1985, VI–VIII.

7 Brooks-Davies, *Dunciad*, 63, 73–4.

8 D. Money, *The English Horace*, Oxford: OUP for the British Academy, 1998, 146, 176.

9 H. Erskine-Hill, 'Literature and the Jacobite cause', in E. Cruickshanks ed., *Ideology and Conspiracy*, Edinburgh: John Donald, 1982, 51.

10 A. Grosart, *English Jacobite Ballads, Songs and Satires from the Mss at Townley Hall*, Manchester: Privately printed, 1877, 3.

11 Grosart, 7, 101–4.

12 PRO SP 35/65/116.

13 Money, 190–92.

14 See for example, *Paving and Lighting: A new song to the tune of Chevy Chase* in E. Lord, *Derby Past*, Chichester: Phillimore, 1996, 58.

15 A. Boyer, *The Political State of Great Britain*, London: 1716, Vol. XI, 747.

16 HMC, *Calendar of the Stuart Papers belonging to HM the King preserved at Windsor Castle*, Vol. VII, 1923, 146.

17 Monod, 47.

18 PRO SP 35/33(3).

19 R. Samuel, *Theatres of Memory*, London: Verso Press, Vol. I, 1996, 22.

20 W. Donaldson, *The Jacobite Song, Political Myth and National Identity*, Aberdeen: Aberdeen University Press, 1998, 3.

21 W. Gibson, *Dilston Hall*, London: Longman, 1850, 62–3.

22 Grosart, 109.

23 H. Paton ed., *The Lyon in Mourning*, Edinburgh: Scottish Academic Press, First published 1895, facsimile reprint 1978, 359.

24 Grosart, 86.

25 Grosart, 37–41.

26 Grosart, 86.

27 Grosart, 84.

28 Grosart, 77–8.

29 Grosart, 71.

30 CRO 588Z/16.

31 HMC, *Calendar of the Stuart Papers in the Possession of His Majesty the King at Windsor Castle*, Vol. III, 1907, 182–4.

32 J. Hoppit, *A Land of Liberty? England 1689–1727*, Oxford: OUP, 2002, 180–82.

33 D. Macrae-Daniel, *Daniel Defoe and the Jacobite Movement*, Salzburg: Institute für Englisch und Amerikeristik, 1980, 3; See for example PRO SP 35.30/67.

34 CRO 588/Z/12–3.

35 J. Byrom and R. Thayer, *Manchester Vindicated*, Chester: E. Adams, 1749.

36 E. Cruickshanks and E. Corp, eds, *The Stuart Court in Exile and the Jacobites*, London: The Hambledon Press, 1995, xx.

37 R. Parkinson ed., *The Private Journal and Literary Remains of John Byrom*, Manchester: Chetham Society, 1854, 29.

38 For a discussion on portraits of the Stuarts in exile see E. Corp, *The King Over the Water. Portraits of the Stuarts in Exile after 1689*, Edinburgh: Scottish National Portrait Gallery, 2001.

39 In possession of HM the Queen.

40 R. Nicholson, *Bonnie Prince Charlie. A Study in Portraiture*, London: Associated Universities Press, 2002.

41 Scottish National Portrait Gallery.

42 National Portrait Gallery, London.

43 HMC, *Calendar of the Stuart Papers in the Possession of the King at Windsor Castle*, Vol. IV, 1910, 554; Vol. VI, 19169, 337.

44 HMC, *Calendar of the Papers in the Possession of the King at Windsor Castle*, Vol. II, 1904, 169–70.

45 R. Sharp, *The Engraved Record of the Jacobite Movement*, London: Scolar Press, 1996.

46 Sharp, 111.

47 British Museum, Department of Prints and Drawings, Satires 2833.

48 Sharp, 224.

49 HMC, *Calendar of Stuart Papers at Windsor Castle in the Possession of HM the King*, I, 1902, 77.

50 *Stuart Papers* I, 165.

51 *Stuart Papers* II, 74–5, 116.

52 *Stuart Papers* II, 223.

53 F.A. Skeet, *Stuart Papers, Pictures, Relics, Medals and Books*, Leeds: John Whitehead and Son Ltd, 1930, 72–5.

54 F.A. Skeet, *Catalogue of Jacobite Medals & Touch Pieces in the Collection of Miss Maria Widdrington*, Leeds: John Whitehead & Son Ltd, 1938, 10–12.

55 Skeet, *Stuart Papers*, 75.

56 P. Clark, *British Clubs and Societies 1580–1800*, Oxford: Clarendon Press, 2000, 13.

57 B. Lillywhite, *London Coffee Houses*, London: George Allen & Unwin Ltd, 1963, 63, 254, 432, 496.

58 F. Lole, *A Digest of Jacobite Clubs*, Royal Stuart Papers, Vol. LV, 1999, 5, 10.

59 R.G. Francis, *The Romance of the White Rose*, London: John Murray, 1933, 226–31; S. Jones, *Jacobite Imagery in Wales: Evidence of Political Activity*, Royal Stuart Society Papers, LIII, 1998, 1–2.

60 Jones, 7–10.

61 W.J. Hughan, *The Jacobite Lodge at Rome 1735–7*, Torquay: Lodge of Research, 1910, 35.

62 Hughan 14, 18, 16, 21, 52.

63 Hughan, 25–6.

64 M. Baigent and R. Leigh, *The Temple and the Lodge*, London: Jonathan Cape, 1989, 174, 177, 183.

65 N. Paton, *The Jacobites. Their Roots, Rebellions and Links with Freemasonry*, Fareham: Sea Green Ribbon Publications, 1994, 23.

66 Paton, 29–30, McLynn quoted in Paton, 37.

67 J.P. Jenkins, 'Jacobites and Freemasons in 18th century Wales', *The Welsh Historical Review*, Vol. 3, 1979, 392, 402.

68 J. Hancox, *The Queen's Chameleon*, London: Jonathan Cape, 1994, 67, 71.

69 G. Seddon, *The Jacobites and their Drinking Glasses*, Woodbridge: Antique Collectors Club, 1995, 230–47.

70 Seddon, 139, 158, 174.

71 Hancox, 183, 210.

CHAPTER 9

• • • • • • • • • • • • • • •

Sir John Hynde Cotton: the Jacobite and the Tory party

'Pox! The world is come to a fine pass, indeed, if we are all fools except a parcel of Roundheads and Hanover Rats! Pox! I hope times are a-coming that we shall make fools of them and every man shall enjoy his own. I hope to see it, sister, before the Hanover rats have eat all our corn, and left us nothing but turnips to feed upon.'[1] So roars Squire Western in Henry Fielding's novel *Tom Jones*. The novel is set in 1745, but Fielding only lets this slip incidentally, and it was published in 1749. Squire Western is the Whig Fielding's caricature of the Tory Jacobite squire who goes to bed each night 'generally so drunk he could not see', whose life was dedicated to his dogs and hunting, who is a JP with no knowledge of the law, who swears and farts and drinks to 'the king over the water'.[2]

Western is a larger than life character. Is he based on another larger than life character, Sir John Hynde Cotton of Madingley Hall, Cambridgeshire? Even if he had not met him personally, Fielding must have known about Sir John and his exploits. His great girth was frequently seen about the streets of London, and evidence of his substantial haunches can be seen in his tartan suit, on display in the National Museum of Scotland. Indeed, Sir John could also be the model for John Trott-Plaid, the fictional author of Fielding's satirical periodical *The Jacobite Journal*, in which characters such as Tory Rory, John Pudding and Humphrey Gubbins appeared, and which included frequent references to the Jacobite Country Squire wearing plaid at every opportunity.[3]

Fielding's figures had some basis in reality. He was pillorying the Jacobite gentlemen who sported their plaid waistcoats and ribbons at Lichfield Races, but perhaps it was unfortunate for the cause that two of the leading English Jacobites, Sir John Hynde Cotton and Sir Watkin Williams Wynn, were so large, loud and colourful, enabling Fielding to create a stereotype of the Tory squire based on them. Other Jacobite gentry were more retiring, keeping their prejudices within their own circle and their home. They knew they had to be circumspect or lose their estates, even their heads.

The Jacobite gentry

Identifying the Jacobite gentry, or the gentry with some Jacobite sympathies, is difficult because after the failure of the 1745 rising it would seem that incriminating papers were destroyed. There is some information in the Stuart papers and the French Foreign Ministry archive but these are often the result of wishful thinking, and those named as Jacobite supporters were not always as committed as the Stuarts hoped. When it came to taking up arms for the cause, they put their family and their estates first, and erred on the side of caution.

Who were the gentry? They were 'gentlemen' but not ennobled. They had the right to bear a coat of arms, and could be knighted or inherit a baronetcy, although some, like Squire Western, bore no honorary title. It did not matter much as baronets and knights were thick on the ground in the mid-18th century; there were at least 1226 baronetcies in existence.[4] At the end of the 17th century Gregory King had estimated that there were about 16,400 landed gentry families, with a further 1200 lawyers and eminent merchants and tradesmen. According to King their average annual income was between £200–800, but this is an underestimate.[5] Most landed estates produced a larger income than this not only from the land but from rents, stocks and shares, but many estates were heavily encumbered by charges on them. Annuities to family members, widows' jointures, daughters' marriage portions all had to come out of the estate income.

The lifestyle of the gentry varied from the hunting, drinking and swearing Squire Western to the cultivated humanism of his neighbour Squire Allworthy. In general, in real life the rural gentry were the social leaders of their community. They acted as Justices of the Peace, they served on the Grand Jury at the Assizes, they attended local assemblies, balls and race meetings. In the larger counties they owned property in the county town where they stayed during assize week, and their presence helped to boost the local economy.

The 18th-century gentry were conspicuous consumers. The inventories of their houses are replete with silver, china, and glass, pictures and musical instruments. They refurbished their houses to the latest fashion, and landscaped their parks using the foremost garden designers of their day such as Capability Brown or Humphrey Repton. In doing this they were looking towards the future. They would not live to see the trees they had planted grow to maturity, or the result of the fully formed planned landscape they had paid for, while the luxury goods inside their homes would be listed as family heirlooms by following generations. These were items that were to stay within the family.

Planning in advance for the future of the family estate shows a confidence in the continuation of the family bloodline in conjunction with its own territory. Entails were set up to ensure that the land passed intact down the male line. Planning for the future, and the maintenance of the family estate may have been one reason that the English Jacobite gentry stayed at home in 1745. In April 1744 a bill was introduced into the House of Commons that would on the one hand attaint Prince Charles for treason the moment he landed, and on the other extend the forfeiture of estates of those who supported him, to their sons. This could be seen as an active deterrent to treason as it would ruin the family, but it would also give an opportunity to those who wished to extract themselves honourably from an engagement with the Jacobites. As Lord Hardwicke who introduced the bill observed, 'No man will acknowledge himself a coward: but no man is afraid of saying he has a great regard for his wife and children.'[6]

Lawyers, merchants and entrepreneurs also laid up stock for the future of the family name. They purchased country estates to which they could retire at the weekend and summer, and the counties near London became popular retreats, with an increase in land prices. A good example of this trend of moving out of London comes from the Houblon family, related by marriage to the Hynde Cottons. The Houblons were financiers, and connected to the Bank of England. They purchased an estate at Hollingbury, Essex, while the London brewing family Parsons, also related by marriage to the Hynde Cottons, purchased Reigate Priory in Surrey.

Although their country estates provided their income and many of their leisure activities, it was in London that county and city gentry coalesced, transacted their business, purchased their clothes and arranged their marriages. London was the acknowledged cultural and social centre of England, attracting to it gentry from all over the country. In order that they could keep in touch with affairs at home, county societies were formed which met to discuss county business in convivial surroundings, and each county had its own gentry network formed by kinship, marriage and political affiliations.

In the north west of the country there was a further gentry network of Catholics, who intermarried and often worshipped together. Their houses were the magnets where Catholics gathered to hear the mass, and to discuss the politics of the day. Catholic gentry were barred from holding offices such as justice of the peace or member of parliament, so much of what they discussed was connected to restoring their civil rights, and in some instances this bordered on treason.

An example of a north-eastern recusant family who were part of a network that encompassed trade and land were the Brandlings. They first appeared in the 16th-century records of Newcastle upon Tyne as merchants, and soon became members of the Hostmen and corporation. As recusants they lost their offices in the 17th century, but continued to rise socially. By the 18th century they were connected to some of the leading Catholic gentry families of the north east, including the Collingwoods and Widdringtons. They were also connected to a wider network in Lancashire through marriages with the Leghs, and to Yorkshire via a marriage into the Constable family. This locked them into a Jacobite network that a marriage to the Protestant but Jacobite Forster family helped to cement.[7]

The Catholic Eyres of Hassop in Derbyshire were also related by marriage to Lancastrian Jacobite families, through a union with the Blundells of Ince, while the infamous John Lunt who accused the Lancashire plotters was allegedly christened by a Catholic priest at an ale house near to Hassop. Rowland Eyre was arrested by the Duke of Devonshire in 1690, but was released before coming to trial. After that he tried to avoid politics, but he was a member of the quasi-Jacobite Mock Corporation of Walton le Dale, and although not directly involved in the 1715 rising, as a Catholic he had to register his estates and pay fines on these following its failure. To prevent the forfeiture of his estates he settled these on trustees and made himself and his male heirs life tenants. The Hassop estate was given an annual value of £1115.14s.1d three farthings in 1717, for which he was fined £84 a quarter.[8]

The Eyres of Hassop could easily have joined Prince Charles Edward when he was in Derby in 1745. Significantly they stayed at home, and while historians examine the careers of more eminent Jacobites and create apologies for them not taking up arms in 1745, they could equally well direct attention to those gentry in Derbyshire on the Jacobites' route from Manchester to Derby who did not take up arms, or even visit Derby to pay homage to the Prince.

In Yorkshire a well-known Catholic Jacobite family were the Constables of Everingham. They were related to the Radcliffes, and Sir Marmaduke Constable left the Earl of Derwentwater £1000 in his will, and was probably sending funds to the court in exile. Constable's estate was worth £1073 a year. Due to his generosity and the charges on the estate he was forced to sell some of his land to pay off his debts, appoint an estate manager, and live on the continent.[9]

Not all Jacobite gentry were Catholics, and not all Catholic gentry were Jacobites. Protestant Jacobite gentry were usually high church, patrons of deprived non-juror clergy, and Tories. Many of them were members of parliament, and held local offices such as justice of the peace. Sir Watkin Williams Wynn, Sir William Wyndham and Sir Henry Goring were examples of this type of Jacobite. But the figure who stands out as epitomising their breed was Sir John Hynde Cotton, third baronet, of Landwade and Madingley Hall in Cambridgeshire.

The Hynde Cottons and Madingley Hall

The Hynde Cotton family came into existence when two great gentry houses of Cambridgeshire were united by marriage in 1647. Jane Hynde (1631–92), the heiress of Madingley Hall, married Sir John Cotton (1615–59), first baronet of Landwade and Exning. Both came from high church Royalist families.

The Cottons of Landwade's original estate was at Exning, and they acquired Landwade in the 14th century through the marriage of Sir Thomas Cotton and Alicia de Hastings.[10] They were an old landed family. The Hyndes' background was different. Their fortune came from the work of a successful lawyer Sir John Hynde who became a judge of common pleas. He already had some land in Madingley, and in 1543 an Act of Parliament granted him Madingley manor in return for an annual rent to be paid to the shire or county that owned the manor. Prior to this, in 1537, at the Dissolution of the Monasteries, he had purchased Anglesey Abbey that lies to the east of Cambridge. Some of the material from the abbey was carted across to Madingley to build a hunting lodge, which eventually became Madingley Hall. In c. 1632 the last male heir of the Hyndes died, and the marriage of Jane Hynde and Sir John Cotton united their estates and their family names.

The first to bear the double name, who confusingly was the second baronet, was also an ardent Royalist and collector of civil war pamphlets. He married Elizabeth Sheldon, the daughter of a Lord Mayor of London. One of Sir John II's daughters Catherine married William Sancroft, the nephew of the non-juror Archbishop of Canterbury. This tied the Hynde Cottons firmly into the high church non-juror clique, and although Sir John took the oath of allegiance he was the patron of at least one non-juror clergyman. Sir John II was MP for the borough of Cambridge 1695–1705, a member of Cambridge corporation, and recorder of the town, thus setting up a tradition of public service that his son the Jacobite Sir John was to follow. Father and son also shared antiquarian interests. The Hyndes were connected by marriage to the Stukeley family, one of whose members, William Stukeley, was one of the best known 17th-century antiquarians. Sir John III was to pay Thomas Carte, the Oxford non-juror antiquarian, to catalogue his father's collection of Civil War pamphlets, and subscribed to Carte's unfinished *History of England*. Carte was a Jacobite agent.

Madingley Hall was described by William Coles in 1763 as being 'a noble pile of buildings, partly old and partly modern'. It was surrounded by an enclosed park formed in 1743–44 after a jury of neighbouring gentlemen and clergy met to alter and exchange some of the lands belonging to the church 'which lay in his [Sir John Hynde Cotton's] way, and incommoded the design'.[11]

Cole suggests that Sir Francis Hynde pulled down St Etheldreda's church in Histon and took away the lead, timber, stones and bells and either sold them or used them at his house at Madingley.[12] This means that Madingley Hall contains in its fabric the remains of two plundered churches, Anglesey Abbey and Histon parish church.

The earliest buildings consisted of the great hall, now the dining hall, a kitchen reached through a serving passage and a turret. The turret shows that Sir John was a man of substance who could afford solid oak stairs and the central newel post made out of a single imported Norwegian pine. The turret room contains 16th-century murals that include a bear baiting scene and a boar hunt. A long gallery was added to the hall at the end of the 16th century, and as tastes changed a saloon was created in the upper hall with a plaster ceiling designed by James Gibb. After his marriage in 1724 Sir John Hynde Cotton III purchased tapestries and paintings for the saloon, and placed his arms above the fireplace, and on the bay windows. Visitors to the hall in 1740 approaching the saloon from the small dining room and withdrawing rooms created out of the old long gallery would pass through wooden Ionic columns forming a proscenium arch, to an oak staircase leading to an upper gallery and the saloon. These were all the work of the Jacobite Sir John, who was obviously planning for the future.

An inventory of the contents of Madingley Hall taken in December 1734 shows that it contained 36 rooms. The rooms that the family used were furnished in the height of luxury and fashion. For example the drawing room where the ladies sat after dinner waiting for the men to finish their port had:

3 pieces of Indian silk hangings
6 chairs and a settee covered with Indian silk
2 pair of silk window curtains
a gilt table
a peer glass, carpet, and a steel hearth with silver fire implements.

The family and guest bedrooms, usually with dressing room attached, were named according to the colour of their furnishings: for example the yellow bed chamber, the red and blue damask chamber, and so on. Household offices included a kitchen, dairy, bread-making room, and a laundry, all containing a great deal of up-to-date equipment.[13] This was not the old-fashioned dark and uncomfortable house of a Squire Western.

Inventories of plate and china show that the Hynde Cottons were conspicuous consumers of epic proportions. Their china included Minton, Chelsea and Delftware, and a 1737 inventory lists over 100 pieces of silver.[14] When the Madingley Hall inventories are compared with the Dilston inventories of the Earl of Derwentwater, it can be seen that Madingley Hall was by far the most comfortable. The Hynde Cottons were well entrenched in local society, and they had a large acquaintance outside the locality. They leased a house in Westminster, convenient for a sitting member of parliament, and the inventories show that silver and china were packed and transported to London, so that Sir John could make a fine show there as well.[15]

Sir John's son, another John, transformed the gardens from a 17th-century formal Dutch garden with clipped box hedges into the wild yet managed landscaped garden and parkland of the 18th century. Capability Brown visited the Hall and an agreement was drawn up that listed what Brown would do and how much he would be paid, in this case £500. As well as demolishing the Dutch garden he was to dig a new lake in the front of the house, make a new carriage road and plant such trees as were necessary. Gravel walks were to be laid out round the garden. Hynde Cotton was to find horses, carts, wheelbarrows, trees and shrubs at his own expense.[16] Again this was planning for the future as this landscape would not mature until many years after Hynde Cotton's death. For the present he planted fruit trees in walled gardens, and a kitchen account book for the late 18th century shows that each year a large amount of fruit was preserved for the household, including melons, pineapples, apricots and peaches in brandy, as well as more mundane fruits such as strawberries, blackcurrants, raspberries and plums, which were made into jams, jellies and fruit cheeses. Apple and blackcurrant juice was bottled for the store cupboard, and raspberry vinegar made for the cook.[17] This suggests that the family led what was for the 18th century a healthy lifestyle with plenty of vitamin C from the fruit they grew. But we also know that the Jacobite Sir John liked the bottle, and in that he does match the Squire Western model. A bill for three days' stay at an inn on the road to London came to £57.7s, an enormous amount for the 18th century. It included breakfasts, bread and beer for the servants, and port and claret for Sir John.

Sir John and his family did not stint themselves when it came to dress and jewellery. In 1736–37 the draper's bills came to £120.7s.1d, and the following year to £200.9s.11d and a halfpenny. This amount was paid in instalments.[18] At the time of his son's wedding Sir John purchased a lady's hairpiece containing 85 brilliants in it valued at £70, and earrings costing £250. The lace man's bill for rich silver spangles for Sir John's waistcoat and gold point lace for his over coat came to £31.3s.6d, and for relaxing at home he purchased a blue and gold damask gown lined with nankeen at the cost of £43.16s.6d.[19]

This finery made Sir John an outstanding figure in more ways than one. But he was living beyond his means, and this may have been the reason for his own marriage into the City of London, and that of his children into trade and finance. It may also have been one of the reasons for him wishing for the return of the Stuarts. In 1713 in the reign of Queen Anne when the Tories were in power he was one of the commissioners for trade. For this he received the healthy sum of £1000 a year.[20] He lost this on the accession on George I when the Tories fell from grace and were barred from holding government posts. Sir John was eventually to take out mortgages on the estate with the Duke of Bolton and Sir Nathaniel Curzon.[21]

Was Sir John a Jacobite for the money and power that would return to him, or from political conviction? Let him stand as a representative for all the other English Jacobites who corresponded with James Stuart; who listened to his agents and promised support; who sent invasion plans and ideas, and sometimes even money to the court in exile; but in 1745 when the time came to put their promises into practice, who did nothing.

Sir John Hynde Cotton III – a Jacobite's life

It is generally assumed by historians that the lack of incriminating evidence among the records of the English Jacobite gentry means that these were destroyed in 1745. What we know about them comes from lists of supporters and reports of conversations sent by agents to the court in exile. These lists may represent wishful thinking on behalf of the agents. But while it is true there is little open Jacobitism in Sir John's papers, there are hints embedded in them, and the gigantic tartan suit he was given is evidence enough of his espousal of the Jacobite cause. But how much of this was bluster remains to be seen.

Sir John Hynde Cotton III was born in 1686 and inherited the baronetcy when his father died in 1712. He was educated at Westminster School and Emmanuel College Cambridge, matriculating in 1701 and achieving his MA in 1705. He was a high churchman and a Tory, described by Horace Walpole as having 'wit and the faithful attendant of wit, ill nature'.[22]

Like his father before him, he was to enter Parliament as a Tory MP: for Cambridge borough in 1708–22, for the shire in 1722–27, for the borough again in 1728–34, and for the pocket borough of Marlborough, Wiltshire in 1741–52, after he fell out of favour with the Cambridge borough electors because of his stinginess.[23] Following the 1715 election Sir John and his fellow Tory candidate Thomas Slater were accused of corruption, and the election was inspected by the parliamentary Committee of Privileges, Sir John was cleared of the charge of bribery.[24] While the Tories were in power under Queen Anne he rose with them. All this was to be lost on the accession of George I.

Sir John was not only a country gentleman and owner of a country estate, he was also a shrewd businessman who had no qualms about marrying into trade. His first wife, Lettice Crowley, was the daughter of Sir Ambrose Crowley, a non-juror Northumbrian iron master. Lettice brought with her a dowry of £10,000. When she died in 1718 leaving a son and daughter, Sir John spent six years as a widower, then to the surprise of friends and enemies alike he married Margaret Trefusis, the widow of Samuel Trefusis of Cornwall and the daughter of Samuel Craggs, the brother of the Whig secretary of state.

Was this an astute political move by Sir John, giving him access to confidential information and inside knowledge of what the government knew about Jacobite conspirators or, as was more likely, was it a match made for economic reasons? Margaret owned considerable real estate, and personal effects that under the marriage settlement were conveyed to trustees for her to use for life, and were then to pass to Sir John and his male heirs. She also possessed £17,000 of capital invested in stocks and a large amount of jewels and plate.[25]

At what point did Sir John become a Jacobite? His sympathies probably always lay with the old regime. He came from a family with Royalist sympathies who supported the Stuarts. But although both he and his father were patrons of non-juror clergy there is no evidence that suggests that they did not take the oath of allegiance, and though they were high church they were staunchly Protestant. However, by 1713 Sir John was a member of the ultra-Tory 'Loyal Brotherhood', a semi-masonic organisation that met at the Cocoa Tree Coffee House. This organisation may have raised funds for the Jacobites, but it was primarily a Tory rather than a Jacobite club although known Jacobites belonged to it such as Sir William Wyndham, the Earl of Orrery and Sir Watkin Williams Wynn.[26]

Sir John avoided being implicated in the Atterbury plot, but Sedgwick suggests that his name was first sent to the court in exile as a possible supporter in 1721.[27] It is possible that Sir John was reviewing his position with regard to his future allegiance as early as 1713. Among his papers for December 1713 to February 1714 is a list of the ordnances, engineers and gunners in England and Edinburgh as laid down by the Duke of Marlborough, and apparently passed to Sir John by James Craggs.[28] This would have been valuable information to pass to the Jacobites, and we should ask why he had this and what he was going to do with it. It should be noted that it predates the Hanoverian accession, and it may show that Sir John was considering his options once Queen Anne died.

Sir John became one of the leaders of the Tory opposition, manipulating the voting, and provoking Sir Robert Walpole on every possible occasion.[29] This kept him in the notice of the Jacobites, and in 1739 he was approached by the Jacobite agent Colonel Brett to see whether he would support James if he was accompanied by a French invasion.[30]

From 1740–45 Sir John was involved in a dangerous double game. On the one hand he received Jacobite envoys, who reported him as being 'shy' but one of James's most ardent supporters who should be put on any regency to run the country for James;[31] on the other hand he was jockeying for a government post as Walpole lost his ascendancy. Sir John was reputed to have told Jacobite agents that he would back a restoration attempt provided it was accompanied by a body of troops able to bolster the support of the English Jacobites and confront government troops. If this could be guaranteed Sir John would meet James when he landed, and it was claimed he offered to act as a clearing house for messages from the continent to be distributed across the country.[32] How far this was what Sir John promised, and how far the agents had misunderstood his real intentions is not clear. In 1744 when the French sent their own envoy to find out the actual numbers of Jacobite supporters in England, his name was prominent among them, although he appeared in the French list as 'Monsieur Cotton'. There is a problem with linking this to Sir John. There were three Cottons who were potential Jacobite supporters at this time. To confuse the issue they all came from eastern counties. There was Sir Robert Cotton of Steeple Gidding in Huntingdonshire and his son John, as well as Sir John of Madingley. The two John Cottons were exact contemporaries, and as the hyphenated Hynde was not always applied it is easy to confuse the two. For example, it would be easy to assume that the John Cotton who joined the rebels at Preston was Sir John of Madingley. In fact it was the Huntingdonshire John Cotton, although it would appear that the French agents were not always aware of this. So the question we must ask is whether the John Cotton who appears in the French archives is really Sir John of Madingley.

Sir Robert Cotton and Sir John were friends, and in 1731 Sir John became one of the first trustees of the Cotton Library that Sir Robert gave to the nation. Another trustee was William King, the Oxford Jacobite, and Thomas Carte the Jacobite agent drew up the plan for preserving the library.[33] Here was a nest of Jacobites who could use trustees' meetings as ideal cover for plots.

In 1740 there was a revival of Jacobite plots, based around the idea of a French invasion close to London. These plans were revealed to the government by a double-agent Francois de Bussy, who sold his information about the plot for £2000. He named the Duke of Beaufort, Lord Barrymore, Sir Watkin Williams Wynn and 'Monsieur Cotton' as its main instigators in England. But when asked if Monsieur Cotton was Sir John Hynde Cotton the MP, he replied that it was the Cotton who had escaped from Preston in 1715,[34] thus adding to the confusion as to the depth of Sir John Hynde Cotton's involvement with the Jacobites.

In 1742 Walpole's power was in decline, politically and physically. On 12 February 1742 the whole opposition including Whigs, Hanoverian and Jacobite Tories met at The Fountain Inn, in the Strand. The Duke of Argyle set himself up as their leader, and proposed that they amalgamate to form a coalition and bring the Walpole government down. They could then form their own government that would unite Whigs and Tories, and reinstate the Tories to office. This would be a 'broadbottomed' administration. Accordingly Sir John and other leading Tories went to kiss the king's hand.

The term 'Broadbottom' was to heap ridicule on the new administration when it took power in 1744, as it described exactly the figures of Sir John and his fellow Tory Jacobite Sir Watkin Williams Wynn. Scurrilous cartoons and satirical prints appeared playing on the term, displaying Sir John's substantial rear end as the major feature. Sir John hoped to be given a lucrative office, preferably in the Admiralty. The king refused this, and the Duke of Argyle resigned. Immediately, Lord Barrymore started overtures to him to bring him into the Jacobite camp and James, seeing an opportunity to get more supporters from the ranks of disappointed Tories, sent a message that all their offices would be restored after a Stuart restoration. This suggests that James was well aware that self-interest was one of the motivating forces of his support in England.

In July 1744 Sir John visited Scotland. On 20 July he was made a burgess and gild brother in Edinburgh, and on the 24th a freeman of Glasgow, and three days later a burgess and freeman of the borough of Hamilton.[35] *The Caledonian Mercury* shows that he was travelling with the Earl of Strafford. Strafford was one of the Tories who had kissed the king's hand with Sir John, and if not an actual Jacobite had a tendency to support them. What were they doing in Scotland at this time? It is possible they were seeing for themselves the strength of support for the Stuarts, and conferring with Scottish Jacobites. But the inauguration of them as freemen of Scottish burghs suggests that they may have travelled in an official capacity as members of the Broadbottom coalition. Edinburgh was known as a Jacobite city, so it was no surprise that it gave the freedom to Sir John, but Glasgow at this time was strongly Presbyterian and anti-Jacobite, so for that city to give the freedom to Sir John reinforces the idea that they travelled as official representatives. It was at this time that Sir John acquired his tartan suit, with a view to wearing this when he met his king, James III.

The Broadbottom Administration eventually took office in December 1744. On the 24th of that month Sir John received 'letters patent' making him Lord Treasurer of the Chamber. Although Cruickshanks claims he refused to take an oath to the king on this occasion, the letters patent among his papers are endorsed 'sworn and admitted'.[36] He was paid a retainer of £133.13s.8d and £22 a year, a far cry from the £1000 a year he had received at the Board of Trade. Nevertheless, there was scope for making more from the office by taking gifts from those who wanted employment in the royal household. The Lord Treasurer of the Chamber paid the wages of such exotic personnel as Thomas Philips the royal historiographer, Colley Cibber the poet laureate, Stephen Slaughter keeper of the king's pictures, John Gower rat-killer, Alice Bill strewer of herbs in the privies, and John Clother, court drummer.[37] Some thought this housekeeping role was beneath Sir John's dignity, and Horace Walpole wrote to the Duke of Newcastle in March 1745 that he thought Sir John would resign the post soon.[38] But Sir John did not render his final account until midsummer 1746, when it showed a deficit of £1693.6s.11d halfpenny. The words 'and he is quit' were not added until 30 November 1748.[39]

It would appear that even whilst holding a crown office Sir John was hedging his bets and entering into plots with the Jacobites. In January 1745 he and Sir Watkin Williams Wynn sent a message to France pointing out that the cream of the English army were out of the country, and this would be an excellent opportunity for an invasion. They asked the French to send 10,000 men and arms for 30,000 more, and suggested that they should land at Maldon in Essex, as being convenient for London.[40]

1745 was a busy and expensive year for Sir John. His son's marriage to Anne Parsons took up a great deal of time, his estate had to be surveyed before the marriage settlement could be made, and he spent a great deal of money on the wedding and its accoutrements. The expenses of the wedding itself came to £1209.14s.3d.[41] His accounts for 1745 show that he purchased horses, pistols and leather breeches, which may have been in preparation for action.[42]

When Prince Charles landed in July 1745 Parliament was in recess and Sir John at home in Cambridgeshire, where he remained until Parliament was recalled. He was back in London by October 1745 when he was in the House to vote against the suspension of *Habeas Corpus*. Before leaving Madingley tradition suggests that he buried three miniatures of Prince Charles and his brother Henry in the garden.[43] Lady Houblon, who was descended from Sir John's daughter, suggests that at the time of the landing Sir John was asked to resign his office, and that tradition says he was sent to the Tower. Cruickshanks also suggests that he was arrested, questioned and released, although there is little evidence for this.[44] He kept his office and his head. He was present in London during pro-Jacobite riots, and in the panic that ensued once the rebels reached Derby. This success may have encouraged him to join with Lord Barrymore to send a message to the French urging them to land in Essex where 'they would be met by loyal gentlemen'.[45] However, neither would give firm assurances that they would join the Prince. They claimed that this would expose them too early and suspicion would be roused if they left London; this would render them useless to the cause.

The French clearly did not trust the English Jacobites, and although they agreed to prepare an invasion force, they decided to land on the south coast rather than the east, and not to tell Barrymore and Sir John about the change of plan. In the event Admiral Vernon found out about the plan from a French ship he captured, and the invasion never took place.[46] Sir John never had to use his new pistols in anger.

What do his actions in 1745 tell us about Sir John? He was shrewdly playing a waiting game. If he declared for the Jacobites and joined them in the north, and the rebellion failed he would be attainted as a traitor, hung, drawn and quartered and his estates lost to his family. If he waited until a French invasion force arrived he could join in with more confidence of success. But there was no guarantee that either he or his fellow English Jacobites would join a French force. At the start of the rebellion much of the British army was overseas. By December 1745 most of them were back, and supplemented by 6000 Hessian troops. Although there were pro-Jacobite elements in London, the trained bands came out in force to defend the capital against the rebels, and from the shires and counties loyal addresses flooded into the King, and voluntary associations of gentlemen raised troops. Once Prince Charles had withdrawn from Derby there was no point in declaring for him and being branded a traitor.

To historians interpreting some of the sources written at the time it might seem as if there was massive public support for the Jacobites and a Stuart restoration. Other sources, such as the Minute Books of the Baptists' General Congregation and the diaries of non-conformist ministers, show this was far from being the case. They dreaded the restoration of a Catholic monarchy and all it stood for. They saw the return of the Inquisition and the burning of heretics. And where was the Catholic support for the rebels? Apart from a few Lancastrian Catholics, they stayed firmly at home. Someone as shrewd as Sir John would have realised that by December 1745 the rebellion was a lost cause, and quietly faded into the background.

After Culloden there was still the matter of high-born prisoners brought to London for trial who had incriminating evidence against Sir John and his English Jacobite colleagues. John Murray of Broughton, who turned King's evidence, said he had met Sir John in 1740 and before meeting him had been told by Viscount Bolingbroke that the English Jacobites 'only vent that Loyalty which their Claret inspires'.[47] He claimed to have had several meetings with Sir John, including one at Lichfield Races, and that he and Lord Barrymore had told him that they were ready to embrace the cause at every opportunity. Barrymore had promised large subscriptions, and pledged his support, but Sir John was more circumspect. When the French agent Butler was compiling his list in 1744, Sir John refused to see him. Murray speculated that this might have been through timorousness.[48] Lord Traquair, on trial for treason, said he hardly knew Sir John and the others and denied he spoke to them about the rising. He had met them once or twice in London, in coffee houses or taverns, but always in public places.[49] Sir John insisted on attending the trials, probably to proclaim his innocence, and there is an eye-witness account of his reaction to the accusations against him. Elizabeth Yorke, Lord Chancellor Hardwicke's daughter, was also at the trial. She knew Sir John well, Madingley and Wimpole being near neighbours. She wrote daily accounts of proceedings to her brother Joseph who was with the army. 'Murray said the first steps towards the conspiracy had been to procure assurances from the Pretender's friends in England, and that he had frequent conversations with Lord Barrymore, Sir John Hynde Cotton and Sir Watkin Williams Wynn, and that Sir John Hynde Cotton was very shy on the subject'.

At this point Sir John Talbot stood up and said this was inadmissible, hearsay evidence, calumniating persons. A great altercation followed between the trial managers and Talbot, and Murray was told he need not name anyone unless it was in actual connection with the rebellion.

You will easily imagine that Murray's evidence made a great deal of noise, and it is not unlikely that it will have further consequence. Two of the persons he named were absent, but our neighbour (Sir John) had affectedly placed himself in the first row of the Commons, and attempted

to turn off what was said in a most audacious behaviour of grinning
and laughing. However, the next day there was a meeting of about 40
Tories to consider what they should do upon the occasion, and it was
apprehended that they should take notice of it in the house; but as this
has not yet been done some people are disposed to surmise that they are
afraid of making bad worse, of which there does indeed appear to be a
danger, as this has certainly opened up a new scene, and it is not easy
to see where it will end.[50]

In the Commons, Thomas Prowse suggested that those who had been accused by Murray should be allowed to speak in their own defence. The Speaker replied that as far as he knew they did not choose it,[51] and he was right. Silence and the diversion of the public gaze was their best defence.

So Sir John and his fellow English Jacobites escaped from the 1745 rising without harm. Why was this allowed to happen when, to some at least, their culpability was obvious? Their treason was, if anything, worse than that of the Highlanders who fought to reclaim a separate nation and were far removed from public office. After all, Sir John and his colleagues had kissed the king's hand. The reason for their treatment must surely lie with the government intelligence service. They knew that no real preparations were being made by Sir John and his colleagues, and that the French did not trust them either. Those acquainted with the English Jacobites would have been aware that much of what they promised was bluster. Sir John might parade in his tartan suit but if it looked as if his estate and family fortunes were threatened, he would very quickly take it off. The political situation had changed as well. A contemporary of his, George Bubb Dodington, suggested that Sir John and his party were sitting and waiting to see what would be offered to them under James, if a French invasion was successful.[52] Sir John had tasted power once more as a member of the Broadbottom administration, and he had another political string to his bow. Frederick, Prince of Wales had fallen out with his father and created a new political alliance. Sir John was to join this in 1746.

Was Sir John Hynde Cotton Squire Western? He was far more urbane than Fielding's squire. But glimpses of his behaviour do suggest some similarities with Squire Western. His personality has come down to us through the reports of people who knew him as larger than life. William Coles who was at college with Sir John's son and a frequent guest at Madingley, described him as 'the tallest, largest, best-looking man I ever remember to have seen; and I have been told that when he was younger than when I knew him he was one of the handsomest men of his time.'[53]

The tartan suit was made for a man of six feet four inches, and close examination of it reveals that the trousers had been let out at least once. Here was a big man of almost mythical proportions, and myths about him and his love of the bottle proliferated. A story was told about him that when informed by his doctor that his gouty leg would only recover if he drank less than his daily allowance of six bottles of claret, he replied that if that was the case the leg was no use to him.[54] Sedgwick attributes this tale to Coles, but it does not appear in *Gens Cottoniana* and is surely too disrespectful to have been recorded by a family friend, so it is more likely to have come from Whig propaganda. However, Sir John's accounts show he was partial not only to claret, but to white wine, port, sack and rum.[55]

More evidence about his character comes from a series of incidents involving Samuel Shepherd, a fellow Cambridgeshire MP. Shepherd was the son of an East India merchant, who purchased an estate in Exning in Cambridgeshire, where the Cotton family also had land. This may account for some of Sir John's dislike of him, as a rival landowner, and his pretensions. Lady Hynde Cotton wrote that Shepherd was resolved to become a Cambridgeshire gentleman. Another reason for antipathy between the two men may have been Shepherd's morals. He was living with a woman he never married, and no matter what Sir John's other faults were, sexual immorality does not seem to have been one of them. Among Sir John's personal papers are notes dated 1731 on Shepherd's personal life, recording his adultery for many years with a woman that Shepherd had purchased from her husband in a form of conveyance.[56]

But the real reasons for Sir John's dislike was political. Up to 1715 Sir John and Shepherd had been joint MPs for Cambridge borough in perfect amity, but in 1714 Shepherd declared for Hanover. Defeated in the 1715 election he took out a petition against Sir John and his fellow MP but although the Committee of Privileges declared for the sitting MPs, through his persistence Shepherd had one of them, John Slater, unseated, and took his place. From then on he was a valuable ally for Sir Robert Walpole, and he and Sir John were sworn enemies.[57]

Shepherd went out of his way to annoy Sir John. He found an ancient statute that showed that Madingley had been granted to the Hyndes in 1543 with the provision that they pay £10 to a year to the knight of the shire. When Shepherd was elected for the shire he took out a claim against Sir John for this.[58]

Matters came to a head at the Easter quarter sessions of 1726. Several versions exist describing what happened. There are the depositions of witnesses, the evidence of those involved, and the deliberation of the justices who head the resulting court case. There are also notes made by Sir John in his distinctive large round hand that appear to be an *aide mémoire* to himself about what happened.

The dispute arose over the restoration of the chief constable of the county who had been dismissed over an accusation of corruption. Sir John thought the accusation had not been proved, and that the constable should be restored. Shepherd thought he should not, and when Sir John asked why, would give no reason. Sir John said that the only reason the constable was accused was because Shepherd had corrupted him at the last election. Shepherd said Sir John lied. Sir John said he could not hear him. Shepherd repeated 'I tell you before the face of the county you lie', to which Sir John shouted 'Flesh and blood can bear it no longer' and struck Shepherd with his cane. Or at least that was Sir John's version.

A number of witnesses under oath had a different version. They claimed that Sir John made a speech claiming that if the constable was not restored 'None of us will be safe in our Rights, our Liberty, and our Property will be invaded and taken from us'. He then turned to Shepherd and said 'You have been guilty of Bribery and Corruption of the whole County at the last election.' Shepherd protested and said Sir John should not utter such words in a public place and should be more temperate. 'Thereupon Sir John did swear he could not bear it and did with his fist or arm with great violence strike Shepherd to the ground and having in his hands a cane stepped back for a better swing of the cane and beat Shepherd who was in a ducking posture almost back to the ground. 2 or 3 blows to the head with great force and violence.' At this point their fellow justices, who had been frozen to the spot, regained the use of their limbs, leapt off the bench and dragged Sir John away.[59]

When Sir John came before the bench the justices agreed with the witnesses about the manner of his attack on Shepherd, but agreed with Sir John that Shepherd had called him a liar. They added that they thought Sir John's behaviour was 'Rash, violent and unacceptable'.[60] The justices were in an awkward position. They could find no precedent for punishing justices of the peace fighting in the courtroom, and they were aware that sending Sir John to gaol would bring the bench into disrepute. They decided on a compromise that made it look as if both men were guilty. Shepherd was to say to Sir John, 'Sir; I am sorry the provocation you gave me should induce and provoke me to answer you in a language unbecoming to a gentleman.' To which Sir John was to answer, 'Then I am very Sorry for the Rash and Inconsiderate action I was guilty of, and I heartily ask your pardon.'

These words were to be spoken in the presence of four members of parliament, two nominated by Sir John and two by Shepherd. The men were then asked to give their word of honour that all further resentments would cease.[61]

Sir John remained politically active for the rest of his life. He was probably at Lichfield Races when the Jacobite Tories wore token tartan waistcoats and the Duke of Bedford, seen as a traitor to the cause, was attacked. Sir John died at his house in London in 1752, and was buried in Landwade church. His epitaph recalled his 'Attic wit, British spirit, Roman virtue'. It described him as devoted 'to the service of his country as a British Senator above the desire of ill-got power; Untainted with the itch of tinsel titles. He lived, he died – A PATRIOT'.

The Tory party and the English Jacobites

Sir William Wyndham became leader of the Tory party in 1715, and remained leader for most of its time in opposition. With Sir John and other Jacobite Tories he continually spoke and voted against government motions, and refused to endorse addresses of loyalty to the Hanoverians. This does not mean that all the Tories were Jacobites, even though Whig propaganda suggested this.

In entering into the debate about the strength of Jacobitism within the Tory party the historian is entering dangerous ground, and liable to be caught between the fire of two notable historians, Eveline Cruickshanks and Linda Colley. Cruickshanks believes that after their proscription in 1714 the Tory party only survived because of its adherence to the Stuart cause.[62] Colley challenged this, pointing out that the Tories had other options open to them, and that there never was a time when the whole party consisted of Jacobites.[63] J.C.D. Clark takes a different view. He argues that Tory Jacobitism could be used when necessary as a political lever. Its strength lay in its ideological principles on the significance of kingship, order and religion.[64]

Looking at the Whig and Tory manifestos from the distance of the 21st century, it becomes obvious that there was little difference between them. Both wanted to protect property, the established church and to maintain law and order. Whether they would have gone about this in radically different ways we do not know, because after 1714 the Tories were always in opposition. But like the Whigs the Tories were a product of their age, and would have had no compunction about putting more capital crimes on the statute book to protect property, or bolstering the Church of England by proscriptive measures against non-conformists.

The Tory party were, on the whole, the country party; elected in the shires and the pocket boroughs. In the 1715 election they fared badly, and the flight of two of their leaders Bolingbroke and Ormonde into the bosom of the Pretender did not improve their image, or help to unite the party. Although there were a substantial number of Jacobite Tories, there were also a number of Hanoverian Tories, as well as others caught in the middle. This was a nightmare for party managers trying to organise a viable opposition in the House of Commons. The situation was not helped by the Jacobite Tories receiving advice from the court in exile on how they should vote. It could be argued that rather than sustaining the Tory party, the Jacobite Tories helped to keep it in opposition, and involved the party in internecine struggles. However, the party did not entirely crumble away; it survived its years in opposition, and emerged back into office with the Broadbottom administration, which was an excellent example of pragmatic politics.

Did Jacobite Tories espouse the cause because they had a burning desire to see the Stuarts restored, or because they saw this as the only way in which they would be restored to power? In other words, was self-interest the motivating force of Tory Jacobites? Finally we must ask whether Sir John Hynde Cotton's Jacobitism was all bluster? He came from a background that made him a natural conservative, from an old Royalist family pre-eminent in local society. In 1714 he lost a considerable increment to his annual income, and this may have pushed him into the cause. What is not clear is how he would have coped with a Catholic monarch. He was a staunch upholder of the Protestant church, and it appears that what he and his fellow Tories really wanted on the death of Queen Anne was a Protestant successor who did not come from abroad. In May 1748 he wrote:

> *Sir*
>
> *A company of old Fellows of us were lately lamenting the Duke of Gloucester, Queen Ann's(sic) son and our mournful remembrance was a discourse on the Debts and misfortune which have been bought on this nation by a succession of Foreigners. Had Marcellus lived the Evils of a reign of Tiberius would never had happened and had the Duke of Gloucester succeeded to his Mother, and been blessed with English progeny, we should not have lamented the Partial attachment of a Prince to his foreign dominions.*[65]

Sir John probably expressed the wishes of many Jacobite Tories struggling to make themselves heard in a Whig world.

Notes

1 H. Fielding, *The History of Tom Jones*, London: Penguin, 1994, 272.

2 Fielding, 284.

3 *The Jacobite Journal*, Saturday 20 August 1748, 374.

4 J. Beckett, *The Aristocracy of England, 1600–1914*, Oxford: Blackwell, 1998, 96–7.

5 P. Laslett, *The World We Have Lost*, London: Methuen & Co, 1979, 35–8.

6 P.C. Yorke, *The Life and Correspondence of Philip Yorke, Earl of Hardwicke*, Cambridge: CUP, 1913, 327–8.

7 E. Walsh and A. Forster, 'The Recusancy of the Brandlings', *Recusant History*, Vol. X, 1969–70, 35–64.

8 R. Meredith, 'The Eyres of Hassop', *Recusant History*, Vol. IX, 1967–68, 5–52.

9 P. Roebuck, 'The Constables of Everingham Estate Correspondence, 1726–43' *Yorkshire Archaeological Society Transactions*, 1974, Vol. CXXXVI, 2–8.

10 CRO 588/F43 *Gens Cottoniana*, A collection of the very antient Family of Cotton of Landwade and Madingley in the County of Cambridge. Collected by W. Coles.

11 *Gens*, 129.

12 *Gens*, 130–31.

13 CRO 588/E13.

14 CRO 588/A6.

15 CRO/T330.

16 Copy of contract between Sir John Hynde Cotton IV and Lancelot 'Capability' Brown at Madingley Hall.

17 CRO 588/A6.

18 CRO 588/A53–6.

19 CRO 588/A53–6.

20 W. Shaw ed., *Calendar of Treasury Books. Jan–July 1714*, London: HMSO, Vol. XXVIII Pt. II, 1969, 136.

21 CRO 588/T360.

22 R. Sedgwick ed., *The History of Parliament – The House of Commons 1715–1754*, London: HMSO, 1970, 584.

23 Sedgwick, 584.

24 C.H. Cooper, *Annals of Cambridge*, Cambridge: Metcalfe & Palmer, 1852, Vol. IV, 1852, 126–7.

25 CRO 588/F40.

26 L. Colley, 'The Loyal Brotherhood and the Cocoa Tree: the London organisation of the Tory party 1727–1760', *The Historical Journal*, 20, 1977, 77–95.

27 Sedgwick, 517.

28 CRO 588/E13.

29 W. Cobbett, *Parliamentary History 2 Geo I 1716*, London: 1815, 374, 588, 626.

30 Sedgwick, 584.

31 E. Cruickshanks, *Political Untouchables*, London: Duckworth, 1979, 36–40.

32 Sedgwick, 584.

33 CRO 588/Z210 a–f.

34 Cruickshanks, 57–8.

35 CRO 588F/6–8.

36 CRO 588/O7.

37 CRO 588/O7.

38 Cruickshanks, 72.

39 CRO 588/O7.

40 Cruickshanks, 77.

41 CRO 588/A26; CRO 588/A55.

42 CRO 588/A26.

43 L. Eardley-Simpson, *Derby and the 45*, London: Philip Allan, 1933, 59.

44 A. Archer Houblon, *The Houblon Family*, London: Archibald Constable & Co. Ltd, 1907, 55; Cruickshanks, 91.

45 Cruickshanks, 94. No obvious reference is given for this information.

46 Cruickshanks, 96.

47 F. Fitzroy Bell ed., *Memorials of John Murray of Broughton*, Edinburgh: Scottish Universities Press, 1898, 49.

48 Murray 55, 381.

49 Murray, 451, 456, 465, 470.

50 P.C. Yorke ed., *The Life and Correspondence of Philip Yorke, Earl of Hardwicke*, Cambridge: CUP, 1913, 582–4.

51 Cruickshanks, 104.

52 J. Carswell ed., *The Political Journal of George Bubb Dodington*, Oxford: Clarendon Press, 1965, 107.

53 *Gens*, 61–2.

54 Sedgwick, 585.

55 CRO 588/A61.

56 CRO 588/O15.

57 Sedgwick, 421.

58 Sedgwick, 420–21.

59 CRO 588/O15.

60 CRO 588/O15. '

61 CRO 588/O15.

62 Cruickshanks, 6.

63 L. Colley, *In Defiance of Oligarchy*, Cambridge: CUP, 1982 see especially chapter 2.

64 J.C.D. Clark, *English Society, 1688–1832*, Cambridge: CUP, 2002, 141–61.

65 CRO 588/C17.

CHAPTER 10

1745

The 1745 rebellion is one of the best-known and most romantic episodes in the history of Britain. It was the last desperate throw of the House of Stuart to regain the throne, and it was led by the handsome and charismatic Prince Charles, whose exploits quickly passed into legend. It has produced a vast number of historical novels, films and plays, and speculations about 'what if' Prince Charles had advanced from Derby. Tory/Stuart historians see his scratch army of Highlanders as a disciplined and efficient force, while the government forces were ill fed, badly disciplined and barely trained. Whereas the Highlanders advanced with enthusiasm, the local militia fled before them like cowards. The rebel commanders were masters of strategy, the government commanders ineffective, wandering about and offering no resistance to the rebels. The rebels were volunteers, full of ideological zeal, the government army were professionals fighting for money, with no idealistic aim.[1] Notwithstanding the plaudits, the rebellion failed. It failed partly because the English Jacobites stayed resolutely at home, claiming that they were waiting for a French invasion that never came, and partly because it was too late. As far as England was concerned dynastic wars interfered with the process of modernisation, industrialisation and the accumulation of capital. The rebels came out of the mists into a modern country, and disappeared back into the past. The Stuarts' day was over.

1740–44

James III and his advisers thought that by 1740 the time was ripe for another attempt at the British crown. This shows how far out of touch they were with British politics and personalities. They took the denunciation of the Whig government and the Hanoverians for revolutionary zeal, rather than political discontent and the general dissatisfaction that attends any government that has been in power for a long time. Furthermore, they did not realise that the English Catholics and Jacobites were no longer synonymous. By the 1740s the English Catholics wanted religious toleration through constitutional means rather than the violent restoration of the Stuarts. The Scots, however, still smarted under the disarming of the clans following the 1715 rebellion, the continued military presence in the Highlands, and the Act of Union that took away their Parliament. But not all Scots laboured under these resentments. There were Scots who feared a Stuart restoration – the Presbyterians for example felt they would suffer should this happen – and there were those who had seized the Act of Union as an opportunity for trade and had grown rich, and there were city governments like Glasgow which strongly supported the Hanoverians.

Despite the nuances of the situation on the ground, Jacobite agents continued to send reports of discontent in Britain back to the court in exile, and convinced them that the time was good for an attempt to restore the Stuarts. Chief among these agents was Lord Sempill. Of Scots descent, he had been born and brought up in France, and had only a tenuous grasp of British politics and society.[2] Another agent was John Murray of Broughton; the younger son of a Peebleshire baronet, he had been educated at Leiden and from there went to Rome to offer his services to James III. He was sent to Scotland to organise an association of Jacobite leaders.[3]

Sempill was in Britain in 1738 on a mission to arrange concurrent risings in England and Scotland. He contacted key people whose names he had been given including Lord Barrymore, Sir Watkin Williams Wynn and Sir John Hynde Cotton. They told him that a rising would be impossible without a foreign invasion, otherwise they would be at the mercy of a professional army. They asked for a foreign army to land in the south as a rallying point for the English Jacobites, and they would then march on

London, declare themselves and seize all arms and ammunition in the city arsenals. Then and only then should the Scots rise.[4] This response should have warned the court in exile. It shows that the English Jacobites realised that a volunteer force would come off worse against a professional army, and that the English Jacobites could not raise a large feudal army to fight the government forces in the same way that the Highland clans could. A few tenants and servants would be the sum total of their resources. They also asked Sempill to get Colonel Cecil, a Jacobite agent in London, removed. Sir John Hynde Cotton claimed that Cecil was not only a traitor but a fool while Murray of Broughton, who disliked Cecil, found him resentful and discontented, but worse still, old and forgetful.[5]

Cardinal Fleury, the French foreign minister, wanted exact information about how many Jacobite supporters there were in England, and there the plan hung fire until Fleury died in January 1743. Sempill hoped the new administration would be more favourable to a Stuart restoration, and returned to France to solicit French help once again. The French remained sceptical about the commitment of the English Jacobites, and sent over a French agent, James Butler, ostensibly to buy horses for the French king, but in reality to ascertain the strength of English support for the Jacobite cause. Butler, an Irishman, claimed to have been feted by the English Jacobites, entertained by 200 members of the Corporation of London, and Jacobite gentlemen, including Members of Parliament. In September 1743 Butler attended Lichfield Races, a traditional Jacobite meeting place, where he discussed invasion plans. He was to take back to France with him what he claimed was a comprehensive list of English Jacobites, divided into counties, and including London aldermen.[6]

The numbers on this list heartened the Jacobites and removed some of the French qualms, but others still had doubts about the strength of support. Lord Traquair remarked that Sir John Hynde Cotton was 'shy at first', and that the Scots thought the English 'would do nothing, but make a noise and complain of their oppression.'[7] Balhady and Murray of Broughton also travelled to England in 1743, and Balhady compiled his own list, which he claimed was 'an exact list of all the gentlemen of the city who were the King's friends'. Murray was scornful of the list, claiming that anyone who had any inkling about English politics could have compiled the list. Whilst in England they met up with Lord Traquair and leading Jacobites. They found Sir Watkin Williams Wynn especially enthusiastic, 'ready to embrace the cause at every opportunity'. They claimed he promised £10,000 to the funds.[8]

Do these lists reveal a true account of the state of English Jacobite support? Butler's 'comprehensive list' shows some research, as it reveals the annual income of each so-called supporter. Those he named included the Dukes of Beaufort, Bedford, Norfolk, Rutland and Somerset. In 1745 Bedford was to raise his own regiment to fight the rebels, and Norfolk pointedly attended the Hanoverian court. None of the others turned out to support Prince Charles. Cruickshanks points out the majority on the list were Tory peers or MPs, Whigs opposed to the government and Roman Catholics, who might reasonably have been expected to support the Stuarts. The list is meant to imply a general indication of intent and not actual pledges of support.[9] There is no mention in the lists of any popular support.

Another Jacobite agent in England was the Duke of Perth, who was stationed in York. On 11 March 1743 Murray wrote to James III that the Duke of Perth had assured him that the mayor and aldermen of York had freely opened their minds to him on a Stuart restoration, and wished to convey their loyalty to the cause. If they heard of James approaching they guaranteed to raise 10,000 men to support him.[10]

Support seemed assured, but one cannot get away from the suspicion that the agents were telling the French what they wanted to hear in order to stimulate action. The French themselves wanted to provoke the Hanoverian government as they were about to engage in war with Britain. The English Jacobites asked for 10,000 men and arms for 10,000 more who would be led by half-pay officers in the British army, (although of course once Britain and France were at war they would be on full-pay again, and no longer available to the Jacobites). They asked that the French be led by Prince Maurice of Saxony, a Protestant, and that the landing be at Maldon. When the invasion started the Earl Marischal would raise the Scots so that there would be invasion on two fronts. At the same time the tin-miners of Cornwall would rise, and Sir Henry Slingsby would start a rising in Yorkshire.[11]

A regency council was formed to govern the country until James arrived. At this point no involvement of Prince Charles was envisaged. The council would consist of the Duke of Bedford, the Earl of Westmorland, Lord Barrymore, Lord Cobham, Sir Robert Abdy, Sir John Hynde

Cotton and Sir Watkin Williams Wynn. James added Lord Chesterfield, Sir John St John Aubyn, Sir Henry Slingsby and the Lord Mayor of London, although eventually only the first six names were to form a putative council. Cruickshanks claims that correspondence between the council and the continent was made possible with the connivance of the post-master general John Le Febvre, a closet Jacobite.[12] It was more likely that Le Febvre, who had helped to uncover the Atterbury plot, was a double agent.

The regency council drew up a declaration to be distributed when the invasion started. It pointed out that the country was groaning under harsh taxes, its treasure decimated by the demands of the state of Hanover, and its public offices filled with foreigners. Foreign wars had led to the decay of manufacture and trade. The Stuarts, they promised, would issue a general pardon to all who had opposed them in the past, they would support the Church of England, allow free parliaments, disperse the standing army and make peace with France. The result would be a resumption of prosperity for all. Exhortations were made to show the people the depth of their misery under tyrants, 'which like oxen, yoked to the plough, they seem to labour under'. They were called to assert their liberties like 'free born Englishmen'.[13]

The French started to amass their troops near the channel ports in November 1743, but things were going too fast for the English Jacobites. Sir John Hynde Cotton asked the French to put back the timing of the invasion until after the parliamentary debates on taking Hanoverian troops onto the British pay roll. He pointed out that if he and other Jacobite Tories absented themselves from this it would raise suspicions, and they would be arrested. He added that the debate would add to propaganda against the Hanoverians. He asked for the invasion to be put back to February 1744. Lord Barrymore argued against this as the weather would be worse then, and this might prevent some turning out, including 'fat Sir John'.[14]

The French were not amused at this delay. They were ready, and Prince Charles, who was now included in the plans, was on his way from Rome to France, travelling in secret, but tailed by government spies. A good opportunity would be lost. The French troops continued to gather at the channel ports, and the regency council suggested that they aim for Tilbury rather than Maldon, and promised to raise London once the invasion had started.

At what date the government discovered the plot is not clear. Colley claims that one of the regency council was feeding information to the Admiralty, but Cruickshanks suggests that this happened later.[15] The breakthrough for the government came when Jacobite spy number 101, Francois de Bussy, sold Jacobite secrets to the Duke of Newcastle for £2000. De Bussy named Beaufort, Barrymore, Sir Watkin Williams Wynne and Monsieur Cotton as the main instigators of the plot. The government announced their discovery of the invasion plot on 14 February and arrests followed, but not of those named by de Bussy. However, Colonel Cecil was arrested on 24 February and Barrymore was placed under house arrest. Philip Yorke reported that the others treated the accusations with ridicule.[16] Meanwhile a storm dispersed the French fleet and the invasion plan was over.

Balhady was back in England in the spring of 1744 to try to get support for another invasion plan. He report to Murray of Broughton that the original plan could be revived, but should be timed to coincide with George II's annual visit to Hanover. Murray responded that he thought any invasion should concentrate on Scotland.[17] He returned to Paris to try to persuade the French to help. In Paris he found Prince Charles ready for action, and lodged with a Scottish banker Aeneas MacDonald. Murray persuaded him that Scotland was his best option but the French, having been thwarted once, refused to help. Tired of inactivity and convinced that a successful attempt on his own part would enlist French support, Prince Charles decided to act on his own. He borrowed money from MacDonald, and evading the surveillance of the English agents moved to Nantes. On 5 July 1745 he set sail for Scotland.[18] The 1745 rebellion had started, and the English government and the English Jacobites were taken by surprise.

Prince Charles Edward's progress to England

The Prince sailed on board the *Dentelle*, escorted by a small French frigate, the *Elisabeth*. Tradition suggests he was accompanied by seven men. The Duke of Atholl, exiled since the 1715 rising, George Kelly, an Irish clergyman who had been involved in the Atterbury plot, Sir Thomas Sheridan, the Prince's governor and leading adviser, John Strickland, who came from a Westmorland family with land in Ireland, John

Sullivan, a French officer, Aeneas MacDonald the banker, and an Italian valet. Only Sullivan had any military experience.

West of the Lizard the little fleet was attacked by HMS *Lion*, a frigate exactly the same size as the *Elisabeth*. A six-hour exchange of fire followed in which both ships were badly damaged, and both had to return to port. The loss of the *Elisabeth* meant the loss of essential supplies and money, but notwithstanding that Prince Charles sailed on up the west coast of Britain.[19] He landed at Eriskay on 24 July 1745. Eriskay is isolated so he set sail again down the coast, landing at Glenfinnan, provocatively close to the government stronghold of Fort William. Here he raised the Royal Standard, signalling his intentions to George II and Britain.[20]

Johnstone and Blaikie claim that news of his landing did not reach Edinburgh until 8 August, and that it was several weeks before the news filtered through to London.[21] Panic followed because the English were unprepared for the invasion. However, this assumes that the government were not aware of the passengers being escorted by the *Elisabeth*, that the entire population of the Western Highlands were friendly towards the Jacobites, and that there were no patrols out from Fort William shadowing his movements. A proclamation issued on 1 August placing a price of £30,000 on Prince Charles's head shows that the government knew he had landed by that date.

Government troops were recalled from the continent, and the country placed on alert. As Parliament was in recess most of the leading English Jacobites were on their country estates at this time, but they quickly reconvened in London, and on 20 August the Earl Marischal sent a memorandum to the French Foreign Ministry naming the English leaders who had offered assistance to the Jacobites, providing this was backed by a French invasion. They asked for five cannons and four frigates of 34 guns and 10,000 men to be led by the Duke of Ormonde.[22] The French, now officially at war with Britain, saw an invasion as an excellent enterprise. They began to move troops from Flanders to the channel coast.

Meanwhile in Scotland, owing to the ineptitude of the government commander in Scotland, Sir John Cope, the Prince moved southwards unopposed, joined by clan chiefs and their clans as he went. He entered Edinburgh on 18 September, meeting no resistance, and took up residence in Holyrood House. There followed a stand-off between Prince Charles in the south of the city, and the government troops in the strongly defended castle which could easily bombard the town, and Sir John Cope and his troops approaching the city from the east.

On 21 September the Jacobite army surprised the government troops at dawn as they camped at Prestonpans 20 miles east of the city, and defeated them. When the news of this reached London there was panic. A run on the Bank of England nearly paralysed the country's economy, and more troops were recalled from the continent and sent north with Marshall Wade.

Pro-Jacobite historians suggest that combined with the panic, and a core of Jacobite sympathisers in the city of London, the capital could have easily fallen into the rebels' hands. This ignores the 160 carriages carrying merchants to pledge their loyalty to the king, and the loyal addresses sent in from cities and towns across the country, including Edinburgh, and the Jacobite stronghold of Oxford. The militia was raised on 13 September and on the 27th the Duke of Cumberland was recalled from the continent and given high command of the government forces. Papists were disarmed, and suspicious Irish watched or arrested.[23]

In York where there had been an influx of refugees following the Battle of Prestonpans, Archbishop Herring, a staunch Whig and Hanoverian supporter, denounced the rebellion and helped to raise a volunteer regiment which became known as the Royal Regiment of Hunters.[24] The Duke of Perth had promised that York was a Jacobite centre and would rise to greet the invasion. This was clearly wishful thinking. Loyal regiments were raised in Liverpool and other towns, and everywhere town defences were strengthened. This was not a country that was going to welcome the Jacobites with open arms, and although it has been suggested that religion no longer played a part in the dynastic struggle, there is evidence that the non-conformists viewed the resumption of a Catholic monarchy with dread.[25]

After the victory at Prestonpans, Prince Charles returned to Holyrood where he was to remain for six weeks. This may have been to allow the French time to complete their invasion plans and to give time for more Highlanders to join the army. But the delay exhausted his financial resources, and a body of bored Highlanders encamped in Edinburgh and wanting action or permission to return home was becoming a problem. The clansmen's customary way of campaigning was a short sharp action and away home. They felt they had been from their homes too long.

Prince Charles also wanted more action. On 30 October he called a war council to decide on the next course of action. He declared his intention to march south. Lord George Murray and the clan chiefs thought this was too risky. Prince Charles argued that this would give chance for their friends in England to join them, but Murray said they had delayed too long in Edinburgh, they should have marched directly after Prestonpans. Their delay had given Cope time to regroup his troops, and for the English to muster.[26] This difference of opinion between Lord George and the Prince was a portent of things to come. Lord George was to argue with the Prince over every decision to be made, and usually Lord George had the backing of the clan chiefs who resented the Prince's reliance on Irish and French officers. However, this time they agreed to march south.

The next difference of opinion was on what route to take. The Prince wanted to take the east coast route and confront Marshall Wade at Newcastle. He argued that this would draw their supporters in north-east England to join them, whilst those in the north west could protect their flank. Lord George wanted to take the western route via Carlisle, which was not so well defended as Berwick, a route they would have to take before going on to Newcastle. He argued that if they took the western route they could keep Cumberland guessing as to where they were going, London or Wales, and they had many supporters who would join in Manchester. The clan chiefs who trusted Lord George's judgement over that of the Prince said they would only advance if they took the western route. Eventually it was agreed that the main army should take the western route, but a diversionary column would set out on the eastern route, but turn west to join the rest.[27]

The rebels left Edinburgh on 1 November, the Dukes of Atholl and Perth going west via Peebles and Moffat, and the Prince and Lord George going east via Kelso and Jedburgh.[28] McLynn believes that the decision to invade England was taken in the belief that there was a large body of support there,[29] but no contact had been made with the English Jacobites and they had made no effort to contact the rebels. Although the Prince assured his generals he had pledges of support, this was a falsehood. The English Jacobites had no intention of declaring for him until they were assured of certain success through a French invasion. Even then their support was doubtful. Sir John Hynde Cotton and Sir Watkin Williams Wynn were elderly men, and by all accounts unfit for active service.

Others who had been named as supporters such as the Duke of Bedford had already declared for Hanover, and the Duke of Beaufort would do nothing to endanger his estates.[30] The only possible active support were the Lancastrians who had been out in 1715, and might rise again. The rebels must make for Lancashire.

Into England – Carlisle to Manchester

The government expected the Jacobites to make for Carlisle and the north west. Carlisle was told to strengthen its defences, and the county militia was called out. The city had sent a loyal address, and the government was reasonably confident it would not be taken by the rebels.[31] Prince Charles crossed the Esk into England on 8 November, the advance guard was at Carlisle by the 9th and the rest of the army arrived on the 10th. They found the gates closed against them. Like Edinburgh, Carlisle had a military citadel, the castle, within the city. From there operations were directed by Colonel Duval. His main problem was to fire on the rebel army without hitting the town. He assumed that Marshal Wade was on his way from Newcastle to give help, and that he would only need to withstand a siege for a few days. Prince Charles sent a message to the mayor that if he surrendered there would be no bloodshed, but if he did not and the town was taken it would be sacked. The mayor did not reply, and the Jacobites started to dig siege trenches around the town, while the Prince and his party retired to Brampton to spend the night. The Jacobites also expected Wade to attack from Newcastle, but there was extremely bad weather on the east side of the Pennines and Wade got no further than Hexham. When the Jacobites realised this they redoubled their efforts to take the town. One account suggests that they created a human shield of women and children to stop the garrison firing on them, and force the mayor to open the city gates.[32] Prince Charles remained at Brampton, sending part of his army out to take all the horses and carts they could find and destroy all crops they could not carry,[33] a scorched earth policy hardly likely to win support from the local populace.

Where was the local support for the Jacobites? Troops were not flocking to the standard, and in fact no English Jacobite had appeared to join them since they crossed the border. The Prince decided to mobilise

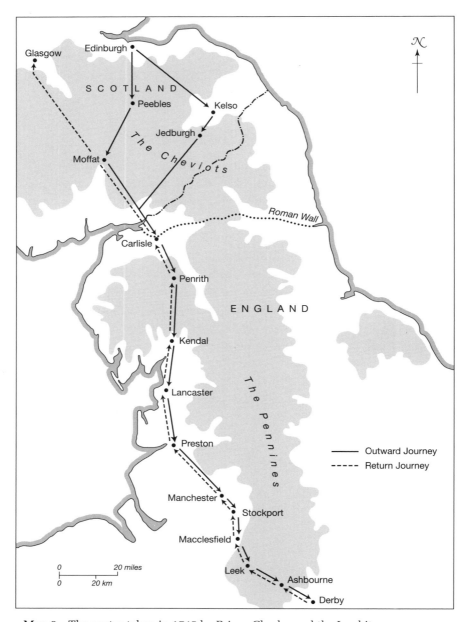

Map 3   The routes taken in 1745 by Prince Charles and the Jacobites

the English Jacobites through Lord Barrymore. He wrote a note to him, pointing out that they had come this far without opposition, and after taking Carlisle they would be on their way to London and victory. The note was given to Peter Pattison, a grocer from Cockermouth, who may have been a Jacobite supporter, but was more likely an innocent bystander. He took the letter to Barrymore's Cheshire residence and gave it to Barrymore's eldest son, Lord Buttevant. Buttevant was no supporter of the Jacobites, and he handed it over to the government.[34] Thus the only attempt made to contact the leaders of the English Jacobites failed.

The absence of any local support raised the question as to whether it would be better to withdraw back to Scotland. The bad weather had crossed the Pennines and the men were cold and tired; morale was low. Morale was low inside the city as well. The men of the Cumberland and Westmorland militia refused to fight, and the garrison in the castle citadel consisted of 80 elderly and invalided men. On 15 November the mayor rode to Brampton to offer to surrender, and to pay £2000 to prevent the town from being sacked.[35]

The militia are often derided as cowards who fled in the face of the enemy.[36] But these were amateur soldiers without training in arms, ploughboys and labourers who had to face armed clansmen used to bearing arms and settling feuds by blood. The militia were only obliged to serve for a month, and they wanted to get home, while the treatment they received in Carlisle did not encourage them to defend it. They were forced to pay for board and lodgings at the highest price for the worst possible accommodation.[37] They had some excuse for not engaging the Jacobites in battle. On 18 November the Prince made a triumphal entry into Carlisle, riding a white horse and accompanied by bagpipers. King James was proclaimed in the market, and the Jacobite leaders retired for a council of war. Once more retreat back to Scotland was mooted. Lord George Murray and the clan chiefs complained about the lack of English support, and the failure of the French to invade. The Prince told them he had assurances from the English Jacobites, and the French government. If they marched onto London they would see that support would come.[38] The Prince prevailed and the rebel army left Carlisle on 20 November. It numbered about 4–5000 at this time, plus women and other camp followers.[39]

The rebels reached Penrith by 21 November, and Kendal on the 23rd. They were now following the fatal route into Lancashire taken in 1715, and heading for Preston. But in Lancashire they hoped that the Catholic gentry and their tenants would flock to join them. They entered Lancaster on 25 November. James was proclaimed king, and in his name excise money was confiscated. There was no influx of English Catholics to join them. One Englishman who did join them was John Daniel, who met up with the Jacobites on the road between Garstang and Preston. His father had been out in 1715, so he came of an old Jacobite family. He was immediately given a commission by the Duke of Perth, and the task of drumming up recruits by dispersing the Prince's manifesto round the neighbourhood, which called on people to assert their liberties.[40] Few joined. His next task was to confiscate any arms found in the neighbourhood. By the time he caught up with the rest of the army at Preston he had acquired 39 recruits whom he presented to Perth. It appears that Perth had forgotten all about him, but offered him another commission and the command of his recruits.

The army left Preston on 28 November. Already it had come further than in 1715, but although the local communities turned out to watch it pass, none would join it, and the doors of those who had been out in 1715 remained resolutely closed. Lancashire had changed during the thirty years since 1715. It was in the early stages of industrialisation, and had concerns other than a dynastic war. A new order was emerging, based on trade and industry and a new capitalist leadership. The old recusant families had withdrawn to their estates, where they hoped to be allowed to worship in their chosen religion in peace. In the towns the non-conformists were gaining strength, and by 1745 the county was much more urbanised than it had been in 1715. It was on the brink of a new era. Liverpool had become a booming port, and was a staunchly Whig town. It raised a loyal regiment, the Liverpool Blues, but Manchester, home of non-jurors and Tories, was a more promising destination. This was the Jacobites' next goal.

In London the Jacobite MPs had been recalled to attend Parliament. The government suspected they were meeting in coffee houses to conspire, and kept a close eye on them.[41] The Prince's manifesto that had been secretly distributed was gathered up by government agents and burnt. Whig families began to leave the capital, and the roads became clogged with fugitives.[42] Sir Watkin Williams Wynn moved back to Wales, and rumours began to circulate that he was planning a rising there, which only needed a French invasion to be activated. Things seemed dire for the Hanoverians and the government.

The government commander-in-chief, the Duke of Cumberland, was at Lichfield where, contrary to accounts by some pro-Stuart historians, morale and confidence were high.[43] Colonel Joseph Yorke with Cumberland's army wrote to his brother Charles that it was impossible for the rebels to know anything of the strength drawn up at Lichfield, and that the men were in high spirits. He added perceptively that the rebels 'by advancing into the kingdom they have given their friends here an opportunity of showing themselves if they had the spirit for great enterprises. Their friends have failed them.'[44]

The position on 29 November when the Jacobites entered Manchester was that the main government force was spread out on a line south of the Trent. The eastern flank was covered by the Yorkshire volunteers, and the Liverpool Blues were breaking down the bridges across the Mersey, and the Derbyshire Blues led by the Duke of Devonshire were smashing up the road from Manchester to Buxton. Troops were arriving from the continent and the militia regiments from the south of England were gathering in London.

The English Jacobites were eagerly awaiting a French invasion, the Duke of Beaufort was on his estates on the Welsh marches, and Sir Watkin Williams Wynn was in North Wales. What both the Jacobites in the south and the government wanted to know was whether the Jacobites would proceed to London via the Derbyshire route, cross the Pennines and go down the Great North Road, or march into Wales to meet up with Wynn and Beaufort and approach London from the west, via Oxford, thought to be a fruitful Jacobite recruiting ground.

Both Cumberland and the Prince's generals were left guessing about his intentions. But in the meantime the Jacobites would enjoy some rest and relaxation in Manchester, which they considered to be a friendly town full of their supporters.

Manchester

There are a number of contemporary accounts of the Jacobites' stay in Manchester. These include the reminiscences of men accompanying the army such as John Daniel and the Chevalier de Johnstone, and citizens caught up in events like Elizabeth Byrom, or the unlucky constable of the town, Thomas Walley. Elizabeth Byrom's account is biased toward the Jacobites and especially the Prince, whom she saw as a romantic figure. Elizabeth Byrom was the daughter of John Byrom, who is alleged to have been a Jacobite. However, his long and detailed diary gives little hint of this, and we know he taught his version of shorthand to the Duke of Cumberland. A poet, mason and caballist, it has been suggested by Joyce Hancox that Byrom had an 'affair' with Caroline of Anspach, the wife of Frederick, Prince of Wales, and that she was a secret Jacobite.[45] Byrom's main connection with the Jacobites came through his friendship with Thomas Deacon, a non-juror, whose three sons were to enlist with the Jacobite army. Walley wrote his version in case he was ever called to account for his actions at the time.

The interpretation of events in Manchester suggests that the town was solidly behind the Jacobites. In fact the Whig families had left, taking their possessions with them. James Clegg, a non-conformist minister, noted that fugitives were arriving at Chapel-en-le-Frith from Manchester on 25 November, and as the rebels grew nearer some fugitives fled across the Pennines to Sheffield. By 27 November Chapel and the surrounding villages were full of refugees.[46]

All contemporary accounts agree on the peculiar nature of the Jacobite entry into Manchester. Elizabeth Byrom (alias Beppy) wrote that on 28 November 'about three o'clock came into town two men in Highland dress, and a woman behind one of them with a drum on her knee'.[47] The Chevalier de Johnstone's account provides more details on this extraordinary advance party: 'One of the Highlanders was a Sergeant Dickson, a young Scotsman as brave and intrepid as a lion. He asked permission to set out for Manchester a day ahead of the army to start recruiting, and quitted Preston with a horse, Johnstone's drummer and his mistress to beat up for recruits.' Johnstone claimed that on entering Manchester the sergeant was surrounded by a tumultuous crowd who would only let him go on his way after he threatened to shoot them, and those inhabitants attached to the house of Stuart flew to his assistance, so that he was soon escorted by 5–600 men.[48]

This is not corroborated by Elizabeth Byrom, but she did note that the sergeant continued to beat up for recruits, offering 5 guineas in advance, and 1s a day. She listed those who joined: Mr J. Bradshaw a barber, 'Tom

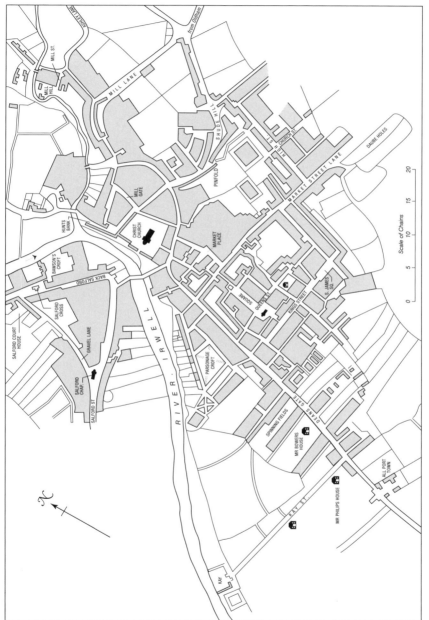

Map 4 Manchester and Salford in the 18th century

Syddall whose father had been executed in 1715, Tom Deacon, George Fletcher a linen draper, and Tom Chaddock the son of a chandler, and several others have enlisted, above eighty men by eight o'clock, when my papa came home to tell us that there was a party of horse come in, he took care of me to the cross, where I saw them all. . . . They are my Lord Pitsligo's Horse.'[49]

Meanwhile the hard-pressed constables were being given instructions on what should be prepared for the Prince's arrival. The church bells were to be rung, and the bellman was to go round the town telling people to illuminate their houses. Although Elizabeth Byrom reported that the Jacobites were extremely civil to the townsfolk, the constables were threatened and abused by them, and given the unenviable task of finding billets for 10,000 men and confiscating 180 carriage horses.[50] The justices who should have stood between them and the rebels had fled.

The Prince entered Manchester at 3 o'clock in the afternoon of Friday 29 November. Elizabeth Byrom went to the Cross to see him come in and described him as attired in a plaid and wearing the garter sash, and a Scotch bonnet with a white rose in it. He went directly to lodgings in Market Street. Later Elizabeth heard King James proclaimed and the Prince's manifesto read out.[51] What she was not aware of was what had gone on behind the scenes. The constables had been ordered to read the proclamation but this was an act of treason, which they wanted to avoid, and they did everything they could to impede it. Constable Foden said he could not read the proclamation because his spectacles were at home. Thomas Walley claimed it would be impossible for him to read it as he had a speech impediment. Eventually, in near-farcical conditions, the Jacobites read out each sentence to Foden and he had to repeat it to the crowd.[52]

Recruitment to what was to become the Manchester Regiment continued. Much to John Daniel's pique David Morgan, a barrister from Monmouth, was given the task of inspecting new recruits, including those Daniel had brought in from Preston. Daniel described Morgan as aged about 51, mean looking and bad tempered.[53] As well as being a barrister Morgan was also a poet. He was the author of a 630-line satirical poem *The Country Bard and the Modern Courtier*, dedicated to the 'Prince of Wales'. A preface by Sir Watkin Williams Wynn left no doubt as to which Prince of Wales this referred to.

Daniel not only objected to Morgan taking over the recruiting proced-
ure, but also to the colonel appointed to lead the Manchester Regiment,
Colonel Francis Townley, who came from the Lancastrian recusant
family who owned Townley Hall. Townley had served in France with
the Duke of Berwick, but had returned to Britain to live in Wales. In
1744 a French commission had been sent to him, which in theory if
captured by the government troops made him a prisoner of war rather
than a traitor. Importantly, he was one of the few Jacobite officers
with military experience.[54] Daniel claimed that the Manchester men persuaded the Prince to stay in the town for an extra day, promising that
more recruits would join. In fact there were more pressing matters that
had to be addressed before they could move on. The Liverpool Blues had
destroyed the bridges across the Mersey, and these had to be restored.
The hapless constables were sent to find timber and workmen, and scouts
were sent out to see if the river could be forded at any point, and to ascertain the position of the government troops.[55]

Elizabeth Byrom was besotted with the Prince and all things Scottish. On 29 November she stayed up until one in the morning making
St Andrew's crosses for the following day. The next morning a Highland
officer took her and her aunt to see the Prince. They observed him come
out of his lodgings and mount his horse; 'a noble sight it is, would not
have missed it for a great deal of money . . . he was received with much
joy and shouting . . . '. The officer took Elizabeth and her aunt to see the
artillery, and then to view the Prince at supper. They were taken into a
room where the officers were dining:

> they were all exceedingly civil and almost made us fuddled with
> drinking the Prince's health for we had no dinner, we sat there until
> Mr Secretary Murray came to let us know the Prince was at leisure and
> had done supper, so we were all introduced and had the honour to kiss
> his hand; my papa was fetched prisoner to do the same, as was Dr Deacon,
> then we went out and drank his health again in the other room.[56]

Elizabeth reveals that John Byrom was more circumspect than his daughter, and had to at least put on a show of resistance before acknowledging
the Prince.

The Prince's generals were in conference. They asked if David Morgan
could reach Manchester from Wales, where was Sir Watkin Williams

Wynn and his promised host? They pointed out that apart from the men in Manchester no other English Jacobites had joined them. Once more they advised retreat back to Scotland. The Prince assured them that if they proceeded into England, the English would join them, and reluctantly they agreed to advance. But which route should they take? The Duke of Cumberland would have liked to know this. There were several options open to them, they could go via Cheshire into North Wales, or they could cross the Pennines and take the north-eastern route, or make for Derby and the Swarkestone crossing of the Trent. And if they took the latter route would they go via Buxton or Leek? Up in Chapel-en-le-Frith James Clegg also wanted to know the route the rebels would take. He had sent his men to help the Duke of Devonshire break up the turnpike from Manchester to Buxton at Waley bridge, but he confided to his diary he did not think this would do any good, and it was bad for legitimate travellers.[57]

Although historians assume that the government did not know which route the rebels would take, Chancellor Hardwicke was sure they would make to Derby and then on to London. He had a route plan taken off a ship stranded at Montrose that indicated that route. Nevertheless, Hardwicke's son Joseph, with the government troops at Lichfield, thought the rebels would make for Wales because the government troops stood between them and London if they took the other route.[58] Other intelligence reports to the government suggested the route would be across the Pennines to Sheffield, and Marshall Wade was ordered to go to Halifax to cut off the Pennine passes.[59]

It has to be remembered that these events were taking place in late November and early December. Daylight hours were limited, and the weather was extremely cold, with heavy snowfall on the Pennines and hard frosts. The Pennine route would be difficult, but at that time of the year any route from Manchester to London would be difficult.

The Jacobites left Manchester on 1 December at six in the morning. Elizabeth Byrom got up to watch them go, and reported that a last desperate effort had been made to get recruits, and that the inhabitants of Manchester did not know which route they would take. But four men came in from Bagueley in Cheshire and said they had not seen them, so they knew they were not taking that route. At four o'clock the town was thrown into panic by rumour that government forces were on their way. This proved to be false.[60]

The last of the Jacobites had left Manchester by 10.30. The main army crossed the Mersey at Stockport, the artillery and baggage at Didsbury. They were reunited at Macclesfield.

Macclesfield to Derby

At Stockport the Prince had been greeted by 'loud huzzas and demonstrations of zeal for his success'.[61] But the citizens of Macclesfield showed little enthusiasm for him. There were no bonfires or cheering to greet him, only sullen and frightened faces in the crowd. No arrangements had been made for billeting the army and the result was chaos. Some of the English Jacobites who had joined at Manchester were beginning to have second thoughts, and one at least had to be bribed not to desert.[62]

While the quartermaster pillaged the town for food and fodder, the commanders held a council of war to decide where to go next. Should they go into Wales or proceed towards London and if the latter, which route? Derby was suggested again, as were Wolverhampton, Birmingham and Oxford where they knew there was support for them. But Cumberland's troops were guarding the Trent at Newcastle under Lyme, Stone, Stafford and Lichfield. The Derby route that was just to the west of Cumberland seemed the best option.

In order to give the infantry and baggage train more time to get on the road, Lord George Murray decided to make a feint westwards to draw off Cumberland. He took the cavalry to Congleton, a mere nine miles from Cumberland at Newcastle under Lyme. A troop of Murray's horse was sent within three miles of Cumberland, where they 'accidentally stumbled upon home of Mr Wear a government spy', whom they captured and sent back to Macclesfield.[63]

Lord George's ruse was a success. Government troops stationed at Congleton fled back to Newcastle under Lyme, and Cumberland began to reconnoitre for a suitable site for a battle that would stop the rebels reaching Wales and end the rebellion. With Cumberland occupied in the west it was safe for the rest of the Jacobites to proceed to Leek.

The road they were to travel was difficult and slow, and it was late afternoon before they reached Leek. So far their route had taken them close to a number of homes of potential supporters, the Leghs of Lyme Park, the Davenports at Gawsworth and the Leveson Gowers at Trentham

Hall. Not one of them joined the rebels. In Leek the reception was similar to that in Macclesfield. The population was resentful but not defiant.[64] Even more difficult was the moorland road from Leek to Ashbourne. This was unmetalled, but luckily a frost had made the surface hard. They reached Ashbourne at daybreak the next morning.

Now a small and rather isolated market town, in the 18th century Ashbourne was a key place in the communications network. It stood on the main coaching route between London and Manchester, and its strategic position had been recognised following the 1715 rising when a garrison was posted there. The difficulties this caused the local population are described earlier in this book. In 1716 Ashbourne and Squire Boothby were seen as potential Jacobite supporters and troublemakers. Now the town was violently anti-Jacobite, and trouble broke out between the citizens and the advanced guard. King James was proclaimed in the market place to a silent crowd.[65]

Derbyshire might well have been considered a county favourable to the Stuart cause, and one where gentry sympathisers were likely to join the cause, bringing their tenants with them. Notable among this potential support were the recusant family the Eyres of Hassop, whose tenants were almost all Catholic. In his unashamedly pro-Jacobite book *Derby and the Forty-Five*, L. Eardley-Simpson has an optimistic list of Tory gentry who supported the Jacobites. These included the Curzons of Kedleston Hall, the Harpers of Calke Abbey, and the Poles of Radbourne. Remarkably the list includes the Gells of Hopton, the descendants of the Parliamentarian general John Gell, and a family antipathetic towards the Stuarts. Eardley-Simpson takes his names from Butler's list for the French, and this shows how inaccurate it was. Furthermore the major landholder of the county, the Duke of Devonshire, was a Whig, a strong upholder of the government and organiser of the Derbyshire Blues. Thomas Carte thought that the town of Derby would support the Jacobites. But the corporation was dominated by Whigs, which Eardley-Simpson puts down to corruption and manipulation.[66]

There are two routes from Ashbourne to Derby. Eardley-Simpson thinks that the Jacobites took the northern route via Hulland and Hulland Ward, and past Kedleston Hall. He suggests that the Prince left the line of march to take 'luncheon' with the Pole family at Radbourne. The Poles were recusants, and before the old hall was pulled down in 1760 the panels of the room where the Prince allegedly dined were preserved. Eardley-Simpson describes Jacobite artefacts and portraits in Radbourne Hall, a bust of the Prince in the 1750 uniform of a dragoon, strategically placed beneath a bust of Britannia, and a portrait known as 'The Gentlemen in Red' was in fact the Prince. Eardley-Simpson was told by Colonel R.W. Chandos-Pole before he died in 1930, that the estates had been mortgaged to send funds to the Prince.[67]

There is no evidence for the Prince's diversion, although Eardley-Simpson speculates as to who might have been at the hypothetical lunch party and concludes that it would have been leading Derbyshire Tories, and the Vernons from Sudbury in Staffordshire. He explains their failure to join the rising as a 'wait and see' attitude.[68] These gentlemen were more likely to have been the parties of sightseers lined up along the hilltops to watch the army pass. They were mistaken for government troops and the Jacobite army was drawn up in battle position before they realised their mistake.[69]

On hearing of the rebels' approach to Derby, and knowing he could not defend the town, the Duke of Devonshire withdrew the Derbyshire Blues to Nottingham. Whig families fled in that direction too. The rebel quartermaster and his staff arrived in the town just before midday, and took possession of the George Inn in Irongate. Ironically the George Inn, as its name suggests, was the meeting place of the Whig loyal association. From here the quartermaster set about finding billets for 9000 men.

London and the south

News that the Jacobites had reached Derby sent London into panic. There was a run on the Bank of England, and it looked as if the country's economy would fail. The elite prepared to flee abroad, and troops were rushed north. Guards were placed at strategic points in the capital and Catholic homes were searched, but not it would seem the homes of known Jacobites such as Sir John Hynde Cotton. Irish emigrants were seen congregating in the East End, and there were some public disturbances that may have been pro-Jacobite, but may have been against high taxes. Many of those arrested for rioting were Catholics, but few of them were convicted. The government played up the Catholic dimension, reminding the capital of the horrors of Mary Tudor's reign and the Spanish Inquisition.[70] On the whole the capital remained loyal but frightened.

The leading Jacobites, Lord Barrymore and Sir John Hynde Cotton, were in London at this time. They sent a message by Dr Barry to France requesting troops be sent to invade England, but when asked for assurances that they would join the invasion they refused to commit themselves. Sir John offered to resign his position of Treasurer of the Chamber, and suggested that when he did that this would be a signal to the French that all was ready.[71] The French had good reason to be sceptical about this as it was Sir John who had ruined the last invasion plan, but as they were at war with England, an invasion was sound strategy. They agreed to mount an invasion, but changed the prospective landing place from Maldon to the Kent coast, without telling Sir John and his colleagues.[72]

Prince Charles's brother Henry, Duke of York, was made nominal commander of the invasion force, and he wrote to Sir Watkin Williams Wynn suggesting that it would be useful if the English Jacobites could capture a seaport in readiness for the French. The invasion was to start on 14 December.[73] Renewed panic hit London when it became known that a large embarkation force was gathered at Dunkirk. Beacons were set up and all British navy ships and friendly privateers were put to sea.[74]

With the government in the south expecting an invasion, the population terrified and London in panic, the Jacobites were in a strong field position, especially as a party of Highlanders took Swarkestone Bridge and Causeway. This was an essential crossing point over the River Trent and its flood plain. It had been identified as one of the country's key strategic points by the Earl of Shrewsbury in 1540. He estimated he would need at least 10,000 men to hold it.[75] It was the gateway to the south and London, and it was in Jacobite hands.

Derby

John Daniel described Derby in 1745 as a 'large and handsome town'.[76] By 1745 it had a thriving silk industry and market. The Jacobites hoped for support in the town, but Daniel described the town as being 'terrified'.[77]

There are several descriptions of the main Jacobite army entering Derby, including those in the local newspaper the *Derby Mercury*, the Jacobites themselves and a government spy Eliezer Birch who left an account of his adventures in Derby in December 1745. He rode into the town just in front of the rebel army in order to send details of what was happening to Nottingham. In order to estimate the number of rebels he hit on the ingenious idea of taking a handful of peas, and put one in his pocket for every hundred men. He watched the army enter from a chamber overlooking the road from Ashbourne.[78] Bells were rung in the town and bonfires lit. The horse arrived at about 3 o'clock, followed by the main body six or eight abreast with about eight standards, most white flags with a red cross, accompanied by bagpipers.[79] These standards bearing the cross of St George rather than the Saltire of Scotland must have been made on the march, and were designed to attract English supporters. James was proclaimed in the market place before the Prince arrived on foot at dusk and went straight to lodgings in Exeter House on the bank of the Derwent.[80]

When he went to sleep that night he could be confident that his way was clear for the march to London. Taking Swarkestone Bridge had opened the route into Leicester, and he had got this far into England without opposition. Morale was high and the passwords for the night were 'James' and 'London'. Before going to bed the Prince discussed what he should wear for his triumphal entry into London.[81]

The next morning the Highlanders went shopping for shoes, and queued up to get their dirks sharpened. Some were accused of taking goods without payment, but on the whole they were good-natured. Some wrote letters home, letters that would get no further than the post office. Others collected excise money and forage. Unfortunately for him, Eliezer Birch was recognised and taken to Exeter House to be examined. Birch escaped by jumping from a window, and claims to have swum down the icy river Derwent to Alvaston, where naked and shivering he was given shelter.[82] More importantly another government agent, Dudley Bradstreet, was on his way from London. First he went to consult with Cumberland at Lichfield, and then made his way to Derby. What his precise instructions were is not known, but he went to Derby to pose as one of the missing English Jacobites.

The Prince and his generals attended a service in All Saints church. Following the service a council of war was held to decide what to do next. The Prince wanted to proceed to London; Lord George Murray argued against this on the grounds that there were four government armies in the field against them: Cumberland across the Trent, whom they might have to fight, and the force gathering in London which they might meet already having lost 1000–1500 men in battle. Wade was in their rear, and Devonshire and other loyal associations were massing to the east.

The Prince ignored Murray and began to discuss the order of the march, until Murray stopped him and pointed out that nothing was decided, and reiterated that they must withdraw to Scotland. Other generals agreed with Murray. The Prince tried to persuade them by emphasising the strategic advantage of holding Swarkestone Bridge, and showing them a letter from Scotland that intimated that Lord John Drummond had landed there with a small French force, proof positive of French support and an imminent French invasion.[83]

But there was a missing piece to the jigsaw. Where were the English Jacobites? So far only a few hundred men had joined, and there was no sign of the promised support of the Jacobite aristocrats and gentry. Lord Elcho expressed the sentiments of his colleagues that they would only advance if they had some evidence that the English Jacobites would join them. The Duke of Perth, who had spent much of the meeting with his head on the fireplace, now suggested a compromise. Why not make for Wales and meet up with Sir Watkin Williams Wynn and Welsh rein-forcements and approach London from the west?[84] With that the meeting broke up.

The Prince spent the afternoon trying to attract the Derbyshire gentry to his standard, so that he could show his war council concrete evidence of English support. He knew that sooner or later he would have to admit he had no promissory letters from the English Jacobites, or any evidence at all that they would support him. He rode from house to house, to Calke Abbey, Radbourne Hall and Foremark Hall. He was greeted politely, but no help was forthcoming.[85]

The Prince's absence gave Bradstreet the chance to start his propaganda. Gaining admittance to the Duke of Perth he told him that not only did Cumberland have 8000 men with him at Lichfield, but a further (fictitious) 9000 at Northampton. When he retold this story at the council meeting in the evening it stiffened Lord George Murray's resolve to return to Scotland. This and the failure of the Prince to produce any evidence of English support swung waverers over to his side, and the decision to retreat was taken.[86]

There has been much speculation about this seemingly foolish decision to retreat from Derby when the way to London was clear, Cumberland's army confused, and Wade miles away in the rear and making slow progress. Surely they would have succeeded in getting to London, and the Prince would have been welcomed; the Stuarts would have been restored. Even Smollet writing in the 18th century thought that the Prince might have 'made himself master of the metropolis, where he would have been certainly joined by a considerable number of his well-wishers.' Then he adds, 'But London was well defended and would not have fallen without resistance, and whilst fighting their way into London, Cumberland and Wade could come up in the rear.'[87] Besides the Jacobites at Derby had no way of knowing that Bradstreet's account of the troops at Northampton was a fabrication. Although, they had met with no opposition in England, they had not been welcomed in many of the towns they passed through, and people had not flocked to their standard. Taking the long view, which the Prince was probably incapable of doing but Lord George was, if they succeeded the Stuarts would be faced with a resentful population, and civil war would probably be inevitable. If they could hold on to Scotland they could revoke the Act of Union, separate the two kingdoms again, and reinstate a Stuart monarchy in Scotland. McLynn agrees that there were 'compelling' military reasons for withdrawal. He suggests that the Scots were not happy so far from their homeland, but Lord George Murray was defeatist with no imaginative flair. McLynn thinks that with support for the Jacobites in London and the West Country, and with the government troops in confusion, the Prince would surely have succeeded.[88]

At daybreak on Friday 6 December 1745 the Jacobites began to leave Derby, heading back the way they had come. The Prince left on horseback about 9 am and by 11 am the last Jacobite had left.[89] Derby had not welcomed the Jacobites but it had accepted them, giving them billets and food. Sightseers had come in from the country to see the Prince, and he had held a court in the Assembly Rooms. Here the press of people overturned and broke the royal standard, which John Daniel saw as an unfortunate omen.[90]

Only four men joined the army at Derby. Humphrey Cook a blacksmith, who was executed for his pains, Edward Hewitt a butcher, who fought at Culloden, was taken prisoner and executed, James Sparkes a framework knitter, who was taken prisoner at Carlisle, and Charles Webster, also taken prisoner but acquitted.

Eardley-Simpson claims that Richard Barry and Sir Watkin Williams Wynn arrived in Derby two days after the Prince had left. However, the letter that mentioned this was written two years after the event.[91] In any case they were too late; the Jacobite faces were set to the north.

The retreat

At first the Jacobite army was kept in ignorance of the retreat. One party of horse was sent across Swarkestone Bridge to shadow them on the south bank of the Trent, and the Highlanders were issued with powder and shot as if they were going into action. But at Ashbourne they realised they had been fooled and were 'extremely dejected'.[92] On the advance morale had been high, discipline good and the populace frightened. On the retreat morale plummeted, discipline broke down and the populace, reinforced by returned Whigs, was hostile.[93] McLynn claims that it was the Manchester Regiment that let the rest of the army down, stealing horses and ransacking Okeover Hall.[94] The Prince spent the night at Ashbourne Hall, the home of the much put-upon Boothby family. During the night many deserted, including David Morgan, and in Ashbourne the Highlanders shot dead two men.[95]

From Ashbourne they pressed on to Leek and Macclesfield, reaching there on 8 December. Up to then Cumberland had suspected they were making for Wales; when they turned north at Macclesfield he knew Scotland was their destination and he set out in pursuit.[96] John Daniel describes the bells ringing in towns to welcome the government army as soon as they had left it. He claims that accounts of them pillaging their way back to Scotland was Whig propaganda. But at Macclesfield the army helped themselves to what they needed, while the local population retaliated by cutting the throats of any sick or sleeping Jacobite they found. The militia, grown bolder now that the Jacobites were in retreat, began harassing them.[97] The hostility they received on the retreat must have reassured them that those who had argued for withdrawal because the local population would not support them were right, and had they stayed a civil war would have been the result.

In Manchester the mayor planned to give the Jacobites a different welcome to the one they had received a few days earlier. By order of the Mayor and justices, the bellman went round the town giving notice to all inhabitants to arm themselves with any weapons they could get, and stop up the ends of the town with barriers and trenches. Reinforcements were summoned from the countryside and they flooded into the town, so that a 'tumultuous mob' was raised, and the bellman had to ring to send them home again. The Jacobites arrived on Monday 9 December at about two in the afternoon. Mud and stones were thrown at them, and the Jacobites wheeled and threatened to fire on the crowd. The Prince enforced a curfew and forbad more than two persons to meet together.[98] This time there was no assembly or chance to meet the Prince, instead the Jacobites demanded the town raise £5000 as 'a fine for the insolence of the mob'. £5000 was a large sum for the town to find, but eventually it was scraped together, and on 10 December the Jacobites left Manchester. As they crossed Salford Bridge the last man in the column was shot by someone in the crowd. The army turned back and the onlookers fled in fear, but when five guineas' compensation was offered all was well. Two days later Elizabeth Byrom, who had idolised the Prince, was taken to see the Duke of Cumberland enter the town.[99]

Most of the English Jacobites with the army came from Manchester, so this was the last chance they had to say goodbye to their families, or to melt away into the back streets. In the south of England the Jacobites were in a quandary. Once they heard about the retreat from Derby they too wanted to melt into the background. But there were still rumours of a French invasion; should this happen they might be expected to join an invading army of a foreign force at war with their country. If the Prince was no longer coming to London this could mean the French would take control and Britain become a French dominion. Their qualms increased when rumours reached London on 14 December that the French had actually landed, and Cumberland was recalled from his pursuit of the Jacobites in the north to take command. Of course the rumours were incorrect; the French, hearing about the Prince's retreat, lost interest in the project.

Retracing their former footsteps the Jacobites passed through Wigan, Preston and Lancaster. They were received with hostility at all these towns, but at Kendal the reception was not only hostile but violent. The

Duke of Perth's advanced guard was greeted by a hale of stones, mud and manure, and attacked by men with clubs. Perth's men fired into the crowd and killed four bystanders. In order to prevent further bloodshed Perth then withdrew to Shap, and went back to Scotland leaving the main body of the army at Lancaster. When the main army arrived at Kendal discipline broke down, and houses were looted.[100] The citizens of Kendal retaliated by stealing as many Jacobite horses as they could, and setting them loose in the countryside.

The next stage for the main army was to reach Penrith over Shap Fell. Their passage was hampered by wind and rain that turned the roads into muddy rivers, and prevented the movement of the baggage wagons and artillery, forcing them to stay on Shap overnight. The rear guard had hardly begun to leave Shap the next morning, 18 December, when government troops appeared and shadowed them as they made for Penrith, eventually blocking their passage at Clifton. 'We heard at the same time a prodigious number of kettle drums', wrote the Chevalier Johnstone. At the foot of Thrimby Hill the Jacobites resolved to rush upon the enemy, 'sword in hand, and open a passage to our army at Penrith . . . We darted forward with great swiftness, running up the hill as fast as our legs would carry us'. Lord George Murray in the rear ordered the Highlanders to make a flanking movement: 'They ran so fast they quickly reached the top of the hill, and the government forces who numbered only 300 fled. One unfortunate trooper who had fallen from his horse was cut to pieces by the Highlanders'.[101] A little further on, when they halted to repair their equipment, a larger body of government troops appeared. Luckily the Jacobites were on a road with high thorn hedges on either side, so the government cavalry had difficulty in manoeuvring and were repelled by the Highlanders. But they returned to harry the Jacobites until they reached Clifton Hall, three miles from Penrith, and the Jacobites drew up in battle order, again protected by thorn hedges. The Highlanders cut through the hedges to get to the English: 'a necessary precaution as they wore no breeches only a petticoat to the knee'. Johnstone claimed on the approach of the Highlanders the government troops fled, Joseph Yorke with the government troops that it was the rebels who fled.[102]

The Jacobites continued to Carlisle where on their outward journey they had left a garrison. They decided that a Jacobite garrison should remain there to hinder Cumberland's pursuit. Those chosen to man the

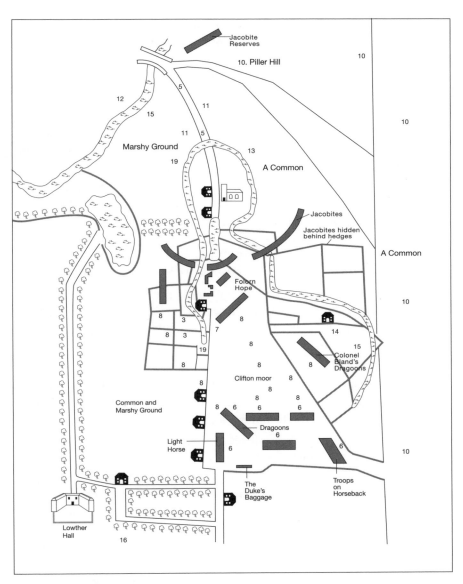

Map 5   Plan of the fight at Clifton

garrison were the Manchester Regiment and those too sick to march any further. Only a handful of English Jacobites accompanied the army back into Scotland.

Carlisle surrendered to Cumberland's troops on 30 December 1745. About 382 prisoners were taken. Most of them came from Lancashire (103), with a handful from Northumberland (4), Cumberland (3), Derbyshire (3), and one man each from Wales, Cheshire, Shropshire, Staffordshire and Nottinghamshire. Apart from Manchester, Wigan was well represented, and there was a strong urban bias amongst recruits, whereas in 1715 there had been a rural bias. Most of the Manchester Regiment's other ranks were connected with the cloth trade.[103] For them the rebellion was over with disastrous results.

The Jacobite invasion of England: conclusion

Whig historians tend to underplay the strength of the Jacobite threat in 1745, Tory historians to exaggerate it, and to over-estimate the strength of support in England for the Jacobites. Jeremy Black suggests that more English Jacobites joined the army than were ever counted, as many of them went home after Derby. He suggests that the militia's reluctance to confront the rebels was probably evidence of lack of enthusiasm for the Hanoverians and the Whig government, and the failure of the population of towns to rise against the Jacobites can be seen as tacit approval of their cause.[104]

But we must remember the social background to the 1745 rebellion. England's citizens had no training in arms. They relied on a professional army, which they paid for out of their taxes, to protect them. When the Jacobites arrived they were confronted by people the English considered barbarians – a feudal army of clansmen, accustomed to settling disputes by blood. Furthermore, the citizens had wives and families to protect. They did this by accepting, rather than approving the Jacobites' presence.

The English gentry had no feudal tenantry to call out. For example, had Sir John Hynde Cotton risen, who could he have taken with him? A few servants, tenant farmers and labourers, who might well have refused to accompany him, and have denounced him to the nearest justice.

The country as a whole had had thirty years of stability under Walpole. Gentility, civility, conspicuous consumption and industrialisation were the order of the day. The Jacobites were a feudal army, out of time, invading a modern country. McLynn describes the Jacobite campaign in England as an outstanding military exploit. He thinks that if the Jacobites had continued south from Derby they would have been successful. He agrees with Cruickshanks that Lord George Murray by forcing the retreat threw away the chance of a Stuart restoration.[105] Strategically, however, Murray's estimation of the situation was correct, and his distrust of the English Jacobites was justified. When faced with the reality of joining an engagement in arms, they stayed at home. They might also have thought that there was no guarantee that the French would leave the restored Stuarts alone, or even have restored James at all. Britain and France were at war, and had the French invasion been successful, they could have kept Britain as a conquered territory, and not handed it over. Had the Jacobites succeeded undoubtedly the country would have been plunged into civil war, and its move towards industrialisation and social change delayed for decades.

The Stuarts and their feudal army were too late. They were an anachronism in a modern world. Dynastic wars in Britain were a thing of the past. They were defeated by modernity.

Notes

1 See for example, F. McLynn, *The Jacobite Army in England 1745*, Edinburgh: John Donald Publishers Ltd, 1983, p. 64.

2 W. Blaikie ed., *Origins of the '45*, Edinburgh: Scottish Academic Press, 1916, repr., 1975, xxviii.

3 R.F. Bell ed., *Memoirs of John Murray of Broughton, 1740–47*, Edinburgh: Scottish Historical Society, 1898, 1–4.

4 Blaikie, xxxii.

5 E. Cruickshanks, *Political Untouchables*, London: Duckworth, 1979, 39; Murray, 47–8.

6 See 'Butlers List of Lords and Gentleman' at the end of this book.

7 Cruickshanks, 42; Blaikie 23.

8 *Murray Memoirs*, 49.

9 Cruickshanks 45, 115.

10 Blaikie, 36.

11 Cruickshanks, 43–4.

12 Cruickshanks, 47.

13 Blaikie, 169.

14 Cruickshanks, 53, information based on Archives Etrangers, Ms 76, 219–20, 290, 369.

15 Cruickshanks, 54. Cruickshanks suggests that this co-operation was at a later date.

16 P.C. Yorke, *The Life and Correspondence of Philip Yorke, Earl of Hardwicke*, Cambridge: CUP, 1913, 328.

17 *Murray Memoirs*, 94.

18 C.S. Terry, *The Last Jacobite Rising, 1745*, London: David Nutt, 1900, 19.

19 Chevalier de Johnstone, *A Memoir of the Forty-Five*; first published London: 1746, new edition London: Folio Society, 1958, 23–8.

20 W.B. Blaikie ed. *Itinerary of Prince Charles*, Edinburgh: Scottish Academic Press, 1897, repr. 1975, 2.

21 Johnstone, 25; Blaikie, 2.

22 *Murray Memoirs*, 510–11.

23 *The Gentleman's Magazine*, 1745, 478–83.

24 C. Collyer, 'Yorkshire and the Forty-Five', *Yorkshire Archaeological Society Journal*, Vol. XXXVIII, 1955, 71–95.

25 F. McLynn, 'Issues and motives of the Jacobite Rising of 1745', *The Eighteenth Century*, 1982, Vol. 23, No. 2, 100–104; for non-conformist comments on the 1745 rising see for example, V. Doe ed., *The Diary of James Clegg of Chapel-en-le-Frith*, Derbyshire Record Society Series, III, 1979; or Dr Williams Library Mss 38.84.

26 *Murray Memoirs*, 231–3.

27 *Murray Memoirs*, 235–6; Johnstone, 47.

28 *Murray Memoirs*, 236–7.

29 McLynn, *Jacobite Army*, 14.

30 PRO SP Dom 78/83.

31 Blaikie, *Itinerary*, 8.

32 S. Towill, *Carlisle*, Chichester: Phillimore, 1991, 65.

33 McLynn, *Jacobite Army*, 38.

34 R.C. Jarvis, *Collected Papers on the Jacobite Risings*, Carlisle: Cumberland County Council, 1972, ii, 85–6.

35 Towill, 65.

36 For example Cruickshanks, 89.

37 Towill, 65.

38 *Murray Memoirs*, 243.

39 D. Beattie, *Prince Charles and the Borderland*, Carlisle: Charles Thomas & Son, 1928, 218; J.A. Wheatley, *Bonnie Prince Charlie in Cumberland*, Carlisle: Charles Thomas & Son, 1903, 35.

40 J. Daniel, *A True Account of Mr John Daniel's time with Prince Charles Edward in the Years 1745 and 1746*, in W. Blaikie ed., *Origins of the '45*, 169–70.

41 PRO SP Dom 75/25.

42 Cruickshanks, 91; Yorke, 469.

43 For example McLynn, *Jacobite Army*, 104.

44 Yorke, 469–70.

45 J. Hancox, *The Queen's Chameleon*, London: Jonathan Cape, 1994, 41–4.

46 *Clegg Diary*, 588.

47 R. Parkinson ed., *The Private Journal and Literary Remains of John Byrom*, Chetham Society Publication, Vol. II, ii, 1854 'Elizabeth's Journal', 389.

48 Johnstone, 55–6.

49 Parkinson, 'Elizabeth's Journal', 390.

50 J. Earwaker, 'Manchester and the Rebellion of '45', *Transactions of Lancashire & Cheshire Antiquarian Society*, Vol. VII, 1889, 152–3.

51 Parkinson, 'Elizabeth's Journal', 392–3.

52 Earwaker, 155.

53 Daniel, 172.

54 Daniel, 174.

55 Earwaker, 156.

56 Parkinson, 'Elizabeth's Journal', 393–4.

57 *Clegg Diary*, 558.

58 Yorke, 472–3.

59 McLynn, *Jacobite Army*, 107.

60 Parkinson, 'Elizabeth's Journal', 345–6.

61 *Murray Memoirs*, 247.

62 McLynn, *Jacobite Army*, 112.

63 *Murray Memoirs*, 247–8.

64 L. Eardley-Simpson, *Derby and the '45*, London: Philip Alan, 1933, 92;
W.S. Parker-Jones, 'The Forty-Five in Staffordshire', *North Staffs Field
Club Transactions*, Vol. LVIII, 1924, 90.

65 C.F. Broughton, *A History of Ashbourne*, Derby: 1839, 30–31.

66 Eardley-Simpson, 16–17.

67 Eardley-Simpson, 122–8.

68 Eardley-Simpson, 129.

69 Daniel, 175.

70 N. Rogers, ' Popular Disaffection in London during the Forty-Five',
The London Journal, 1, May 1975, 7–8.

71 Cruickshanks, 93–5. No direct reference is given for this information.

72 Cruickshanks, 96–7.

73 Cruickshanks, 98.

74 Yorke, 477.

75 E. Lord, *Derby Past*, Chichester: Phillimore, 1996, 42.

76 Daniel, 175.

77 Daniel, 175.

78 R.G. Potter, 'A government spy in Derbyshire during the "Forty-Five"',
Derbyshire Archaeological Journal, LXXXIX, 1969, 26.

79 *The Gentleman's Magazine*, 1745, 708; *The Scots Magazine*, 1745, 615.

80 Lord, 40.

81 Eardley-Simpson, 157.

82 Potter, 27, 30–31.

83 McLynn, *Jacobite Army*, 124–6.

84 McLynn, *Jacobite Army*, 126.

85 Eardley-Simpson, 191–2.

86 Lord George Murray's Journal, quoted in C.S. Terry, *The Rising of 1745*,
London: David Nutt, 1900, 96–7.

87 Terry, 97–8.

88 McLynn, *Jacobite Army*, 130–31.

89 Lord, 42.

90 Daniel, 178.

91 Eardley-Simpson, 214.

92 Maxwell of Kirkconnell, Narrative, in Terry, 98–9.

93 Daniel, 180; Parkinson, 'Elizabeth's Journal', 397.

94 McLynn, *Jacobite Army*, 140.

95 *The Derby Mercury*, 12 December 1745.

96 Yorke, 477.

97 Daniel, 179–80.

98 Parkinson, 'Elizabeth's Journal', 397–8.

99 Parkinson, 'Elizabeth's Journal', 398–401.

100 McLynn, *Jacobite Army*, 167, 172.

101 Johnstone, 67–8.

102 Johnstone, 66–70; Yorke, 484.

103 Yorke, 536; Earwaker, 154.

104 J. Black, 'The Forty-Five Re-examined', *Royal Stuart Papers* XXXIV, 1990, 3.

105 McLynn, *Jacobite Army*, 175; Cruickshanks, 100.

CHAPTER 11

· · · · · · · · · · · · · ·

Culloden and after

The handful of English Jacobites who remained with the army into Scotland set off in two columns. The Chevalier de Johnstone with the cavalry went to Dumfries where 'a town of fanatical Calvinists' had seized ammunition wagons on the way out. Now they were made to pay a punishing fine.[1] The other column made for Glasgow arriving there on 25 December 1745, where they learnt of the fall of Carlisle and that all the garrison were now Cumberland's prisoners. Johnstone speculated as to why they had been left behind in Carlisle when it was obvious that it would need 4000 men to defend the city against Cumberland.[2] The reason may have been to maintain a Stuart presence in England, and for this the garrison, mainly Englishmen, was sacrificed.

The Jacobite army left Glasgow on 2 January to lay siege to Stirling Castle, which was in the hands of government troops. They stayed at Stirling until General Hawley and government troops appeared in their rear. The bulk of the Jacobite army turned round and marched to face them at Falkirk on 27 January 1746. Both sides claimed victory for this engagement. Johnstone describes the ground strewn with bodies, over which he had to climb to find the government cannon.[3]

The government troops returned to Edinburgh. Johnstone thought they should have pursued them and retaken the city, but instead they returned to the siege of Stirling Castle. On 30 January 1746 the castle defenders disabled the Jacobites' gun battery, and on the same day they heard that the Duke of Cumberland had arrived in Scotland to take command. The Jacobites abandoned the siege and fled northwards, ending up four months later tired and hungry at Inverness.[4]

The Duke of Cumberland, who could strike fear into Jacobite hearts, was exactly the same age as Prince Charles. But he was an unprepossessing short, stout figure, lacking the personal charisma of the Prince. 'Butcher Cumberland' has come down in history as a cruel and unpleasant figure who mistreated his men and maintained discipline by cruelty.[5] He was, however, an able general, and events preceding Culloden show that he did care for the welfare of his troops. Whereas the Jacobites had taken to the mountains, and arrived at Inverness with no food and an empty military chest, Cumberland had allowed his army to rest and retrain. He had reformed the commissariat so that his men had billets and enough to eat, and he set out for the north by sea, so that the government army arrived fresh and rested.

The weather in the Highlands in March and April 1746 was appalling. Wind, snow, hail and ice hit the Jacobites. John Daniel, still with the army, described 'men covered with icicles. Snow up to their horses stomachs'. He had to revive his horse with a nip from his hip flask.[6] In April it turned wet. Culloden Moor, where the final drama was to be played, was waterlogged, making it difficult terrain for the Highlanders to charge across. On Monday 14 April the Prince was at Culloden House, and Cumberland was at Nairn. The Jacobite army was, by this time, desperately hungry and many of them had gone foraging in Inverness. Sergeants were sent to bring them back, as it had been decided to make a surprise night attack on Cumberland, in the hopes of repeating their success at Prestonpans. Lord George Murray opposed this because the men were exhausted.[7] The Prince insisted, and the army moved off at about eight in the evening. The exhausted men moved slowly, and in the dark the columns could not keep in touch. A halt was called, and it was decided that as they would not reach Cumberland's camp before dawn they would return to Culloden Moor. They returned there at daybreak. The men who were to fight the next day had had no rest the night before.

However, they had one advantage. They chose the battleground. Lord George Murray was convinced it was the wrong choice, and Murray and other observers make it clear that the ground and the battle formation were chosen by the Prince's orders and no one else.[8] The Prince's position and conduct during the battle have been a matter of some speculation. Was he in the thick of the fighting, or in the rear so that he was the first to leave when things went wrong? Battles are confused events. Noise and smoke obscure vision, and no one could be sure where anyone else was at any one time during the battle. It is probable that the Prince moved about the battlefield, and only left when he saw the position was hopeless.

Cumberland started the battle with an artillery barrage. He had a clear range of fire, and his artillery killed many Jacobites with every shot. The Jacobite artillery could not respond. After about ten minutes of punishing fire Cumberland began a flanking movement, and changed the artillery to canister shot. Unable to restrain themselves any longer the Highlanders charged.[9]

This last charge of the Highlanders is the symbol of the triumph of modernity over feudalism, as the feudal foot soldiers of the clans charged the modern machinery of a professional army. At first, however, it looked as if the charge had been successful; one wing of the government army began to give way. But Cumberland had studied the way in which the Highlanders fought and had retrained the government troops to cope with this, making them thrust diagonally with their bayonets rather than straight so that neighbours protected each other from the Highlanders' claymores.[10]

The Jacobites outflanked, tired and dispirited, fell. The Prince left the field and the army began to flee. Many were cut down as they fled. Just as the conduct of the Prince is open to question so is that of Cumberland. Did he or did he not issue the famous 'no-quarter' to prisoners order? Eardley-Simpson, a professed Stuart sympathiser, says he did, and that Lord Hardwicke the Lord Chancellor had a copy of the document.[11] There is no trace of this in the Hardwicke papers, nor any trace of the order in Cumberland's papers. There was a copy in the possession of Lord John Drummond, but this appears to be a forgery. Johnstone wrote that Cumberland allowed the cavalry to pursue the defeated army, and that the road to Inverness was strewn with dead, and having allowed the wounded to lie on the field all night, Cumberland sent his men to despatch them the next morning.[12]

After Culloden

Whilst Prince Charles began his famous wandering in the Highlands and islands, John Daniel, who had taken part in the Highlanders' charge, fled into the mountains with Lord John Drummond. They met up with the Duke of Perth and Dr Cameron of Lochiel and the four men travelled together, with only a pound of black bread to sustain them as they made for the west coast. They reached the sea at Arisaig about 20 days after the battle; emaciated and covered with vermin, they hid among rocks waiting for transport. Two French ships were in the loch, belatedly delivering gold for the Prince. While this shipment was being unloaded, Daniel got into a fight with a Highlander who was stealing from it, and another Highlander accidentally blew up a barrel of gunpowder when he knocked his pipe out on it. After a brief engagement between the French ships and English vessels Daniel embarked on the *Bellona*, and despite thinking he would die of seasickness reached France safely.[13]

Johnstone set off down the north east coast in the hopes of finding a passage there. When this failed he continued south through St Andrews and to Edinburgh, where he was hidden for two months by Lady Jane Douglas. Then disguised as a pedlar he set out for London, passing through safe houses on his way to the capital. On his journey he encountered carts taking the wounded from Culloden south, and lines of marching prisoners, some of whom recognised him but did not report him. Once in London he was reunited with a sweetheart, and there he would have stayed, had it not been for the danger of discovery. Eventually, he left for Holland in the company of Lady Jane Douglas, and ended his days in Paris.[14] Daniel and Johnstone were lucky; the English prisoners taken at Carlisle or Culloden were to be made an example of for their countrymen.

Prisoners of the '45

When the 'forlorn hope' garrison at Carlisle surrendered, the officers on loan from the French army were treated as prisoners of war (A list of prisoners from the '45 appears at the back of this book.) The rest were treated as common criminals. The other ranks were sent to a number of different gaols in the north west including Whitehaven, Penrith, Appleby, York and Lancaster. Those at Whitehaven were placed in the House of Correction, where they slept on straw. Each block of 15 prisoners had the following weekly food allowance:

12 lb cheese to the value of 1s 8d
15 gills of ale to the value of 1s 3d
15 loaves at halfpenny each 7d halfpenny
18lb of beef   6s
To the gaoler preparing the meat and bread for breakfast 6d[15]

At Penrith the guards were allowed 21 and a half pounds of candles for the guardroom, and coal to heat it. The prisoners were allowed nothing.[16] Keeping the prisoners was expensive and the government wanted them despatched quickly. The other ranks were gathered up and returned to Carlisle. Of these 251 agreed to enter into a lottery, whereby they could draw tickets that excluded them from trial but gave them the choice of enlisting in the government army or being transported. Thereupon 134 elected to go for trial, of whom 49 were convicted and 33 hung, 19 at Carlisle, 7 at Brampton and 7 at Penrith.[17]

The officers were taken to London. They included Francis Townley and David Morgan, who had been taken in Staffordshire. Nine of them were convicted of treason and sentenced to death, being hung, drawn and quartered on Kennington Common. They were taken there from Newgate on three sledges. Faggots were placed near the gallows and set on fire. No clergy of any persuasion were present but Morgan read from the prayer book. When he had finished they were all hung together. Townley was taken down first. Observing he was still alive before the butchery started the executioner struck him hard on the breast and killed him. Dying with him were David Morgan, Thomas Deacon, the son of the Manchester non-juror, James Dawson, a Cambridge-educated gentleman, John Berwick, a Manchester linen draper, Thomas Chaddock and Thomas Syddall; also Andrew Blood from Yorkshire. Their bodies were taken to Southwark for burial, but Deacon's head was taken to Manchester to be set up. His brother James in Newgate was taken to see the execution.[18] James was transported and died shortly after reaching the West Indies. The third brother Robert died shortly after the surrender of Carlisle.

An English Jacobite who set out to join the rising but never got there was Charles Radcliffe, the Earl of Derwentwater's brother. He had escaped from Newgate in 1716, and had been living on the continent ever since. In 1745 he sailed for Scotland to join the rising with his son. The ship they were in was taken prisoner at Sheerness, and as a returned traitor Radcliffe was sent straight to the Tower of London. From there he followed his brother's footsteps to execution on Tower Hill.[19]

John Murray of Broughton, taken prisoner at Culloden, turned King's evidence in return for his freedom. During his examination at the trials of the Jacobite leaders in London he named the leading English Jacobites as the Duke of Beaufort, Lord Barrymore, Sir John Hynde Cotton and Sir Watkin Williams Wynn. No action was taken against them, but the London crowd attacked Beaufort's London house and broke all its windows.[20]

Although Cruickshanks suggests there was revulsion in London about the execution of the Jacobite officers at Kennington, and considerable sympathy remained in England for the Stuarts, some contemporary sources give a different impression. There was great relief on behalf of the non-conformist congregations, and general rejoicing in the country that it had been spared the return of a Catholic monarchy. Handel composed *Judas Maccabees* to celebrate Cumberland's victory, and in the provinces the local population began to try to get compensation for the horses, carts and forage taken from them by the Jacobite army and the government troops.[21]

In politics the split between Jacobite and non-Jacobite Tories deepened. Jacobite Tories took to wearing tartan waistcoats at all times. Cruickshanks thinks this was to signal their readiness to support another rising[22] but it may also have been as an irritant to annoy the Whigs and their fellow Tories.

In 1748 there was a pro-Jacobite riot in Oxford on the occasion of the younger son of James III's birthday, but the government took little notice of the continued Jacobite support in the university there until 1749. At the opening of the Radcliffe Camera Dr William King, a known Jacobite, made a speech on the theme of *Redeat* (let him or it return), which to those who could understand Latin and the implications of the term was an obvious call to Jacobite arms. The speech looked back to the golden days of Queen Anne, and was translated into English and circulated to the wider public. The crucial phrases read 'Return, with effect return! That the national good may reflourish, with him restored, peace confirmed . . .'. The government retaliated by removing the chancellor of the university Lord Arran, and replacing him with the Duke of Cumberland. King remained a Jacobite supporter until the accession of George III by which time he had lost faith in the cause.[23]

King's disillusionment may have been due to a meeting he had with the Prince when he made a clandestine visit to London in 1750. King met him in Lady Primrose's dressing room. King's assessment of him was that 'in polite company he would not pass for a genteel man. He hath a quick apprehension, and speaks French, Italian and English. The last with a little of a foreign accent. As to the rest little care seems to have been taken with his education . . . I was astonished to find him unacquainted with the history and constitution of England . . . I never heard him express any noble or benevolent sentiments or discover any sorrow or compassion for the misfortunes of so many worthy men who had suffered in his cause. But the most odious part of his character is his love of money.' It was during this visit that it is alleged that the Prince converted to Protestantism. However, King claimed that the Prince had no true religion and was Catholic with the Catholics, and Protestant with the Protestants.[24]

The Elibank plot and the decline of English Jacobitism

Following his well-known adventures in the Highlands Prince Charles returned to France, where he was an unwelcome guest. He had returned with his hopes of a restoration undiminished, and that the French would help him regain the throne for his father. One of the aims for his visit to London in 1750 was to solicit support, and he claimed to have the names of 50 English supporters. In 1751–52 a new plan emerged, this time with the help of Prussia, a long-time enemy of Hanover. In order to promote this plan the Prince travelled around Europe in disguise, creating great anxiety for the British government whose spies lost sight of his movements. However, one government agent known as 'Pickle' had infiltrated the Jacobite network, and was able to inform the government of what was happening, and in particular passed on information about the Elibank plot, which was named after its chief instigator Alexander Murray of Elibank. For its mode of operation it looked back to the early days of Stuart plotting, and took as its model the assassination plot. The conspirators were to rush St James's Palace, and kill or seize the king and the royal family. As Pickle was able to inform the government of all the conspirators' moves, it was easy for them to arrest them. Only Dr Archibald Cameron of Lochiel was executed, and no English Jacobites were implicated.[25]

By 1750 the English Jacobites were decidedly lukewarm towards the cause. The core of Tory Jacobite MPs were elderly or dead, and 1754 was the last general election at which the Jacobite Tories had any influence on the outcome.[26] Those who might have rioted in favour of the Jacobites had other concerns, such as the extension of the franchise through universal male suffrage, which was something the old regime of the Stuarts was never likely to grant.

The Jacobites failed to capitalise on the unrest surrounding the introduction of the 1753 Bill to Naturalise the Jews, or the American War of Independence. Bostonian royalists offered Prince Charles the crown of America if he would go there and lead them, and there is some suggestion that during one of the periods when British agents had lost sight of him, he was in America.

James III died in 1766, and Prince Charles was proclaimed king. European monarchs who once used the Stuart pretenders as pawns in their quarrels and wars did not recognise him, and he lived on as a discontented alcoholic, whose morals and treatment of his wife and mistresses disgusted those who once supported him. In the late 18th century the grandson of the Jacobite Sir John Hynde Cotton was on the Grand Tour; in Italy he was to see 'Charles III':

> We have had for this week past the Pretender with us, his constitution seems broke and they say his understanding is not much better than his constitution. He has four or five gentlemen that accompany him, that have as miserable a time as their Master. Who indeed is an object of pity. They say the Pope has withdrawn his protection and pension from him, and France and Spain have done the same, and that he only has what his brother the Cardinal gives him. I have not heard of his meeting any English, who are all particularly desired by Sir Horace Mann to avoid him.[27]

The Prince died in 1788, his brother Henry IX, a cardinal of the Roman Church, in 1807.

Conclusion

All attempts to restore the Stuarts to the British throne failed. Plots to assassinate William III were foiled by spies, double agents and treachery.

Risings were foiled because the strength of support for the Jacobite cause in England was over-estimated, and the depth of feeling against the restoration of a Catholic monarch under-estimated. A crowd might declare for King James as it ran through Oxford or Northampton, but when it came to taking up arms, that was a different matter. Crowds can be manipulated and bribed. Individuals must make a deliberate choice. The early Jacobite plotters such as Sir John Friend or Sir John Fenwick made this choice – Friend through pique at the loss of his office, Fenwick through principles. Viscount Bolingbroke and the Duke of Ormonde made their decisions to defect to the Jacobites through political reasons, the Earl of Derwentwater made his decision through ideals and a sense of duty to his cousin and his religion.

The later parliamentary Tory Jacobites made their decision through a lust for power, but acting out what they discussed when they toasted the 'King Over the Water' was beyond them. It was the failure of the English Jacobites to act in a coherent and committed fashion that prevented the return of the Stuarts and the triumph of Jacobitism.

Notes

1 Chevalier de Johnstone, *A Memoir of the Forty-Five*, London: Folio Society, 1958, 78.

2 Johnstone, 84.

3 Johnstone, 87–97.

4 Johnstone, 100–107.

5 See for example M. Pittock, *Jacobitism*, London: Macmillan, 1998, 108.

6 J. Daniel, 'A true account of Mr John Daniel's progress with Prince Charles Edward', in W. Blaikie ed., *Origins of the Forty-Five*, Edinburgh: Scottish Academic Press, 1916, repr. 1975, 203.

7 Lord George Murray's Journal, in C.S. Terry, *The Last Jacobite Rising 1745*, London: David Nutt, 1900, 140–41.

8 Lord George Murray, 144–5; John Cameron's Journal in Terry, 146–7; Johnstone, 126.

9 Pittock, 109.

10 Pittock, 110 says this was less successful than claimed.

11 L. Eardley-Simpson, *Derby and the '45*, London: Phillips, 1933, 286–7.

12 Johnstone, 129.

13 Daniel, 213–23.

14 Johnstone, 168–249.

15 R.C. Jarvis ed., *The Jacobite Risings of 1715 & 1745*, Cumberland County Council, Record Series 1, 1954, 343.

16 Jarvis, 351.

17 Jarvis, 351–2.

18 F. Douglas, *The History of the Rebellion in 1745 and 1746*, Aberdeen: 1755, 294–332.

19 Mrs Thomson, *Memoirs of the Jacobites*, London: Bentley, 1845, Vol. III, 480–509.

20 P.C. Yorke, *The Life and Correspondence of Philip Yorke, Earl of Hardwicke*, Cambridge: CUP, 1913, 582–4; E. Cruickshanks, *Political Untouchables*, London: Duckworth, 1979, 105.

21 Cruickshanks, 105–6; V. Doe ed., *The Diary of James Clegg of Chapel-en-le-Frith*, Derbyshire Record Society, Vol. II, 1979, 561; R.C. Jarvis ed., *The Jacobite Risings of 1715 and 1745*, Cumberland County Council Record Series 1, 1954, 275–91.

22 Cruickshanks, 106.

23 D. Money, *The English Horace*, Oxford: The British Academy, 1998, 207; *The Monthly Review*, Vol. II, 1 November 1749, 70.

24 W. King, *Political and Literary Anecdotes*, London: 2nd edn, 1819, 235–6.

25 For a full account of Pickle see A. Lang, *Pickle the Spy*, London: 1897.

26 D. Greenwood, *William King*, Oxford: Clarendon Press, 1969, 182.

27 CRO 588/C16.

CHAPTER 12

Studying the English Jacobites

Sources for the study of English Jacobites

The charismatic adventurer Prince Charles quickly passed into legend. Within a few months of Culloden memoirs and fictional accounts were in print, and since then a vast amount of paper has been devoted to his exploits and the '45 rebellion. The English Jacobites are more difficult to trace, but with persistence sources about them can be found and a narrative compiled.

The evidence can be divided into manuscripts, printed sources, pictorial representations and artefacts. It has to be emphasised, however, that the repositories where one would hope to find information about individuals are often bare of direct evidence, and indirect evidence has to be compiled about involvement with the Jacobite cause. This may be because it was destroyed when it looked as if John Murray of Broughton's evidence would condemn many English Jacobites, or it never existed in the first place. Information gathering and dissemination may have relied on word of mouth and have never been written down. In view of this and because the English Jacobites were operating in secrecy, the historian can be very grateful for the state intelligence gathering system and especially to Sir Robert Walpole's vigilance, which although there is a great deal of bias in this, does give a base to move from. The results of the state intelligence gathering can be found in the State Papers Domestic Series, National Archives class mark SP. These contain a wealth of different types of information about English Jacobites, including accounts of pro-Jacobite riots, confiscated seditious papers, poems and journals, lists of Jacobite prisoners and their petitions for mercy, letters from informers and confiscated coded letters.

Accounts of the estates of Jacobite prisoners found guilty of treason can be found in the records of the Forfeited Estates Commission, NA FEC 1 and 2, while the manuscript accounts of their trials are in NA KB. However, there are printed transcripts of these trials in T.B. Howell, *A Complete Collection of State Trials*, 1816. Less exalted prisoners were tried at the assizes. Accounts of their trials can be found in NA ASS1 41–47, and CHES 21 & 24, DURH 17 & 19, and Lancaster PL 25–28 for the Palatine counties.

There is a large amount of information about English Jacobites in the Royal Stuart Papers in the Royal Archives at Windsor Castle. The early papers have been calendered by the Historical Manuscripts Commission. Further information appears in the French Foreign Ministry archives in Paris. Much of this has been reproduced in publications about the Jacobites. There are papers pertaining to the Jacobites in the British Library, for example Stowe Mss 232 which is copies and abstracts from intercepted letters, Add. Mss 39923 and Add. Mss 22221, the Strafford papers, includes letters from Sir John Hynde Cotton. The Carte and Rawlinson collections at the Bodleian Library are an invaluable source for the student working on English Jacobites and the eighteenth century.

There is also a large number of contemporary printed sources by and about the Jacobites. Many of these are included in the bibliography, and an additional bibliography can be found in Terry's *The Rising of 1745*.[1] Printed material ranges from newspapers, journals, pamphlets and memoirs. Especially interesting for the historian working on the English Jacobites are the accounts of those who turned King's evidence in 1715 and 1745, but the historian using printed materials must be aware that much of this was produced for propaganda. Critical awareness is also necessary when using literary evidence such as poems, and pictorial representations. The latter may either idealise the subject or satirise it. The National Portrait Gallery, Scottish National Portrait Gallery, British Museum and Ashmolean Museum all have good collections portraying English Jacobite personnel and events. One of the best collections of

Jacobite art and artefacts is held by the Drambuie Company in Edinburgh, and the Scottish National Museum has a Jacobite room which includes Sir John Hynde Cotton's tartan suit. A complete gazetteer of genuine Jacobite glasses can be found in G. Seddon's *Jacobite Glasses*, details in the bibliography.

Manuscript material is also available in printed transcripts published by county record societies, for example the transcripts of the trials of the Lancashire plotters have been published by the Chetham Society, as has the Reverend Patten's memoirs of the 1715 rising. John Murray of Broughton's memoirs and evidence has been printed by the Scottish Historical Society, and other societies had produced printed versions of Jacobite evidence. This means that there is a large amount of material easily accessible for the historian to interpret.

Historians and the English Jacobites

'Within the past decade or so, Jacobitism has once more entered the mainstream of eighteenth-century political history. Traditionally the province of the antiquarian, or of the Scottish nationalist or sentimentalist, Jacobitism has become a source of scholarly reinterpretation; challenging a number of post-Namierite orthodoxies'.[2] As Rogers points out, nineteenth- and early twentieth-century authors were more interested in Prince Charles exploits, and in telling a story rather than interpreting the evidence. The Radcliffe brothers also had some attention in the nineteenth century, but the less charismatic figures of English Jacobitism drew little attention. It is only recently that historians such as Eveline Cruickshanks and Linda Colley have drawn attention to the political dimension of English Jacobitism and its importance to the Tory party's development. Similarly, it is only recently that local studies such as that by Rogers on Bristol and Norwich, Gooch on the north east, and McLynn on Newcastle and Nottingham, have started to reveal the extent of local enthusiasm for the cause.

History, however, is a matter of perception and interpretation of the sources. As Youngson points out in *The Prince and the Pretender*, 'All perception is selective. Our grasp of things always incomplete . . .'.[3] Perception and selection has led historians writing about the Jacobites to fall into a number of different camps. Daniel Szechi suggests that this has made Jacobitism into the 'bane of early eighteenth century British historical writing'. From this 'stems the near-mystical view of much of the Jacobite world view'.[4] In a later book Szechi calls the group of historians who have this mystical view of Jacobitism, 'the optimists'. Amongst their number he includes Sir Charles Petrie who wrote that 'Jacobitism was a genuine political movement with a mass following'. Szechi adds that Petrie's enthusiasm overcame his scholarship. Also among this group he places Frank McLynn and Eveline Cruickshanks, whose work on *The History of Parliament* revived an interest in the role of Jacobitism in 18th-century Tory politics.[5]

Cruickshanks' immensely scholarly work has recovered the role of English Jacobites from the mists of time, and her work in British and French archives has revealed their secret world. All historians working on Jacobitism owe a great debt to her pioneering scholarship. Although she promotes the Jacobites in a reasoned interpretation of the sources, other pro-Stuart historians have been less subtle. But it is useful to ask when they were writing, and why they might have espoused the Stuart cause. A good example of this is L.S. Eardley-Simpson's work on Derby in the '45. Eardley-Simpson admits he is pro-Jacobite, and his bile against the Hanoverians leaps off the page. The king is always referred to as the Elector of Hanover, showing that Eardley-Simpson did not recognise the legitimacy of the Hanoverians' claim to the throne. Many pro-Jacobite authors are Catholic, Eardley-Simpson was not, and was at pains to prove that no Catholic mass was held in All Saints, Derby during the Jacobite occupation of the town. He was writing in 1933 as Hitler came to power, and he had served in the First World War. The 'Huns', who by implication included the Hanoverians, were still his enemy.

Eardley-Simpson was a member of the Royal Stuart Society, one of whose aims was 'To teach the true history of our Stuart kings and those right principles of Monarchy, which they in their persons represented'.[6] In its early days the society had a strong Catholic bias, holding masses for the deceased princes of the House of Stuart on White Rose Day, 10 June 1954.[7] But as in the eighteenth century, not all Jacobites are Catholic, and the same is true of the society's membership, whilst the series of papers it publishes have added to the historical debates on Jacobitism.

Szechi suggests that the Whig/Protestant writers on Jacobitism are 'the pessimists', who see Jacobitism as being a 'self-delusory movement with little prospect of success'. Among their number he places Edward Gregg, who challenged the pro-Jacobite notion that Queen Anne favoured a Stuart accession; Bruce Lenman and Nicholas Rogers also belong to this group. Another group Szechi identifies are 'the rejectionists'. They are the pro-establishment Whig historians who take Fielding's Squire Western as symbolising the typical Jacobite Tory squire, 'a bigoted, ignorant, drunken philistine'. Among the rejectionists Szechi places the big names of 18th-century history: G.M. Trevelyan, who saw the Jacobites as being on the margin of 18th-century history, and Sir Lewis Namier who 'could find no evidence for any serious support for Jacobitism in England'.[8] It was partly to redress this school of history that the pro-Stuart optimists emerged.

The clash between these different schools of historians entered the late 20th century with a difference of opinion between Eveline Cruickshanks, David Cannadine and Linda Colley. Cruickshanks claimed that Cannadine was rewriting history for the sake of the welfare state and for the relevance of contemporary Britain. She wrote that Cannadine only wanted to look at success.[9] Cannadine was writing in the 1980s and success was the paradigm of that decade.

The debate between Cruickshanks and Colley hinged on the Tory party's commitment to Jacobitism. Cruickshanks' interpretation of sources led her to believe that the Tory Party only survived for the four decades when it was banned from office by clinging to the Stuarts. Colley pointed out that it had other options open to it, and there was never a Jacobite majority in the Tory party.[10] Colley saw the English Jacobites as wanting a bloodless coup to restore the Stuarts, expressing their allegiance in harmless ways such as drinking to the king over the water. 'This was scarcely a heroic brand of protest'.[11]

Paul Monod has added another dimension to the English Jacobites by placing them into their social and cultural context.[12] It is only when we do this that we can start to understand why the English Jacobites supported the restoration of the Stuarts, and why they failed to act when called upon. In order to understand this fully we need to set Jacobitism into the wider social and economic developments in England during the 18th century, and we can see that Jacobitism was becoming an anachronism. England was moving inexorably to industrialisation and modernisation. It was turning into a society in which 'new men', capitalists, industrialists and entrepreneurs were emerging at the head of urban society, and the old rural ties of obligation were disappearing. The old Jacobite society that 'revolved around kinship and social networks'[13] had disappeared in England, and although this survived in Scotland, industrialisation and land reclamation were to erode it there. The clash of the two cultures, the old absolute monarchy based on obligation and allegiance, and the new industrial society can be summed up by James Clegg's entry in his diary when the Jacobites left Manchester for the last time. 'Blessed be God the silk mill is safe'.[14]

The Jacobites and fiction

It did not take long after Culloden for Prince Charles to appear in a fictional guise as *Ascanius* about his exploits in the Highlands. This was the first of many fictional accounts of his wanderings, whose authors included Sir Walter Scott and Robert Louis Stevenson. Apart from a steady stream of novels on the Scottish Jacobites, there have also been a number on the English Jacobites, perhaps because their elusiveness in the sources allows full reign for the author's imagination. The 17th-century Jacobites appear in Mrs Henry Clark's *In Jacobite Days*, 1903, which described Devon just before William of Orange landed, and Dorothy Moore's *My Lady Bellamy*, 1909, a romance set in the days immediately following 1688. Some actual historical figures appear in this, including Sir George Barclay. The fictional Sir Gervaise Bellamy, a reckless Irishman, gets involved in a Jacobite plot and his wife has to obtain pardon for him. They reappear in *A Lady of Mettle*, 1910, when Sir Gervaise gets mixed up in the assassination plot. The assassination plot also appears in *For Liberty's Sake*, 1873, *A Woman Courier*, 1896, and *Shrewsbury*, 1898, and most notably in *The History of Henry Esmond*, 1852, by William Makepeace Thackeray.[15] The English involvement in the 1715 includes W. Harrison Ainsworth's *Preston Fight*, 1877, in which the Earl of Derwentwater is the central figure. He reappears with his brother Charles and Mad Jack Hall of Otterburn in *The Burning Cresset*, 1908. Other Northumbrian characters that appear in fiction include Tom Forster who is the central character in J. Grant's *Lucy Arden*, 1859. This book contains a complete narrative of the 1715 rising taken from Patten's account, and it makes Forster into a good-natured roué. Forster's sister

Dorothy appears in *Dorothy Forster*, 1884, which is a first-person narrative. Dorothy refuses Derwent-water's hand because of his religion. Another Romeo and Juliet twist comes in *Strained Allegiance*, 1905, in which a Whig loves a fair Jacobite maid. Robert Neill's *Black William* covers the period immediately before 1715. Using the device of an outsider from London, he introduces many of the figures involved in the 1715 including a non-juror parson, the Earl of Derwentwater and William Cotesworth, the government spy.[16]

The period between 1715–19 is covered by *For the White Rose*, 1907 and *Peckover Mill*, 1890 which involves Sussex smugglers in a Jacobite intrigue. Two interesting novels, one set in Lancashire, *The Two-Handled Sword*, and the other in Yorkshire, *The Morning of Today*, introduce us to a Wesleyan revival in juxtaposition with the Jacobites, a theme historians have not explored in detail. More recently Diana Norman in *Blood Royal* has woven a story of a scion of the Stuarts into a scenario that includes appearances of Sir Robert Walpole, highway robbery and the South Sea Bubble.[17]

The '45 rebellion has been a profitable pillaging ground for novelists, including a series of novels written for children such as *The Flight of Georgiana*, 1905, and *The Hearth of Hutton*, 1906. The popularity of the '45 in fiction can be judged by the fact that G. Norway's *The Jacobite Conspirator*, first published in 1895, was in its third edition by 1915. In this an Irish Jacobite is washed up on the shores of Lancashire. Taken in by a Jacobite family he and the son of the house join the '45 rising but, 'Disgusted with the rabble who clustered around the ill-fated Prince', he abandons the rebels at Derby and makes his way to Jamaica where he purchases a plantation.[18]

These are only a sample of the many novels written about the Jacobites, English and Scottish. Details of other novels can be found in Baker's *Guide to Historical Fiction*.[19] Most of the fictional portrayals of the English Jacobites are romances. Although historical personages appear in them, they are invariably the more charismatic figures such as the Earl of Derwentwater; less colourful characters such as Bishop Atterbury are usually absent. This and the concentration of popular history on Prince Charles has helped to give the Jacobite movement a spurious romanticism that it did not possess in reality.

Notes

1 C.S. Terry, *The Rising of 1745*, London: David Nutt, 1900.

2 N. Rogers, 'Popular Jacobitism in Provincial Contexts, Bristol and Norwich' in E. Cruickshanks and J. Black eds, *The Jacobite Challenge*, Edinburgh: John Donald Publishers Ltd, 1988, 123.

3 A. Youngson, *The Prince and the Pretender*, London: Croom Helm, 1985, 3.

4 D. Szechi, *Jacobitism and Tory Politics*, Edinburgh: John Donald Ltd, 1984, 5–6.

5 D. Szechi, *The Jacobites – Britain and Europe 1688–1788*, Manchester: MUP, 1994, 2–3.

6 *The Royalist*, Winter 1959–60, 2.

7 *The Royalist*, April 1954, 12.

8 Szechi, *The Jacobites*, 3–5.

9 E. Cruickshanks and J. Black eds, *The Jacobite Challenge*, 1–2, Edinburgh: John Donald Ltd, 1988.

10 E. Cruickshanks, *Political Untouchables*, London: Duckworth, 1979; L. Colley, *In Defiance of Oligarchy*, Cambridge: CUP, 1982, see especially chapter 2.

11 L. Colley, *Britons*, London: Vintage, 1996 edn, 79–81.

12 P. Monod, *Jacobitism and the English People 1688–1788*, Cambridge: CUP, 1989.

13 Szechi, *The Jacobites*, 24.

14 V. Doe ed., *The Diary of James Clegg, 1708–55*, Derbyshire Record Society, Vol. III, 1980, 559.

15 H. Clark, *In Jacobite Days*, London: 1903; D. Moore, *My Lady Bellamy*, London, 1909; D. Moore, *A Lady of Mettle*, London: Partridge, 1910; W.J. Yeoman, *A Woman Courier*, London: Chatto, 1896; J.B. Marsh, *For Liberty's Sake*, London: Strahan, 1873; S.J. Weyman, *Shrewsbury*, London: Smith, Elder, 1898; W.M. Thackeray, *The History of Henry Esmond*, London: 1852.

16 W. Harrison Ainsworth, *Preston Fight*, London: Routledge, 1877; H. Perse, *The Burning Cresset*, London: Constable, 1908; J. Grant, *Lucy Arden*, London: Routledge, 1859; W. Besant, *Dorothy Forster*, London: Chatto, 1884; R.H. Forster, *Strained Allegiance*, London: Longman, 1905; R. Neill, *Black William*, London: Arrow Books, 1973.

17 F. Badrick, *Peckover Mill*, London: Clutch, 1890; F. Ormerod, *The Two-Handled Sword*, London: Simpkin, 1909; F. Bone, *The Morning of Today*, London: Eaton, 1907; D. Norman, *Blood Royal*, London: Penguin, 1999.

18 S. Neilson, *The Flight of Georgiana*, London: Nash, 1905; W.J. Escott; *The Hearth of Hutton*, Edinburgh: Blackwood, 1906; G. Norway, *The Jacobite Conspirator*, London: Jarrold & Sons, 3rd edn, 1915, 332–3.

19 E.A. Baker, *Guide to Historical Fiction*, London: Routledge, 1914.

Glossary

Assizes The assizes took place in February, March, July and August. Pairs of peripatetic judges left London for the assize circuits to try serious crimes such as murder, rape, arson or burglary.

Attainder Extinction of civil rights when judgement given against someone accused of treason. It involved the forfeiture of property and the right to transmit a title by descent. It was confirmed by a Bill of Attainder, which was a Parliamentary Act.

Augustan 18th-century literary school that derived inspiration from the work of classical authors writing at the time of the Roman Emperor Augustus.

Broadbottom Administration 1744 coalition of anti-Walpole Whigs and Jacobite Tories.

Compounders Supporters of James II who wanted a Stuart restoration as an absolute monarchy.

Convocation An assembly of clergymen.

Darien Disaster This occurred when a Scottish colony was established in Spanish territory on the Panamanian isthmus in 1698. The British government gave an order to its Caribbean colonies not to give them any assistance, with the result that by 1700 most of the settlers were dead through disease or at the hands of the Spanish.

Dissenter/non-conformist Member of a Protestant religious group other than the Church of England, for example the Baptists or Congregationalists.

Entail A settlement made on an estate so that it passed only to specific heirs, usually the eldest son.

Glorious Revolution Arrival of William III in 1688 and the foundation of a constitutional monarchy.

Habeas Corpus The short title of a writ which could be raised to release or bail prisoners imprisoned but not brought to trial: Habeas Corpus Act 1679.

High church Branch of the Church of England that believed in the sacraments and rituals.

Hostmen Members of the Guild of Hostmen, an elite trading company in Newcastle upon Tyne, who regulated coal prices and production.

Impeachment A solemn accusation of a great public offence such as misappropriation of public funds or treason. The House of Commons had to agree that the offence had been committed, and as prosecutors support this in the House of Lords which tried the case.

Keel men Worked the coal boats on the Tyne.

Latitudinarist Church of England clergy who put no store on rituals and the liturgy.

Marriage settlement Deed made before marriage specifying the amount of dowry to be paid and when, the wife's pin money and widow's jointure and the portion of the estate that was to provide the income for these, the annual income of sons other than the heir, and marriage portions for the daughters of the marriage.

Messenger A crown officer who served arrest warrants.

Non-compounders Supporters of James II who wanted a conditional restoration.

Non-juror Cleric, Oxbridge fellow or holder of a public office who refused to take any oath of allegiance following the abdication of James II.

Recusant Roman Catholic.

Riot Act Passed in 1715, it stated that a gathering of 12 or more people comprised a riot. If the Riot Act was read to a gathering of people they had one hour to disperse or be summarily arrested and sentenced to death.

Settlement Deed settling a landed estate on trustees and making the owner and heirs life tenants, so avoiding death duties.

Staithes The coal wharves.

Strict settlement Deed by which land was settled limiting it to specific heirs, and preventing the sale of designated parts of it.

Tory Originally a term of abuse against Roman Catholics. Term first appeared in Ireland in the 1640s and came from the place-name Toraighe. It appeared in England in 1678 when it was used to describe supporters of the divine right of kings. Some but not all of the 18th-century Tory party believed in this. In the 18th century the Tory party was the country party representing the interests of the country squires and gentry.

Whig Came from Whiggance, a force of Scottish covenanting rebels in the 1640s, and was applied to those who defended parliamentary government. In the 18th century the Whig party was the court party.

Gazetteer

Ashbourne, Derbyshire SK 1846

The centre of the town, with the market place where the bonfires were lit in 1716 and King James III proclaimed in 1745, lies at the bottom of a steep hill which was once the main road from Manchester to London. Look for the coaching inns that represent Ashbourne's past. Infill of the market place has produced winding alleys going up the hill. The town boasts many fine 18th-century houses and a 16th-century grammar school, St Oswald's parish church contains the tombs of the Boothby family, including the touching monument to the infant Penelope Boothby who died in 1791.

Bamburgh, Northumberland NV 1834

Bamburgh Castle, which was owned by Thomas Forster, the rebel general in 1715, stands guard above the little town and the Northumbrian coast. Although in private hands, it is open to the public.

Carlisle, Cumbria NY 397563

The citadel with its castle is still clearly demarcated from the rest of the city. The walls were demolished in the 19th century, but the line of Lowther Street follows the line of the eastern wall. Carlisle Castle is managed by English Heritage and contains an exhibition of Jacobite material.

Clifton, Cumbria NY 530271

The fight at Clifton took place on common land; flat ground to the south of the village. There is a memorial to the Hanoverian troops killed in the engagement on Clifton Moor south of the settlement, and a commemorative stone to the Jacobites on Town End to the north of the village. Clifton is two and a half miles south of Penrith on the A6 and easily reached from the M6. Nearby Clifton Hall, a 15th century tower house, is managed by English Heritage and is open to the public.

Derby, Derbyshire SK 3536

Although no longer a market, the open space in front of the new assembly rooms marks where James III was proclaimed in 1745. The George Inn in Irongate still exists, and at the northern end of Irongate is All Saints church where the Jacobites heard divine service. Exeter House by the Derwent, where the Prince stayed, has gone but the city museum contains a Jacobite Room.

Derwentwater, Cumbria NY 2521

Part of Derwentwater where the original Radcliffe family held land on Lords Island, and the origin of their earldom is held by the National Trust. The nearest car park is at Keswick.

Dilston, Northumberland NY 9763

The ruin of the castle at Dilston known as Dilston Castle and incorporated into Dilston Hall when remodelled by the Earl of Derwentwater is all that remains of the Earl's hall. The chapel where he was buried stands close by, and Devils Water lies below the cliff. Permission should be sought before entering the grounds of Dilston Hall.

Holy Island, Northumberland NV 1242

This island off the Northumbrian coast, taken briefly by the Jacobites in 1715, can be reached by a causeway at low tide. The castle lies on its eastern tip, and Lindisfarne monastery in the west.

Ingatestone Hall, Essex TQ 6499

The hall is owned and lived in by Lord Petre, but is open to the public on Saturdays, Sundays and Bank Holidays 19 April–28 September, and in addition to this from 23 July to 5 September on Wednesdays, Thursdays and Fridays from 1–6 pm. It contains the Earl of Derwentwater's scaffold suit and other memorabilia about him and his family.

Lyme Park, Cheshire SK 122NX

Home of Sir Peter Legh where he was arrested in 1692 by the government messenger and John Lunt. Now cared for by the National Trust.

Madingley Hall, Cambridgeshire TL 3960

Home of Sir John Hynde Cotton, the hall is now owned by the University of Cambridge and houses the Institute of Continuing Education. The grounds can be visited on open days.

Preston, Lancashire SD 5429

The fight at Preston is overshadowed by the civil war Battle of Preston for which interpretative boards are provided in the town. However, using the 18th-century map it is possible to trace out the course of the 1715 battle as the lines of the streets in the town centre have not changed. The church defended by the Earl of Derwentwater and his brother is still there, and close to it is the White Bull Inn. The large open market place where the Jacobites surrendered still exists, and is flanked by the Harris Museum.

Romney Marsh, Kent and Sussex TR 0430

Well-drained marshland where sheep graze. From its isolated settlement close to rivers and marshes only flooded at high tide, Jacobites came and went secretly from the country.

Swarkestone Bridge and Causeway, Derbyshire SK 3628

A medieval bridge and causeway over the River Trent and its flood plain. In the 18th century this was one of the most important crossing points from north to south England. Held by the Jacobites in 1745.

Museums and galleries containing English Jacobite material

Border History Museum
British Museum
Carlisle Castle
Derby City Museum

Harris Museum, Preston
Ingatestone Hall, Essex
National Museum of Scotland (Sir John Hynde Cotton's suit)
National Portrait Gallery
Scottish National Portrait Gallery

Was my ancestor an English Jacobite?

This appendix contains the names of English Jacobites who do not appear elsewhere in the book.

Bedford, Hilkiah 1663–1724   Non-juroring bishop. Father a mathematical instrument maker in Smithfield. Educated Bradley School, Suffolk, St John's Cambridge, Fellow 1685, lost in 1689. Seized and fined 1000 marks and given three years' imprisonment for Jacobite allegiance.

Betts, John   Ensign Manchester Regiment, escaped 1746.

Brett, Thomas 1667–1743   County gentry from Wye, Kent. Educated Sandwich Grammar School and Queens' College, Cambridge, but removed by father because of extravagance. Re-entered at Corpus Christi in 1689. 1690 ordained and took the family living at Betteshanger. Refused to take the oath to George I, and was labelled a papist and Jacobite.

Bromfield, Mr/Dr   Pretended Quaker and agent provocateur in 1694. Involved with the Lancashire plotters, travelled between Ireland, Scotland and Northern England. Escaped capture and made commissioner of the Irish mint by James II. Captured 20 June 1695 on a French ship carrying letters from James (Luttrell, 487).

Caryll, Goodman   Actor, involved in the assassination plot.

Chivery, Reginald   Captain of James II's army. Ringleader in the Dog Tavern Jacobite riot of 1695 (Luttrell, 484–5).

Collier, Jeremy 1650–1726   Born Stow cum Quy, Cambridgeshire. Poor scholar at Caius College, 1685 Lecturer at Grays Inn. First to go into print against the 1689 revolution. 1692 imprisoned in Newgate for trying to contact a Jacobite on Romney Marsh. 1696 involved in the assassination plot and visited Sir William Parkin in prison.

Crossgrove, Henry   Printer of the *Norwich Gazette*, a pro-Jacobite newspaper. Son of a Jacobite Irishman from Stepney. 1715 accused of arming 80 men to attack the Whigs in Norwich and pull down dissenting meeting houses. 1716 house ransacked for treasonable papers and arms.

Culcheth, Mary   Daughter of Hugh Dicconson of Wrightlington, Lancashire, married Thomas Culcheth, a Catholic. 1689 involved in plots against William. Ordered five war saddles and hid her five brothers.

Dicconson, William   Brother of Mary Culcheth, tried in 1694 for treason. Lost his estates in 1707.

Dorrell, Captain   Hostler and brewer of Clare Market, London. Went to raise James III's standard at Oxford in 1715. Taken by General Poppau's Dragoons. Tried for treason 22 November 1715, hanged 30 November 1715 (*Ryder's Diary*, 141).

Fitzwilliam, John 1636–1699   Fellow of Magdalene College, Oxford, chaplain to the Earl of Southampton, tutor to Queen Anne. Witness for John Ashton.

Howell, Laurence   Parson and Jacobite. Attended John Hall and William Paul on the scaffold in 1716. Rumours that he wrote Paul's treasonable scaffold speech. Arrested and put into Newgate 1720.

Keyes, Thomas   Trumpeter, present at assassination plot conspirators' meetings and the Rainbow Coffee House. From Glatton, Huntingdonshire.

King, Edward   Reconnoitred for the ambush planned at Turnham Green by the assassination plotters.

Leslie, Charles 1650–1722   Irish with Scottish connections. Became a lawyer in the Temple with the Earl of Clarendon as his patron. Mediator between the non-jurors and James. 1711 visited St Germains and stayed in exile.

Maddock, Samuel   Ensign Manchester Regiment, apothecary, transported 1746.

Paul, William   Vicar of Orton-on-the-Hill, Leicestershire. Captured at Preston in 1715, freed but re-taken by Leicestershire JP and hanged.

Rookwood, Ambrose   Indicted, tried and executed for part in the assassination plot. From Stanningfield, Norfolk.

Scudamore, Richard   Captain in the Guards. Part of the assassination plot.

Sheppard, James   A coachmaker's apprentice who offered to go to Italy to talk to James III if expenses could be paid. Offered to assassinate George I. Told this to John Leake, a non-juror who told the government for £200. Sheppard arrested for treason and hanged.

Snatt, William 1645–1721   Son of Edward Snatt, master of the Free School, Southover, Sussex. Educated Magdalene College, Oxford. Rector of Denton, Sussex. Absolved Sir John Friend and Sir William Parkin on the scaffold in 1696. Arrested and put into Newgate.

Townley, Richard   Of Townley, Lancashire. Out in 1715. Took 60 men with him. Taken prisoner at Preston. Tried at the Marshalsea in May 1716. The judge summed up for conviction, but the jury acquitted him. Francis Townley, the commander of the Manchester Regiment in 1745, was his nephew.

Wagstaff, Thomas 1645–1712   Non-juroring bishop from old Warwickshire county family. Educated at Charterhouse and New Inn Hall, Oxford. Prebend of Lichfield, and held livings of St Margaret Poultry and St Gabriel, Fenchurch Street. Turned to medicine when ejected. Distributed Jacobite money to impoverished non-jurors.

English Jacobites at the court in exile, 1703–20

Baynes, John

Baynes, Richard, kitchen officer

Bede, William

Bedingfield, Michael, king's valet

Bigges, Alexander

Booth, Charles, groom of the bedchamber, m. Barbara Neill

Brown, Elizabeth

Buckenham, Robert, equerry of the chamber

Burch, Winifred

Byerley, Joseph, gentleman of Belgrave, Leicester

Conquest, Henry, paymaster for the household

Copley, John, gentleman usher, m. Henrietta Conquest d. of Henry

Corby, Henry, gentleman of the bedchamber

Crane, William

Dicconson, William

Eden, Richard

Golding, Anne

Leyburne, Charles

Parry, Henry, clerk of the kitchen

Sackville, Thomas

Stone, William, Lord Waldegrave's servant

Strickland, Robert

Symes, Anne

Whetenhall, Thomas

Wyndham, Charles

English Jacobites prisoners after 1715 rebellion

Anderton, William, in Fleet prison 1717

Arkwright, William, Preston, labourer

Begg, Miles, Preston, labourer

Blackburn, Richard, Lancashire, gentleman

Blackwood, James, Preston, gentleman

Blundell, James, Standish, wood turner

Bowyer, Thomas, Chester prison 1717

Burn, James, Fishwick, Lancashire, tailor

Butler, Richard, Myerscough, Lancashire, gentleman

Carus, Christopher, Halton, Lancashire, gentleman

Chorley, Charles, Chorley, Lancashire, Catholic, gentleman

Chorley, Richard, Chorley, Lancashire, Catholic, gentleman

Clark, Hugh, Chester prison 1717

Clavering, John, Northumberland, in Fleet prison 1717

Clulow, James, Chester prison 1717

Cottle, Thomas, Chester prison 1717

Cotton, John, in Fleet prison 1717

Cotton, Robert, in Fleet prison, 1717

Cowpe, Thomas Walton-le-Dale, yeoman

Cowper, Nicholas, Chester prison 1717

Dixon, David, Chester prison 1717

Finch, John, Walton-le-Dale, Lancashire, gentleman

Harrison, William, Burnley, labourer

Hodgson, George, Walton-le-Dale, labourer

Hutchinson, Robert, Chester prison 1717

Jackson, Thomas, Preston, butcher

Jarvis, William, in Fleet prison 1717

Kennard, George, Chester prison 1717

Lane, John, Chester prison 1717

Masterson, John, in Fleet prison 1717

Muncaster, Roger, Garstang, Lancashire, attorney

Ord, Richard, Chester prison 1717

Ord, William, in Fleet prison 1717

Parker, Joseph, Burnley, labourer

Patterson, James, in Fleet prison 1717

Patterson, John, in Fleet prison 1717

Potley, John, Chester prison 1717

Robinson, George, Chester prison 1717

Rowbotham, Henry, Preston, labourer

Rowbotham, John, Claughton, Lancashire, labourer

Sanderson, Alex, Preston, ship's carpenter

Sanderson, George, Chester prison 1717

Sanderson, Richard, Preston, ship's carpenter

Seager, Stephen, Burnley, labourer

Selby, William, Chester prison 1717

Shaw, John, Chester prison 1717

Shuttleworth, Richard, Preston, Catholic, gentleman

Siddall, Thomas, Manchester, blacksmith

Smith, David, Chester prison 1717

Smith, Thomas, Chester prison 1717

Stanley, James, Chester prison 1717

Sykes, Edward, Nether Wyersdale, labourer

Wadsworth, Joseph, gentleman

Walden, Lionel, in Fleet prison 1717

Walmsley, Henry, Preston, gentleman

Walmsley, Thomas, Billsborough, Lancashire, innkeeper

Withington, Richard, Ribbleton, labourer

English Jacobites died in prison after 1745 rebellion

Andrew, John, Lancashire

Bald, James, Wigan

Ball, Thomas, Lancashire

Bendleton, John

Bolton, Thomas, Warrington

Bouston, George

Brindle, Matthew, Lancashire

Chadley, Thomas, Preston

Grenshire, James, Lancashire

Henson, Thomas, Nottingham

Hervey, Thomas, Wigan

Hewit, Edward, Derby, butcher

Hodgson, John

Hunter, William, Newcastle

Lawson, Robert, Lancashire

Lea, Humphrey, Lancashire

Lowman, William, Lancashire

Magnald, John

Marnery, John

Mash, James, Lancashire

Mellin, James, Preston, weaver

Norris, Thomas, Lancashire

Parkinson, Henry, Lancashire

Poor, Thomas

Righley, Thomas, Lancashire

Spencer, William, Lancashire

Thompson, Thomas, Lancashire

Tiercon, Samuel, Chester

Walmsley, John, Lancashire

Wilcock, Edward, Lancashire

Williams, Owen, Wales

English Jacobites enlisted in army to gain pardons after the 1745 rebellion

Brown, Richard, Lancashire, carpenter

Chaddock, James, Wigan

Cook, William, Lancashire

Fulthorpe, Roger, Warrington, barber

Hargreaves, William, Lancashire

Hartley, George, Manchester

Hartley, John, Lancashire, carpenter

Keighley, Thomas

Lackey, William

Lee, Samuel, Lancashire, tailor

Saunderson, John, Lancashire, labourer

Tinsley, Robert, Wigan, weaver

Turner, Thomas, Bury, shoemaker

Turner, Thomas, Walcot, weaver

Walker, John, Lancashire, labourer

Waring, George, Lancashire, weaver

Waring, Matthew, Lancashire, weaver

English Jacobites escaped from prison after the 1745 rebellion

Betts, John, Ensign, Manchester Regiment

Farrier, William

Holker, John, Lieutenant, Manchester Regiment

Moss, William, Captain, Manchester Regiment

English Jacobites executed for part in 1745 rebellion

Townley, Francis, Colonel, Manchester Regiment

Beswick, John, Lieutenant, Manchester Regiment, linen-draper

Blood, Andrew, Captain, Manchester Regiment

Bradshaw, James, Captain, Manchester and Elcho's Regiments

Brady, Michael, Sergeant, Manchester Regiment

Chadwick, Thomas, Lieutenant, Manchester Regiment, tallow-chandler

Clavering, Edmund, Northumberland

Coppack, Rev. Thomas, chaplain, Manchester Regiment

Dawson, James, Captain, Manchester Regiment, student St John's Cambridge

Deacon, Thomas, Lieutenant, Manchester Regiment

Dellard, Michael, wool-comber

Dempsey, William, Sergeant, Manchester Regiment, joiner

Fletcher, George, Captain, Manchester Regiment, linen-draper

Holt, Valentine, Sergeant, Manchester Regiment, clothworker

Hunt, Philip, Sergeant, Manchester Regiment, Wigan, barber

Mathews, Barnabus

Morgan, David, Captain, Manchester Regiment, lawyer, Monmouth

Park, Thomas, Sergeant, Manchester Regiment, shoemaker

Roper, Edmund, weaver, Lancashire

Rowbotham, John, Sergeant, Manchester Regiment

Sydall, Thomas, Adjutant, Manchester Regiment, barber, Manchester

Taylor, Peter, joiner, Lancashire

English Jacobites transported for part in 1745 rebellion

Allan, John, Manchester Regiment

Barton, Lewis, Lancashire, Manchester Regiment

Bibby, Henry, weaver, Wigan, Manchester Regiment

Bold, Thomas, Wigan, Manchester Regiment

Brown, Francis, Lancashire, Manchester Regiment

Burn, John, Northumberland

Charnley, Thomas, weaver, Walton, Manchester Regiment

Cheisley, John, Manchester Regiment

Chesterfield, John

Cottam, John Clifton

Crosby, William, weaver, Whitchurch, Shropshire

Deacon, Charles, died on reaching the West Indies,
Manchester Regiment

Dickenson, William, weaver, Lancashire, Manchester Regiment

Furnivall, John, warehouseman, Manchester Regiment

Johnson, Hugh, weaver, Walton, Manchester Regiment

Leatherbarrow, Richard, Winwick, weaver

Livesay, John, cordwainer, Lancashire, Manchester Regiment

Maddock, Samuel, apothecary, Manchester Regiment

Mills, William, Lancashire, Manchester Regiment

Newton, John, weaver, Lancashire, Manchester Regiment

Ogden, Thomas, weaver, Manchester

Paterson, Robert, Lancashire

Paton, Archibald, joiner, Lancashire, Manchester Regiment

Proctor, Richard, Lancashire, Manchester Regiment

Sanderson, John, overseer, Northumberland

Shorrock, David, weaver, Lancashire, Manchester Regiment

Shorrock, James, tailor, Preston, Manchester Regiment

Singleton, Francis, weaver, Preston, Manchester Regiment

Tickhall, William, tailor, Lancashire, Manchester Regiment

Winstanley, William, weaver, Wigan, Manchester Regiment

Butler's List of Lords and Gentlemen in each county favourable to the Stuart cause, made in 1743

(* = known Jacobite)

Bedfordshire

This county is entirely devoted to the rightful king.
Duke of Bedford, Roger Burgoyne M.P., Butler Chernock M.P.,
John Chester M.P., Charles Leigh of Leighton Buzzard M.P.,
Samuel Ongley M.P.

Berkshire

Lord Abingdon, Lord Craven, Lord de Brook, Lord Stawell, Blagrave,
John M.P., Packer, Howard M.P., Powney, Penistone M.P., Strode,
William M.P.

Buckinghamshire

Duke of Bedford, Lord Bathurst, Lord Chesterfield, Lord Dormer, Lord
Masham, *Lord Orrery, Denton, George, M.P., Fleetwood, James M.P.,
Gore, Thomas M.P., Grenville, George, M.P., Grenville, Richard M.P.,
Marshall, Henry M.P., Selby, James of Whaddon Hall

Cambridgeshire

*Hynde Cotton, Sir John, Landwade and Madingley Hall, M.P.

Cheshire

This county will follow Lords Barrymore, Molyneux and Warrington.
*Lord Barrymore, *Lord Molyneux, Lord Warrington, Cholmondley,
Charles, M.P., Crewe, John M.P., Grosvenor, Sir Robert of Eaton Hall,
M.P., Warburton, Peter, of Arley Hall, M.P.

Cornwall

This county noted for the number of miners living there has always
been attached to its rightful king. The gentry are brave and very zealous.
Lords Arundel of Falmout, Trevice and Wardour, Carew, Sir William
M.P., Cook, George, M.P., Forster, Thomas M.P., Lyddell, Henry, M.P.,
Morris, Sir William, M.P. Nugent, Robert, M.P., Penton, Henry, M.P.,
*St. Aubyn, Sir John M.P., Trelawney, Charles

Cumberland

This is the poorest and most disloyal county in the whole of England;
the greater part of the land formerly belonged to the Crown; and since
the Revolution has been alienated to men who are afraid of losing it
through the restoration of their rightful king only Lord Hilton and
Haggerston, Sir Carneby can be relied on.

Derbyshire

Duke of Rutland, Haddon Hall, Curzon, Sir Nathaniel, has 10,000 miners
at his command. Stanhope, John M.P.

Devon

Duke of Bedford, Courtenay, Sir William M.P., Fortescue, William M.P.,
Lyttleton, George, M.P./Peer, Northcote, Sir Henry, M.P., Sydenham,
Humphrey, M.P.

Dorset

Lord Deerhurst, Brown, John M.P., Chaffin, George M.P., *Pitt, John M.P.
described by Horace Walpole as 'an active Jacobite', Pleydell, Edmund
M.P., Richards, George, M.P.

Durham

This small county has a large number of gentry generally well disposed.
Lord Falconberg, Bowes, George M.P., Tempest, John M.P.

Essex

Lord Suffolk,*Lord Petre,*Lord Waldegrave,*Abdy, Sir Robert M.P.,
Bramston, Thomas M.P., Grey, Charles, M.P., Saville, Samuel M.P.

Gloucestershire

*Duke of Beaufort, Lord Gainsborough, Chester, Thomas M.P., Bathurst,
Benjamin M.P., Berkeley, Norborne M.P., Gage, Viscount, Master,
Thomas M.P.

Herefordshire

*Duke of Beaufort, Lord Foley, Lord Oxford, Cornwall, Velters M.P.,
Foley, Thomas M.P., Harley, Robert M.P., Hopton, Thomas M.P.,
Windford, Thomas M.P.

Hertfordshire

This county is very rich and populous.
Duke of Bridgwater, Lord Exeter, Lord Stanhope, Gore, Charles M.P.,
Houblon, Jacob M.P., Stanley, Hans

Huntingdonshire

Lord Rockingham, Lord Sandwich, Fellows, Coulson M.P., Mitchell,
William M.P.

Kent

One of richest and most populous.
Lord Aylesford, Lord Teynsham, Lord Thanet, Lord Westmoreland,
Dashwood, Sir Francis M.P., Dering Sir Edward Pluckley, M.P.,
Twisden, Sir Roger M.P., Watson, Thomas M.P.

Lancashire

This county is of great extent, and contains a large number of old families, is entirely devoted to its rightful king.
Earl of Derby,*Lord Barrymore, Lord Strange, son of the Earl of Derby, M.P., Curzon, William M.P., Fazackerley, Nicholas, M.P., Fenwick, Robert M.P., Lister, Thomas M.P., Master, Legh, M.P., Shuttleworth, James M.P., Shuttleworth, Richard M.P.

Leicestershire

Duke of Rutland, Lord Huntingdon, Lord Stamford, Cave, Sir Thomas M.P., Wigley, Joseph M.P., Wright, George M.P.

Lincolnshire

Lord Bristol, Lord Haversham, John Mitchell M.P., John Proby M.P., Robert Vyner M.P.

Middlesex

The country people of this rich county, which includes part of London have always been of the right way of thinking.
Duke of Bedford,*Duke of Beaufort, Duke of Somerset, Lord Burlington Newdigate, Sir Roger M.P., Smithson, Sir Hugh, M.P.

Norfolk

The nobility of this county is generally speaking attached to the rightful king, but Sir Robert Walpole has corrupted large numbers of people.
Duke of Norfolk, Lord Andover, Andrews, Sir Francis M.P., Jerningham, Sir George M.P., Woodhouse, Armine, M.P.

Northamptonshire

Lord Rockingham, Lord Thanet, Cartwright, Thomas M.P., Isham, Sir Edward M.P., Montague, Edward Wortley M.P., Parker, Armistead M.P., Shirley, Sewallis M.P.

Northumberland

This county contains many ancient families who have never been perverted.

*Earl of Derwentwater (but not resident in the county in 1743), *Lord Widdrington, Blacket, Walter, M.P., Fenwick, John M. P., Fenwick, Nicholas M.P., Swinburne, Sir John.

Nottinghamshire

Duke of Norfolk, Lord Chesterton, Lord Middleton, Lord Trevor, Levinz, William M.P., Warren, Borlase M.P.

Oxfordshire

This county holds to passive resistance, but has a very large number of gentry zealous for the cause.
Lord Abingdon, Lord Lichfield, Butler, Dr. M.P., Dashwood, Sir James M.P., Dawkins, James M.P., Herbert, Philip M.P., Moore, William M.P., Rowney, Thomas M.P.

Rutland

The towns are hostile.

Shropshire

County unanimously Jacobite.
Astley, Sir John M.P., Corbet, Sir Richard M.P., Kynaston, William M.P., Lister, Richard M.P.

Somerset

The gentry are zealous supporters of their lawful king.
*Duke of Beaufort, Lord Clifford, *Lord Orrery, Lord Stawell, Buck, John M.P., Carew, Thomas M.P., Chapman, Sir John M.P., Doddington, George Bubb M.P., Harvey, Michael M.P., Hoblyn, Robert, M.P., Portman, Henry M.P., Prowse, Henry M.P.

Southamptonshire

The county is generally hostile; nevertheless these are enthusiastic Jacobite supporters and have much influence there.
Lord Dormer, Lord Shaftesbury, Barrington, Sir John M.P., Delme, Peter M.P., Gibbon, Edward M.P.

Staffordshire

This county, situated mainly in the centre of England is unanimous in its attachment to its lawful king. It was at Lichfield races that Mr Butler had the pleasure of seeing more than three hundred peers and gentry, the poorest of whom had nearly £4000 a year who all declared their readiness to follow Lord Barrymore in the restoration of their rightful king.

Lord Audley, Lord Berkshire, Lord Chetwynd, *Lord Gower, Lord Leigh, Lord Stourton, Lord Stamford, Bagot, Sir Wagstaff M.P., Holt, Sir Lister, M.P., *Leveson-Gower, Baptiste M.P., *Leveson-Gower, William M.P., Vernon, George Venables, M.P., Wilbraham, Randle, M.P.

Suffolk

Lord Bristol, Lord Suffolk, Affleck, John M.P., Firebrace, Sir Cordrel M.P., Hanmer, Sir Thomas.

Surrey

The greater part of this county has been acquired by stock-jobbers and supporters of the government, some have high principles.

Lord Aylesford, Lord Butler, brother of the Duke of Ormonde, Lord Mountjoy, Lord St. John, Harvey, John, M.P., Newland, George, M.P., Scawen, Thomas, M.P., Thrale, Ralph M.P., Woodroffe, George M.P. will not be bribed.

Sussex

The government has many supporters in this county, which is one of the most important in the country, but some of the oldest families are faithful to their lawful king.

Duke of Norfolk, Duke of Somerset, *Lord Caryll, Lord Derby, Lord Montacute, Lord Thanet, Campion, Henry M.P., *Caryll, Richard Fagg, Sir William M.P. Goring, Sir Charles, M.P., *Kemp, Anthony, *Middleton of Horsham, Peachy, Sir John M.P., Webster, Whistler M.P.

Warwickshire

Lies in the centre of the country. Has always been one of the best disposed Lord Aylesford, Lord Brook, Lord Denbigh, Lord Hereford,

Lord Middleton, Lord Northampton, Lord Westmoreland, Lord
Willoughby, Berkeley, Rowland, Digby, Edward, M.P., Grove,
William M.P., Mordaunt, Sir Charles, M.P., Perkins, John of Sutton
Coldfield, Sheldon, Edward of Weston Underwell Hall, Throgmorton,
Sir Robert

Westmoreland

This county is the least well cultivated in England. The alienation
of its Crown domains has rendered half the inhabitants hostile.
Sir Philip Musgrave, M.P. is the only man we can trust.

Wiltshire

This county is small but rich, and contains a large number of gentry of
whom the greater part are loyal.
Duke of Somerset, Lord Arundel, Lord Berkshire, Lord Craven,
Lord St. John, Bouverie, Sir Jacob M.P., Crawley, John M.P., Grenville,
James, M.P., Long, Sir Robert, M.P., Pitt, William M.P., Popham,
Edward M.P., Seymour, Sir Edward M.P., Thursby, John M.P., Turner,
Sir Edward M.P.

Worcestershire

The town of Worcester still retains a leavening of Cromwellism, but the
county is well disposed.
Lord Coventry, Lord Foley, Lord Shrewsbury, Foley, Thomas M.P.,
Lechmere, Edward, M.P., Pitts, Edward M.P.

Yorkshire

The county, the largest in England is somewhat tainted on the side
near Hull, but the gentry are, generally speaking, loyal to their rightful
Sovereign, and the country people will follow them.
Duke of Norfolk, Lord Abingdon, Lord Aylesbury, Lord Burlington,
Lord Carlisle,*Lord Gower, Lord Langdale, Lord Shrewsbury,
Aislabie, William, M.P., Berkeley, George, M.P., Fox, George, M.P.,
Pelham, Charles, M.P., Slingsby, Sir Henry, M.P., Stapelton, Sir Miles,
M.P.

Wales

The twelve counties of the Principality are entirely at the orders of the Duke of Beaufort and Sir Watkin Williams Wynn and have undertaken to hold themselves at readiness to take the saddle as soon as the signal is given by Lord Barrymore.

There followed a list of the Corporation of London showing whether they were Jacobites, Patriots, Hanoverians or Whigs. The following wards were deemed to be predominantly Jacobite:
Aldersgate, Aldgate, Bishopsgate, Bridge, Broad Street, Castle Baynard, Cordwainer, Cornhill, Cripplegate Within and Without, Dowgate, Farringdon Within, Faringdon Without, St Dunstan West, Ludgate, Limestreet, Portsoken, Queenhythe and Tower.

Sources

The original lists can be found in the Stuart Mss 253/51 in the Royal Archives at Windsor Castle. This is probably a copy of the French Foreign Office List AEM & D. Ang.
The list has been reproduced in many publications on the Jacobites in 1745, including L. Eardley-Simpson, *Derby in the '45*, and E. Cruickshanks, *Political Untouchables*. Eardley-Simpson annotated his list with information on the members of parliament and the seats they held.

Bibliography

Primary sources – manuscripts
Cambridgeshire County Record Office

588/A6, 26, 53–8, 60–61

588C/7–8, 16–17

588/DR/A/3, 52–9

588/DR/F 6–8, 49–50, 41, 43

588DR/T/297–8, 312, 329–30, 351–4

588/E 9, 13, 24, 55

588/F40, 42

588/L/3

588/O7–8, 15, 17–19

588/T 9, 314, 330, 360

588Z/10a–f, 12–13, 15–16

Dr Williams Library

Mss 38.84

Madingley Hall

Copy of the contract between Sir John Hynde Cotton IV and Capability Brown, 1756

Public Record Office

ADM 76/59–61, 86

ADM 76/60, 70

FEC A.24, B.62

SP 4/44, 47–8, 50

SP 7/78, 83

SP8/118(2)

SP 30/67

SP 35/4/47

SP 35/6/14, 15 (2–8), 42

SP 35/7/1–10, 13–16, 23–7, 33–6, 54–5, 66

SP 8/3, 11, 14, 20, 28, 34, 41–3, 111–12, 119, 123

SP 35/2/18

SP 35/3/18, 54, 79

SP 35/4/1–3, 18, 43–4, 62–2.65(1)

SP35/8/4–5, 9, 12–13, 16

SP 35/9/37, 43

SP 35/15/73, 81, 87, 101, 116, 123

SP 35/15/2, 3

SP 35/16/101

SP 35/17/14.16.33

SP 35/19/2

SP 35/20/19, 27, 54

SP 35/27/82

SP 35/28/7, 9–13, 28, 32, 35, 37, 39

SP 35/29/14–15, 36, 62 (1)

SP 35/33 (3)

SP 35/58/80

SP 35/61/9

SP 35/65/45, 82, 116, 126–7

SP 35/74/66

SP 78/83

Primary sources – printed

An Account of the Riots, Tumults and Other Treasonable Practices Since His Majesty's Succession to the Throne, London: 1716

Ailesbury, Earl of, *Memoirs*, London: Roxburgh Club, 1890

Allerdyce, J. ed., *Historical Papers Relating to the Jacobite Period*, Aberdeen: New Spalding Club, 1895–6

Arnet H. ed., *Extracts from the Records of the Burgh of Edinburgh 1701 to 1718*, Edinburgh: Oliver and Boyd, 1928

Bagley, J. ed., *The Great Diurnall of Nicholas Blundell of Little Crosby*, Lancashire and Cheshire Record Society, 110, 1958

Baker, E. ed., *Calendar of State Papers Domestic William III, 1700–02*, London: HMSO, 1937

Barrell, R. comp. *The French Correspondence of James 1st Earl Waldegrave*, Lampeter: The Edwin Mellor Press, 1996

Beamont, W. ed., *The Jacobite Trials in Manchester*, Manchester: Chetham Society, 28, 1853

Bell, R.F. ed., *Memoirs of John Murray of Broughton, 1740–47*, Edinburgh: Scottish Historical Society, 1898

Berwick, Duke of, *Memoirs*, London: 1779

Blaikie, W. ed., *The Itinerary of Prince Charles*, Edinburgh: Scottish Academic Press, 1897, repr. 1975

Blaikie, W. ed., *Origins of the '45*, Edinburgh: Scottish Academic Press, 1916

Boyer, A., *The Political State of Great Britain*, X, XI, July–December 1715, London: 1716, XXV, 1722

Byrom, J. and R. Thayer, *Manchester Vindicated*, Chester: E. Adams, 1749

Cameron, W.J. ed., *Poems on Affairs of State*, New Haven, Yale University Press, V, 1688–97, 1971

Carswell, J. ed., *The Political Journal of George Bubb Dodington*, Oxford: Clarendon Press, 1965

Cibber, C., *The Non-juror; alias the Hypocrite*, London: W. Griffin, 1769

Clark, P., *The March of the Insurgent Force from Penrith to Preston*, London: 1716

Cobbett, W., *Parliamentary History, 2 Geo I, 1716*, London: 1815

Cowper, S. ed., *Diary of Mary, Countess Cowper, 1714–1720*, London: John Murray, 1864

Daniel, J., *A True Account of Mr John Daniel's Time with Prince Charles Edward in the Years 1745 and 1746*, in Blaikie, *Origins of the '45*

De Beer, E.S. ed., *The Diary of John Evelyn*, Oxford: OUP, 1959

De Saussure, C., *A Foreign View of England in the Reigns of George I and George II*, translated by Madame van Muyden, London: John Murray, 1902

Defoe, D. ed., *A Tour Thro' the Whole Island of Great Britain, 1724–6*, facsimile edn, London: Frank Cass, 1968

Dickson, W.K. ed., *The Jacobite Attempt of 1719, Letters*, Edinburgh: Edinburgh University Press, 1895

Doe, V. ed., *The Diary of James Clegg of Chapel-en-le-Frith*, Derbyshire Record Society Series III, 1979

Douglas, F., *The History of the Rebellion in 1745 and 1746*, Aberdeen: 1755

Ellis, J. ed., *The Letters of Henry Liddell and William Cotesworth*, Surtees Society, 197, 1987

Estcourt, E. ed., *The English Catholics, 1716*, London: Burns and Oates, 1886

Fielding, H., *The History of Tom Jones*, London: Penguin edn, 1994

Gillow, J. and Hewitson, A. eds, *The Tyldesley Diary, 1712–1714*, Preston: A. Hewitson, 1873

Goss, A. ed., *An Account of the Trials at Manchester*, Chetham Society, 61, 1864

Grosart, A. ed., *English Jacobite Songs and Ballads, Songs and Satires from the Mss at Townley Hall*, Manchester: privately printed, 1877

Hardy, W.J. ed., *Calendar of State Papers Domestic, William and Mary 1689–90*, London: HMSO, 1895

Hardy, W.J. ed., *Calendar of State Papers Domestic: William and Mary, May 1690–October 1691*, London: HMSO, 1898

Hardy, W.J. ed., *Calendar of State Papers Domestic: William III, 1697*, London: HMSO, 1927

Hearne, T., *Remarks and Collections of Thomas Hearne*, Oxford Historical Society 1894–98

Historical Manuscripts Commission, *Calendar of the Manuscripts of the Earl of Carlisle*, London: HMSO, 1897

Historical Manuscripts Commission, *Calendar of the Manuscripts of Lord Kenyon*, HMSO, 1894

Historical Manuscripts Commission, *Calendar of the Manuscripts of the Marquess of Townshend*, London: HMSO, 1887

Historical Manuscripts Commission, *The Calendar of the Stuart Papers in the Possession of HM the King at Windsor Castle*, I, London: HMSO, 1902

Historical Manuscripts Commission, *The Calendar of the Stuart Papers in the Possession of HM the King at Windsor Castle*, II, London: HMSO, 1904

Historical Manuscripts Commission, *The Calendar of the Stuart Papers in the Possession of HM the King at Windsor Castle*, III, London: HMSO, 1907

Historical Manuscripts Commission, *The Calendar of the Stuart Papers in the Possession of HM the King at Windsor Castle*, IV, London: HMSO, 1910

Historical Manuscripts Commission, *The Calendar of the Stuart Papers in the Possession of HM the King at Windsor Castle*, VI, London: HMSO, 1916

Historical Manuscripts Commission, *The Calendar of the Stuart Papers in the Possession of HM the King at Windsor Castle*, VII, London: HMSO, 1923

Historical Manuscripts Commission, *The Manuscripts of Lord Kenyon*, London: HMSO, 1894

Historical Manuscripts Commission, *Report on the Manuscripts of the Duke of Portland*, VII, London: HMSO, 1901

House of Commons, *Report from the Committee to whom the books, instruments and papers relating to the sale of the estate of James, Late Earl of Derwentwater were given*, London, 1723

House of Lords, *A Speech in the House of Lords upon the Third Reading of the Bill for Inflicting Pains and Penalties against Francis, late Bishop of Rochester*, London: 1723

House of Lords, *The Whole Proceedings upon the Articles of Impeachment of High Treason against the Earl of Derwentwater*, London: 1716

Howell, T.B. ed., *A Complete Collection of State Trials*, London: Longman Hurst, Vol. XII, 1812

Hudleston, C., *Durham Recusants Estates 1717–1778*, Durham: Surtees Society, CLXXIII, 1958

Hughan, W.J. ed., *The Jacobite Lodge at Rome, 1735–7*, Torquay: Lodge of Research, 1910

Jarvis, R. ed., *Collected Papers on the Jacobite Risings*, Carlisle: Cumberland County Council, 1972

Jarvis, R. ed., *The Jacobite Risings of 1715 & 1745*, Carlisle: Cumberland County Council, 1954

Johnstone, Chevalier de, *A Memoir of the Forty-five*, London: Folio Society, 1958

Jones, C. and Holmes, G., *The London Diaries of William Nicolson, 1702–1718*, Oxford: Clarendon Press, 1985

King, W., *Political and Literary Anecdotes of His Own Time*, London: John Murray, 2nd edn, 1819

Last, C.E. ed., *Jacobite Extracts from the Parish Registers of St Germain-en-Laye*, London: St Catherine's Press, 1910

Letters which passed between Count Gyllenberg and others relating to the design and raising of a rebellion in HM Dominions to be supported by a force from Sweden, London: 1717

Livingston, A., C. Aikman, and B. Hunt, *Muster Role of Prince Charles Edward's Army, 1745–6*, Aberdeen: Aberdeen University Press, 1984

Luttrell, N., *A Brief Historical Relation of State Affairs, 1678–1714*, Oxford: OUP, II 1857, III 1857, IV 1858, VI 1867

Macky, J., *Memoirs of the Secret Services of John Macky*, London: Roxburgh Club, 1895

Macpherson, J., *Original Papers Containing the Secret History of England*, London: 1775

Mahaffy, R.P. ed., *Calendar of State Papers Domestic, 1702–3*, London: HMSO, 1916

Mahaffy, R.P. ed., *Calendar of State Papers Domestic 1703–4*, London: HMSO 1924

Matthews, W. ed., *The Diary of Dudley Ryder, 1715–1716*, London: Methuen, 1939

Newcastle upon Tyne Antiquarian Society, 'Wills of Jacobite Refugees', *Proceedings*, IX, 1920

Parkinson, R.ed., *The Private Journal and Literary Remains of John Byrom*, Chetham Society, 1854

Parliamentary Papers, *Report of the Secret Committee of the House of Lords relative to the Post Office*, Cmnd. 582, 1844

Paton, H. ed., *The Lyon in Mourning*, Edinburgh: Scottish Academic Press, facsimile reprint 1978

Patten, R., *The History of the Late Rebellion*, London: 1717

Payne, J.A. ed., *Records of English Catholics, 1715*, London: Burns and Oates, 1889

Post Boy, May–June, 1715

Rae, P., *The History of the Late Rebellion*, Dumfries: 1718

Register of the Estates of Roman Catholics in Northumberland, Surtees Society 34, 1918

Roebuck, P. ed., 'The Constables of Everingham Estate Correspondence, 1726–43', *Transactions*, Yorkshire Archaeological Society, CXXXVI

Shaw, W. ed., *Calendar of Treasury Books, Jan–July 1714*, London: HMSO, 1969

Smith, M., *Memoirs of the Secret Service*, London: 1699

St James Post, May–June, 1715

Stackhouse, T., *Memoirs of the Life and Conduct of Dr Francis Atterbury*, London: 1723

The Caledonian Mercury, 16 July 1744

The Derby Mercury, 12 December 1745

The Gentleman's Magazine, 1745

The Jacobite Journal, 1748

The Monthly Review, 1749

The Scots Magazine, 1745

The Wandered or a surprising escape, London: 1747

Ware, S.H. ed., *The Lancashire Memorials of the Rebellion, 1716*, Chetham Society, V, 1865

Ware, S.H., *The State of the Parties in Lancashire before the Rebellion of 1715*, Chetham Society, V, 1845

Yorke, P. ed., *The Life and Correspondence of Philip Yorke, Earl of Hardwicke*, Cambridge: CUP, 1913

Secondary sources – books

Archer Houblon, A., *The Houblon Family*, London: Archibald Constable & Co. Ltd, 1907

Arnold, R., *Northern Light*, London: Constable, 1959

Atherton, H.M., *Political Prints in the Age of Hogarth*, Oxford: Clarendon Press, 1974

Baigent, M. and R. Leigh, *The Temple and the Lodge*, London: Jonathan Cape, 1989

Baker, E., *Guide to Historical Fiction*, London: Routledge, 1914

Baynes, J., *The Jacobite Rising of 1715*, London: Cassell, 1970

Beattie, D., *Prince Charles and the Borderland*, Carlisle: Charles Thomas & Son, 1928

Beckett, J., *The Aristocracy of England 1600–1914*, Oxford: Blackwell, 1998

Beeching, H.C., *Francis Atterbury*, London: Pitman & Son, 1909

Beloff, M., *Public Order and Popular Disturbances 1660–1914*, Oxford: OUP, 1938

Bennett, G.V., *The Tory Crisis in Church and State, 1688–1720*, Oxford: Clarendon Press, 1975

Blanning, T., *The Culture of Power and the Power of Culture*, Oxford: OUP, 2002

Brooks-Davies, D., *Alexander Pope. A collection of poetry*, London: Dent, 1996

Brooks-Davies, D., *Pope's Dunciad and the Queen of the Night*, Manchester: Manchester University Press, 1985

Broxap, H., *A Biography of Thomas Deacon the Manchester Non-juror*, Manchester: Manchester University Press, 1911

Broxap, H., *The Later Non-Jurors*, Cambridge: CUP, 1924

Clark, J.C.D., *English Society, 1688–1832*, Cambridge: CUP, 2002

Clark, P., *British Clubs and Societies*, Oxford: Clarendon Press, 2000

Colley, L., *Britons*, London: Vintage, 1996

Colley, L., *In Defiance of Oligarchy*, Cambridge: CUP, 1982

Cooper, C.H., *Annals of Cambridge*, Cambridge: Metcalfe and Palmer, IV, 1852

Corp, E., *The King Over the Water. Portraits of the Stuarts in Exile after 1689*, Edinburgh: Scottish National Portrait Gallery, 2001

Coupe, F., *Walton-le-Dale. A History of the Village*, Preston: Guardian Press, 1954

Cruickshanks, E., *Ideology and Conspiracy*, Edinburgh: John Donald Ltd, 1982

Cruickshanks, E., *Political Untouchables*, London: Duckworth, 1979

Cruickshanks, E. and J. Black, eds, *The Jacobite Challenge*, Edinburgh: John Donald Ltd., 1988

Cruickshanks, E. and E. Corp, *The Stuart Court in Exile and the Jacobites*, London: The Hambledon Press, 1995

Deacon, R., *A History of the British Secret Service*, London: Muller, 1969

Dennistoun, J., *Memoirs of Sir Robert Strange*, London: Longman, 1855

Dickinson, F., *The Castle on Devilswater*, Stocksfield: The Spreddon Press, 1969

Dickinson, H., *Bolingbroke*, London: Constable, 1970

Donaldson, W., *The Jacobite Song, Political Myth and National Identity*, Aberdeen: Aberdeen University Press, 1998

Douglas, H., *Jacobite Spy Wars*, Stroud: Sutton, 1999

Eardley-Simpson, L., *Derby and the '45*, London: Philip Allan, 1933

Ellis, K., *The Post Office in the Eighteenth Century*, Oxford: OUP, 1958

Foord, A., *His Majesty's Opposition 1714–1830*, Oxford: Clarendon Press, 1964

Francis, R.G., *The Romance of the White Rose*, London: John Murray, 1933

Garrett, J., *The Triumph of Providence*, Cambridge: CUP, 1980

George, M., *English Political Caricature to 1792*, Oxford: Clarendon Press, 1959

Gibson, J., *Playing the Scottish Card – the Franco-Jacobite Invasion of 1708*, Edinburgh: Edinburgh University Press, 1988

Gibson, W., *Dilston Hall*, London: Longman, 1850

Gilmour, I., *Riots, Risings & Revolutions. Governance and Violence in 18th Century England*, London: Hutchinson, 1992

Gooch, L., *The Desperate Faction?*, Hull: Hull University Press, 1995

Hancox, J., *The Queen's Chameleon*, London: Jonathan Cape, 1994

Hay, D. ed., *Albion's Fatal Tree*, London: Penguin, 1977

Haydon, C., *Anti-Catholicism in 18th century England*, Manchester: Manchester University Press, 1993

Herman, A., *The Scottish Enlightenment*, London: Fourth Estate, 2001

Hill, P.K., *The Oglethorpe Ladies and the Jacobite Conspiracies*, Atlanta: Cherokee Publishing Company, 1971

Hodgson, J., *The History of Northumberland*, Newcastle upon Tyne, 1827

Holcroft, F., *The Jacobites in Lancashire*, Wigan: Fred Holcroft, 1995

Holmes, G., *The Making of a Great Power 1660–1722*, London: Longman, 1993

Holmes, G., *The Trial of Dr Sacheverell*, London: Eyre, 1973

Hoppit, J., *A Land of Liberty? England 1689–1727*, Oxford: OUP, 2002

Hughes, E., *North Country Life in the 18th Century*, Oxford: OUP, 1952

Ingamells, J., *A Dictionary of British and Irish Travellers in Italy, 1701–1800*, New Haven, Connecticut, 1999

Jones, G., *The Main Stream of Jacobitism*, Cambridge, Mass: Harvard University Press, 1954

Ketton-Cremer, R., *Matthew Prior*, Cambridge: CUP, 1957

Ketton-Cremer, R., *A Norfolk Gallery*, London: Faber, 1948

Lang, A., *Pickle the Spy*, London: 1897

Laslett, P., *The World We Have Lost*, London: Methuen, 2nd edn, 1979

Lathbury, T., *A History of the Non-Jurors*, London: William Pickering, 1845

Lenman, B., *The Jacobite Risings in Britain 1689–1748*, London: Eyre Methuen, 1980

Lillywhite, B., *London Coffee Houses*, London: George Allan & Unwin Ltd, 1963

Lord, E., *Derby Past*, Chichester: Phillimore, 1996

Macrae-Daniel, D., *Daniel Defoe and the Jacobite movement*, Salzburg: Institute für Englisch und Amerikanistik, 1980

Martin, G. and S. McIntyre, *A Bibliography of British and Irish Municipal History*, Leicester: Leicester University Press, 1972

McLynn, F., *The Jacobite Army in England 1745*, Edinburgh: John Donald Publishers Ltd, 1983

Massue, M., *The Jacobite Peerage*, London: Charles Shilton, 1974

Money, D., *The English Horace*, Oxford: OUP, 1998

Monod, P., *Jacobitism and the English People, 1688–1788*, Cambridge: CUP, 1993

Munby, L., *The Common People Are Not Nothing*, Hatfield: Hertfordshire Publications, 1995

Newman, B., *Spy and Counter-Spy*, London: Robert Hale, 1970

Nicholson, R., *Bonnie Prince Charlie. A study in portraiture*, London: Associated Universities Press, 2002

Overton, J., *The Nonjurors*, London: Smith, Elder & Co, 1902

Paton, N., *The Jacobites. Their Roots, Rebellions and Links with Freemasonry*, Fareham: Sea Green Ribbon Publications, 1994

Petrie, C., *The Jacobite Movement. The First Phase, 1688–1716*, London: Eyre & Spottiswood, 1948

Phythian-Adams, C.V. ed., *Societies, Culture and Kinship, 1580–1850*, Leicester: Leicester University Press, 1993

Pittock, M., *Cultural Identities*, Basingstoke: Macmillan, 1997

Pittock, M., *Jacobitism*, Basingstoke: Macmillan, 1998

Rivington, C., *Tyrant: the story of John Barker Jacobite Lord Mayor of York*, York: William Sessions Ltd, 1989

Rogers, N., *Whigs and Cities*, Oxford: Clarendon Press, 1989

Rose, C., *England in the 1690s*, Oxford: Blackwell, 1999

Rudé, G., *Hanoverian London*, London: Secker & Warburg, 1971

Samuel, R., *Theatres of Memory*, London: Verso Press, Vol. 1, 1996

Seddon, G., *The Jacobites and their Drinking Glasses*, Woodbridge: Antique Collectors Club, 1995

Sedgwick, R. ed., *The History of Parliament – The House of Commons 1715–1754*, London: HMSO, 1970

Sharp, R., *The Engraved Record of the Jacobite Movement*, Alderston: Scolar Press, 1996

Skeet, F.A., *Catalogue of Jacobite Medals and Touch Pieces in the Collection of Miss Maria Widdrington*, Leeds: John Whitehead & Son Ltd, 1938

Skeet, F.A., *The Life of the Rt Hon. James Radcliffe, 3rd Earl of Derwentwater*, London: Hutchinson, 1929

Skeet, F.A., *Stuart Papers, Pictures, Relics, Medals and Books*, Leeds: John Whitehead & Son Ltd, 1930

Stone, L., *The Family, Sex and Marriage in England 1500–1800*, Harmondsworth: Penguin, 1982

Sykes, J., *Local Records or Historical Records of Northumberland and Durham*, Stockton-on-Tees: Patrick & Shotton, 1973

Szechi, D., *Jacobitism and Tory Politics*, Edinburgh: John Donald Ltd, 1984

Szechi, D., *The Jacobites – Britain and Europe 1688–1788*, Manchester: Manchester University Press, 1994

Taylor, A. and H., *1715: The Story of a Rising*, London: Thomas Nelson & Sons, 1936

Terry, C.S., *The Last Jacobite Rising, 1745*, London: David Nutt, 1900

Thompson, E.P., *Whigs and Hunters*, London: Allan Lane, 1975

Thomson, Mrs, *Memoirs of the Jacobites*, London: Bentley, 1845

Towill, S., *Carlisle*, Chichester: Phillimore, 1991

Ward, A. and A. Waller eds, *The Cambridge History of English Literature*, Cambridge: CUP, X, 1912

Wheatley, J., *Bonnie Prince Charlie in Cumberland*, Carlisle: Charles Thomas & Son, 1903

Whiting, J., *Commemorative Medals*, Newton Abbot: David and Charles, 1972

Wrigley, E.A. and Schofield, R.S., *The Population History of England and Wales, 1541–1871*, Cambridge: CUP, 1989

Youngson, A., *The Prince and the Pretender*, London: Croom Helm, 1985

Secondary sources – articles

Bennett, G.V., 'English Jacobites: Myth and Reality', *Transactions, Royal Historical Society*, 5th ser, 32, 1982

Black, J., 'The Forty-Five re-examined', *Royal Stuart Papers*, XXXIV, 1990

Cherry, D., 'Sir Nicholas L'Estrange, non-juror', *Norfolk Archaeology*, XXVI, 1968

Colley, L., 'The Loyal Brotherhood and the Cocoa Tree: the London organisation of the Tory party, 1727–1760', *The Historical Journal*, 20, 1977

Collyer, C., 'Yorkshire and the Forty-Five', *Yorkshire Archaeological Society Journal*, XXXVIII, 1955

Cruickshanks, E., 'Lord North, Christopher Layer and the Atterbury Plot', in E. Cruickshanks and J. Black eds, *The Jacobite Challenge*

Cruickshanks, E., 'The Oglethorpes: A Jacobite Family 1689–1760', *Royal Stuart Papers*, XLV, 1995

Cruickshanks, E., 'Religion and Royal Succession', *Royal Stuart Papers*, L, 1997

Dixon, D., 'Notes on Jacobite Movement in Upper Coquetdale, 1715', *Archaeologia Aeliana*, XVI, 1894

Earwaker, J., 'Manchester and the Rebellion of '45', *Transactions, Lancashire and Cheshire Antiquarian Society*, VII, 1889

Erskine-Hill, H., 'Literature and the Jacobite Cause', in E. Cruickshanks ed., *Ideology and Conspiracy*

Farquhar, H., 'Some Portrait Medals Struck between 1745 and 1752 for Prince Charles Edward', *British Numismatics Journal*, 1923–4, and 1927

Fieldhouse, H., 'Bolingbroke's share in the Jacobite intrigue of 1710–14', *English Historical Review*, 52, 1937

Forster, S., 'The Countess of Derwentwater: A note on her fate', *Northern Catholic History*, 18, 1983

Forster, S., 'The Earl of Derwentwater: A note on his last resting place', *Northern Catholic History*, 20, 1984

Francillon, R., 'Underground Jacobitism', *The Monthly Review*, XXI, 1905

Fritz, P., 'The Anti-Jacobite Intelligence System of the English Ministers, 1715–1745', *The Historical Journal*, XIV, 1973

Goldie, M., 'The Nonjurors, Episcopacy and the Origins of the Convocation Controversy', in E. Cruickshanks ed., *Ideology and Conspiracy*

Gooch, L., 'Incarnate Rogues and Vile Jacobites: Silvertop versus Cotesworth, 1718–1723', *Recusant History*, 18, 1987

Gregg, E., 'The politics of paranoia' in Cruickshanks, E. and J. Black, eds, *The Jacobite Challenge*

Gregg, E., 'Was Queen Anne a Jacobite?', *History*, 57, October 1972

Guthrie, D. and C. Grove, 'Forty Years of Jacobite Bibliography', *Journal of Modern History*, XI, 1939

Hay, D., 'Poaching and the Game Laws on Cannock Chase' in
D. Hay ed., *Albion's Fatal Tree*

Hopkins, R., 'The Commission for Superstitious Lands', *Recusant History*, 15, 1980

Hughes, E., 'Some Clavering Correspondence', *Archaeologia Aeliana*, 4th ser. 1956

Jenkins, J.P., 'Jacobites and Freemasons in 18th century Wales',
The Welsh Historical Review, 3, 1979

Jones, S., 'Jacobite Imagery in Wales: Evidence of Political Activity',
Royal Stuart Society Papers, LIII, 1998

Lavelle, T., 'Essex Papists and the Oath of Allegiance, 1715–1788',
Essex Recusant, 1, 1, 1959

Legg, L.G.W., 'Extracts from Jacobite Correspondence 1712–1714',
English Historical Review, 30, 1915

Lole, F., 'A Digest of Jacobite Clubs', *Royal Stuart Society Papers*, LV,
1999

Lonsdale, E., 'John Lunt and the Lancashire Plot', *Transactions*,
Lancashire and Cheshire Historic Society, 115, 1963

Lord, E., 'Communities of Common Interest: the social landscape of
S.E. Surrey, 1750–1850' in C.V. Phythian-Adams ed., *Societies,
Culture, Kinship 1580–1850*

McLynn, F., 'Issues and Motives of the Jacobite Rising of 1745',
The Eighteenth Century, 23, 2, 1982

McLynn, F., 'Nottingham and the Jacobite Rising of 1745',
Transactions, Thoroton Society, LXXXIII, 1979

McLynn, F., 'Unpopular Front. Jews, Radicals and Americans in the
Jacobite World View', *Royal Stuart Papers*, XXXI, 1988

Meredith, R., 'The Eyres of Hassop', *Recusant History*, IX, 1967–68

Miller, J., 'Proto-Jacobitism? The Tories and the Revolution of 1688–9'
in Cruickshanks, E. and J. Black eds, *The Jacobite Challenge*

Monod, P., 'The Politics of Matrimony: Jacobitism and marriage in
eighteenth century England', in E. Cruickshanks and J. Black eds,
The Jacobite Challenge

Newcastle upon Tyne, Society of Antiquaries, *Proceedings*, 3rd ser, VI, 18, 1914

Nicholson, W., 'Catholic Tyneside, 1600–1800', *Northern Catholic History*, 22, 1985

'Observations on the Radcliffe Pedigree', *Archaeologie Aeliana*, N.S. VII, 1876

Parker-Jones, W.S., 'The Forty-Five in Staffordshire', *Transactions*, North Staffordshire Field Club, LVIII, 1924

Petrie, C., 'The Jacobite Activities in the South and West of England in the Summer of 1715', *Transactions*, Royal Historical Society, 4th ser. XVIII, 1935

Pope, T., 'The Ancient Corporation of Cheadle', *Transactions*, North Staffordshire Field Club, LXIV, 1929–30

Porter, J., 'The Non-Juroring Bishops', *Royal Stuart Society Papers*, IV, 1973

Porteus, T.C., 'New Light on the Lancashire Plot, 1692–4', *Transactions*, Lancashire and Cheshire Antiquarian Society, 4, 1934–35

Potter, R.G., 'A government spy in Derbyshire during the "Forty-Five" ', *Derbyshire Archaeological Journal*, LXXXIX, 1969

Purcell, P., 'The Jacobite Rising of 1715 and the English Catholics', *English Historical Review*, XLIV, 1929

Rogers, N., 'Popular Disaffection in London during the Forty-Five', *The London Journal*, 1, 1975

Rogers, N., 'Popular Jacobitism in Provincial Contexts, Bristol and Norwich' in E. Cruickshanks and J. Black eds, *The Jacobite Challenge*

Rogers, N., 'Riot and Popular Jacobitism' in E. Cruickshanks ed., *Ideology and Conspiracy*

Rounding, A., 'William 4th Baron Widdrington, c. 1675–1743', *Northern Catholic History*, 22, 1985

Sharp, R., '100 years of a lost cause: Nonjuroring principles in Newcastle from the Revolution to the death of Prince Charles' in *Archaeologia Aeliana*, 5th ser, III, 1980

Szechi, D., 'The Jacobite Theatre of Death' in E. Cruickshanks and J. Black eds, *The Jacobite Challenge*

The Royalist, 1954, 1959–60

Trevelyan, G.M., 'The Last Rising in the North', *The Northern Counties Magazine*, I, 1901

Winslow, C., 'Sussex Smugglers', in D. Hay ed., *Albion's Fatal Tree*

Walsh, E. and A. Forster, 'The Recusancy of the Brandlings', *Recusant History*, X, 1969–70

Yould, G.M., 'Two Nonjurors', *Norfolk Archaeology*, XXXV, 1972

Zen, B., 'Jacobitism and the Liturgy in the 18th century English Catholic Church', *Royal Stuart Papers*, XLI, 1992

Index